HYBRID CULTURES

HYBRID CULTURES

Strategies for Entering and Leaving Modernity

NÉSTOR GARCÍA CANCLINI

Translated by Christopher L. Chiappari and Silvia L. López

Foreword by Renato Rosaldo

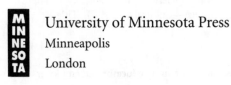

University of Minnesota Press

Minneapolis

London

Originally published as *Culturas híbridas: Estrategias para entrar y salir de la modernidad,* copyright 1989, Néstor García Canclini. Spanish edition published by Editorial Grijalbo, México, D.F., 1990.

Grateful acknowledgment is made for permission to reprint the following figures: 5-7, drawings by Felipe Ehrenberg; 32-39, photographs by Paolo Gori; 40-48, photographs by Lourdes Grobet; 49-50, photographs by Paolo Gasparini; 51-52, drawings by León Ferrari; figures 53-58, cartoons by Fontarrosa.

Every effort has been made to obtain permission to reproduce copyright material in this book. The publishers ask copyright holders to notify them if permission has inadvertently not been sought or if proper acknowledgment has not been made.

Published by the University of Minnesota Press
111 Third Avenue South, Suite 290, Minneapolis, MN 55401-2520
Printed in the United States of America on acid-free paper
Fourth printing 2001
Library of Congress Cataloging-in-Publication Data

García Canclini, Néstor.
   [Culturas híbridas. English]
   Hybrid cultures : strategies for entering and leaving modernity / Néstor García Canclini ; translated by Christopher L. Chiappari and Silvia L. López ; foreword by Renato Rosaldo.
      p.   cm.
   Translation of: Culturas híbridas : estrategias para entrar y salir de la modernidad.
   Includes bibliographical references and index.
   ISBN 0-8166-2314-7.—ISBN 0-8166-2315-5 (pbk.)
   1. Latin America—Civilization—20th century.   2. Civilization, Modern—20th century.   3. Postmodernism.   4. Arts and society—Latin America.   5. Popular culture—Latin America.   6. Latin America—Cultural policy.   I. Title.
F1414.2.G36513   1995
980.03'3—dc20   94-47137

For Teresa and Julián

Personal life, expression, knowledge, and history advance
obliquely, and not directly, toward ends or toward concepts.
That which is sought too deliberately is not obtained.

Maurice Merleau-Ponty

Contents

Foreword

Renato Rosaldo

In his fine synthetic work, *Hybrid Cultures: Strategies for Entering and Leaving Modernity,* Néstor García Canclini explores the tensions, verging on contradictions, between modernization and democratization in Latin American nation-states. These states regard themselves as caught between traditions that have not yet gone and a modernity that has not yet arrived. From its hybrid position between tradition and modernity, the challenge for Latin America is to construct democratic culture and knowledge without succumbing either to the temptations of elite art and literature or to the coercive forces of mass media and marketing. In a work of committed scholarship, the author both interrogates and advocates the development of democratic institutions and practices in Latin America.

Drawing broadly on interdisciplinary social thought from Europe and the Americas, García Canclini seeks to reconceive the larger workings and ethical dilemmas of Latin American societies. Recent economic and political shifts in the United States and western Europe have prepared the ground for this translation of García Canclini's work. The renewed presence of right-wing political movements in the United States, Latin America, and Europe has produced a convergence of analytical and ethical concerns. The upward transfer of wealth and the increasing disparity between the extremely wealthy and the rest, not to mention the expanding number of citizens living in poverty, have deepened the structural parallels between Europe and the Americas. Latin American intellectuals usually attribute such changes to

political and economic globalization as well as to neoliberal economic policies imposed by the World Bank and the International Monetary Fund;
commentators in the United States attribute parallel changes to multina-
tional corporations as well as to neoconservative policies that, in the name
of less government, drastically reduce social programs and state regulation
of capitalism at the same time that they (paradoxically) increase the repressive state apparatus through increases in militarization, police forces, border
patrols, and prison populations.

The structural changes in the Americas just sketched pose a set of central
tensions between economic liberalism and democracy on the one hand, and
authoritarianism and clientism on the other. García Canclini exhorts citizens to resist the conflation of modernization with high cultural modernity,
neoliberalism, authoritarianism, and fascism. The structural changes that
have brought the North and the South onto parallel courses create a profound tension between accelerating economic inequality and a heightened
demand for equality among citizens who make urgent, if contested, demands for social justice.

García Canclini argues that different disciplines complement one another
because they differ in their areas of study, their methodologies, and their
strengths and weaknesses. Central to *Hybrid Cultures* is the notion that anthropology focuses on tradition and sociology concentrates on modernity.
The latter discipline studies the production of social inequalities through the
segmentation of the labor market where differences in jobs, pay, and status
devolve to distinct groups based on such factors as class, gender, and race.
This perspective argues that transnational market forces and the mass media
have reorganized the cultural sphere and it thus questions anthropological
analyses that treat culture as if it were autonomous. Anthropology, on the
other hand, emphasizes differences, diversity, and plurality. It argues against
sociology's metropolitan ethnocentrism that homogenizes society and over-
looks local symbols of conflict and solidarity. In his synthetic work, García
Canclini encompasses the strengths of both disciplinary perspectives.

In a similar manner García Canclini argues for the synthesis of the broad
intellectual trends he equates with Pierre Bourdieu and Antonio Gramsci.[1]
He emphasizes Bourdieu's notion of distinction and his conception of the
long-term social reproduction of social inequalities across the generations.
How, for example, do family socialization and public education teach and
discipline people to play the social roles that re-create the inequalities of
their parents and grandparents? García Canclini values Bourdieu's analysis
of the reproduction of social inequality at the same time that he questions

its failure to study social change and political struggle. He thus argues that Gramsci's notion of the struggles over hegemony provides an important historical and political dimension missing from analyses of social reproduction. Arguably, *Hybrid Cultures* attempts to bring Gramsci center stage in the study of Latin American social formations.

García Canclini contends that Latin American nation-states adopted modernization and national culture as their project. Their attempt to be both modern and culturally pure led to metaphysical versions of the nation's historical patrimony that did more to justify present domination than they did to describe the past. In certain cases, such as in Argentina, the enlightenment project of rationalization and secularization led to prejudice against and the exclusion of (supposedly backward and superstitious) indigenous groups, the nation's original inhabitants. In this context, cultural politics becomes a struggle against ways of appealing to culture and history and thereby legitimating current relations of inequality.

García Canclini similarly opposes the doctrine of evolutionism, especially as it becomes a state ideology. Evolutionism argues that social formations at any single point in time can be ordered chronologically from ancient to modern in a way that corresponds to a parallel moral ordering from inferior to superior. From this perspective, the modern becomes all that is secular, innovative, economically productive, and democratic. The process of modernity involves a movement from religion and metaphysics to art, morality, and science. Hence the ideological equation of the modern with the superiority of high culture and the traditional with the inferiority of popular culture. From García Canclini's viewpoint, the modern and high culture correspond to the hegemonic whereas the traditional and popular culture correspond to the subaltern. In contradictory fashion, he argues, the nation-state ideologically incorporated popular culture into national culture in order to legitimate its domination in the name of the people at the same time that it attempted in its policies to eliminate popular culture in the name of ending superstition.

García Canclini's analysis of tradition and modernity may prove difficult for readers in the United States to apprehend. The gap in comprehension derives from the absolute ideological divide between North and South, between nation-states regarded as having completed their modernization and those that have not yet done so. In Latin America, modernization and development remain vital issues that are named as such in the discussions that reflect and create national self-understanding. In the United States, on the other hand, questions of modernization do not enter the public realm of grappling with vital social issues. Such social issues as poverty and the shameful infant mortality rates among African Americans and the poor, for example, are treated neither as signs of underdevelopment nor as failures of uneven modernization (as they conceivably could be in principle and no doubt would be in Latin America). Thus readers of this translation will need to remember that questions of modernization may not be as alien to them as North/South ideologies would make it appear.

When García Canclini approaches a central theme, that of artistic production in the nineteenth and twentieth centuries, he does so through theories of modernization developed by Max Weber. He investigates Weber's proposition that rationalization must be understood in relation to the autonomous goals of a particular social sector. For example, mysticism may be rationalized through the development of a set of explicitly codified procedures and techniques that increase the likelihood of an individual's achieving a mystical experience. Rationalization in the Weberian sense refers to adjustments in the means of achieving certain ends and not to the ends in themselves (both mysticism and entrepreneurial activity can equally be rationalized).

In opposition to Weber, however, García Canclini argues that artistic production cannot properly be understood as an autonomous realm, despite the insistence to the contrary of such notable artists as Octavio Paz and Jorge Luis Borges. If Paz and Borges understand art to be the product of the creative artist viewed as an autonomous individual, García Canclini sees the artist as one link in a syntagmatic chain that extends from the creations of the artist's studio to the marketplace of private galleries. The multiple stages of artistic production and consumption form a system of mutual influence through which what comes before shapes what comes after and vice versa. To imagine that the artist produces without regard for the market is as foolish as to suppose that the market fails to take the nature of artistic production into account.

When García Canclini turns to folk art, he transforms the syntagmatic chain running from production to consumption by regarding it as a process of entering and leaving modernity. Indigenous producers of folk art (Are they really so different from artists producing for high-culture marketplaces?) appear to live in traditional societies, but their products enter modern marketplaces through a series of intermediate steps, some modern, some traditional. He goes on to speak of different temporalities, meaning that the modern sphere represents a different historical epoch than the traditional sphere. Yet both the modern and the traditional coexist in the late-twentieth-century world. In my view, the issues posed by García Canclini's significant work require discussion in ways that will become increasingly evident as his translated work now enriches new fields of debate.

Much work in Latin America employs the distinction between the modern and the traditional more as an organizing assumption than as a topic for investigation. Yet the distinction is as vexed to me as it is clear to García Canclini. Not unlike notions of the global and the national or the modern and the postmodern, it is evident that both social forces operate in the present and that both are empirically difficult to separate. Indeed, they can more readily be kept separate as approaches to social analysis than as empirical phenomena in the world. To what extent are notions of the modern based on innovations in technology? Is an asphalt road modern? If a traditional peddler is walking on a modern road, does the road become more traditional or the peddler more modern? Both, either, neither?

When García Canclini argues that the processes of production and consumption imply that no realm of cultural production can remain independent of the marketplace (and vice versa), it should follow that entering and leaving modernity deconstructs—indeed, dissolves into hybridity—the very distinction between tradition and modernity that he resolutely maintains. Even if in certain cases commodities can enter and leave modernity with ease and perhaps remain relatively unchanged, human beings usually make such transitions with greater difficulty and emerge transformed to a greater or lesser degree by these late-twentieth-century rites of passage that permeate everyday life.

The term hybridity, as used by García Canclini, never resolves the tension between its conceptual polarities. On the one hand, hybridity can imply a space betwixt and between two zones of purity in a manner that follows biological usage that distinguishes two discrete species and the hybrid pseudo-species that results from their combination. Similarly, the anthropological concept of syncretism asserts, for example, that folk Catholicism occupies a hybrid site midway between the purity of Catholicism and that of indigenous religion. On the other hand, hybridity can be understood as the ongoing condition of all human cultures, which contain no zones of purity because they undergo continuous processes of transculturation (two-way borrowing and lending between cultures). Instead of hybridity versus purity, this view suggests that it is hybridity all the way down (as I would suggest, for example, it is in Paul Gilroy's [1987] work). From this perspective, one must explain how ideological zones of cultural purity, whether of national culture or ethnic resistance, have been constructed. García Canclini never resolves the tension between the two conceptual poles of hybridity, but his analysis favors the former over the latter position.

Debate with *Hybrid Cultures* in the United States will focus not only on the tradition/modernity distinction but also on the notion that the contemporary historical period contains different temporalities (traditional, modern, and postmodern), as if past epochs could persist relatively unchanged into the present. The idea that the present contains distinct historical epochs called traditional and modern seems especially problematic for North American anthropologists who have been critical of ethnographic writing that tacitly equates social with temporal distance.[2] Instead it makes more sense to say that our global contemporaries all equally inhabit a late-twentieth-century world. From this perspective, to speak of certain groups as if they inhabited another century or millennium smacks more of metropolitan prejudice than considered judgment.

Perhaps García Canclini's conception could be interrogated by asking about who determines the designation modern as opposed to traditional. Is the designation made from a metropolitan or a hinterland point of view? Are the two positions congruent or do metropolitan consumers (and intellectuals) disagree with indigenous producers about which social spaces are modern and which are traditional? In either case, what particular characteristics are regarded as modern or traditional? Differently positioned subjects (in this case, metropolitan versus hinterland) could apply the labels traditional and modern to the same objects but for quite different reasons. In my view, the analytical use of the terms traditional and modern should be preceded by an exploration of their usage as folk or vernacular categories. Without such an exploration analytical usage is more likely to reflect the social milieu and biases of metropolitan intellectuals than that of subaltern social realities. In short, the terms tradition and modernity require critical assessment before they can be used in social analysis.

In much the manner that many analysts now recognize that coercive state mechanisms persist alongside an accelerating global political economy, one could argue that García Canclini's analysis potentially opens a set of questions that once appeared to have been left behind by Europe and the United States. His commitment is to study the various, unequal, and contradictory forms of modernity in the broadest possible context. Rather than specialize in distinct social sectors, as different disciplines tend to do, his project aspires to apprehend complex relations within social totalities.

Renato Rosaldo

Notes

1. Commentators making related arguments in the United States would probably have also cited such authors as Anthony Giddens (1979), E. P. Thompson (1966), and Raymond Williams (1977). Williams was especially influenced by Antonio Gramsci.

2. This critique appears with particular clarity in Fabian (1983) and Tsing (1994).

Works Cited

Fabian, Johannes. 1983. *Time and the Other: How Anthropology Makes Its Object.* New York: Columbia University Press.

Giddens, Anthony. 1979. *Central Problems in Social Theory: Action, Structure and Contradiction in Social Analysis.* Berkeley: University of California Press.

Gilroy, Paul. 1987. *There Ain't No Black in the Union Jack: The Cultural Politics of Race and Nation.* London: Unwin Hyman.

Thompson, E. P. 1966. *The Making of the English Working Class.* New York: Vintage Books.

Tsing, Anna. 1994. *In the Realm of the Diamond Queen: Marginality in an Out of the Way Place.* Princeton, N.J.: Princeton University Press.

Williams, Raymond. 1977. *Marxism and Literature.* Oxford: Oxford University Press.

Acknowledgments

This attempt to put into practice intercultural and interdisciplinary studies needed to be nourished in several countries and by working with specialists in a variety of fields. The most constant stimulus was the relationship with graduate students and professors at the National School of Anthropology and History (NSAH) in Mexico, above all those with whom I led the Workshop on Culture and Ideology: Esteban Krotz and Patricia Safa. In studying cultural consumption at the border between Mexico and the United States with Patricia, I understood better the complex relations of family and school in the formation of cultural habits. Alejandro Ordorica, director of the Cultural Program of the Borders, and Luis Garza, director of cultural promotion, supported that research with suggestive reflections and economic resources.

To interpret that vital question in the communication of culture that is the difference between what is offered by institutions and what is received by different groups in the population, the group research conducted with historians of the National Institute of Fine Arts, and with students and professors of the NSAH, was invaluable: Esther Cimet, Martha Dujovne, Julio Gullco, Cristina Mendoza, Eulalia Nieto, Francisco Reyes Palma, Graciela Schmilchuk, Juan Luis Sariego, and Guadalupe Soltero.

To situate these questions in the broader horizon of the crisis of modernity it was necessary to contrast these studies with those of other countries. A grant from the John Simon Guggenheim Memorial Foundation allowed

xx | Acknowledgments

me, in 1982 and 1985, to become familiar with innovations in art, museums, and cultural politics in Europe, to become acquainted with the work of French sociologists (Pierre Bourdieu, Monique and Michel Pinçon) and with Italian anthropologists (Alberto M. Cirese, Amalia Signorelli, Pietro Clemente, and Enzo Segre) who maintain a very open dialogue with what we are doing in Latin America. Another grant, from the French government, and the invitation of the Center for Urban Sociology of Paris to be a visiting researcher there in 1988, gave me access to bibliographic and documentary sources difficult to obtain from Latin American institutions. Also of great help was the use of libraries and the discussion of several chapters of this book while giving seminars at the Universities of Austin and London in 1989. I want to mention several participants: Henry Selby, Richard Adams, Arturo Arias, Pablo Vila, Miguel Barahona, Mari-Carmen Ramírez, Héctor Olea, Patricia Oliart, José A. Llorens, William Rowe, and John Kraniauskas.

In a continent in which cultural information about other countries continues to be obtained mainly through proceedings that are as scarcely modern as personal relations in symposia, citations of those meetings are basic to any list of acknowledgments. I would like to emphasize, above all, what it meant to be able to return several times to Argentina beginning in 1983, and to participate in conferences and seminars that were always filled with the expectations and frustrations generated by the cultural reconstruction and political democratization taking place there. I had the opportunity to present parts of the present text in the symposium "Cultural Politics and the Function of Anthropology" (1987) and the seminar "Popular Culture: An Interdisciplinary Balance" (1988). I remember especially the commentaries of Martha Blache, Rita Ceballos, Aníbal Ford, Cecilia Hidalgo, Elizabeth Jelín, José A. Pérez Gollán, Luis Alberto Romero, and Beatriz Sarlo. Other frequent dialogues with Rosana Guber, Carlos Herrán, Carlos López Iglesias, Mario Margulis, and Juan Carlos Romero contributed to documenting and elaborating my references to Argentina.

Special mention is required of the meetings of the Work Group on Cultural Politics of the Conferencia Latinoamericana de Ciencias Sociales (CLACSO), where we are attempting to combine sociological, anthropological, and communications perspectives in a comparative study of cultural consumption in several Latin American cities. I want to say how much it has helped me to talk with Sergio Miceli about intellectuals and the state in Brazil; to talk with Antonio Augusto Arantes on what it means for an anthropologist to be concerned with historical patrimony as secretary of culture in Campinas; to confront the process of Mexican democratization with the interpretations of Oscar Landi, José Joaquín Brunner, Carlos Catalán, and Giselle Munizaga on Argentina and Chile; to see theater with Luis Peirano in Lima, Buenos Aires, and Bogotá; to know how Jesús Martín Barbero was studying soap operas. Fernando Calderón and Mario dos Santos have been fruitful companions in this and other experiences at CLACSO.

I want to indicate my gratitude to several people for having read parts of this book or for having helped me elaborate some problems: Guillermo Bonfil, Rita Eder, María Teresa Ejea, Juan Flores, Jean Franco, Raymundo Mier, Françoise Perus, Mabel Piccini, Ana María Rosas, and José Manuel Valenzuela; Rafael Roncagliolo and the joint work we carried out in the Institute for Latin America; Eduard Delgado and his Center for Cultural Studies and Resources; the authors and artists cited throughout the text and the many others whom I will not mention so as not to turn this into an unending chapter.

With José I. Casar I was able to clarify some relations between economic and cultural modernization. It also helped that Blanca Salgado proofread this book at the ILET, with very valuable efficacy and patience when one reaches the end of four hundred pages, with many corrections, and is no longer able to look at what one has written. Rogelio Carvajal, Ariel Rosales, and Enrique Mercado helped me not to exacerbate the obscurity of certain problems with that of my writing.

María Eugenia Módena is my closest companion in the task of bringing together both in daily life and in intellectual work what it means to think over the experiences of exile and of taking up roots in new places, the intercultural crosses that form the basis of these reflections.

If this book is dedicated to Teresa and Julián it is for that capacity of children to show us that the cultivated and the popular can be synthesized in mass culture, in the pleasures of consumption that they, without guilt or prejudice, install in daily life as fully justified activities. There is no better way to acknowledge this than by evoking that Christmas in which the National Consumer Institute obsessively repeated, "Give affection, don't buy it," in its anticonsumerist radio and television announcements; Teresa used the word "affection" for the first time, in the wavering language of a four-year-old. "Do you know what it means?" "Yes," she replied quickly, "that you don't have money."

Entrance

What are the strategies for entering and leaving modernity in the nineties?

We phrase the question in this way because in Latin America, where traditions have not yet disappeared and modernity has not completely arrived, we doubt that the primary objective should be to modernize us, as politicians, economists, and the publicity of new technologies proclaim. Other sectors, upon verifying that salaries are returning to the power that they had two decades ago and the products of the most prosperous countries—Argentina, Brazil, Mexico—remained stagnant during the eighties, ask themselves if modernization is not becoming inaccessible for the majority. And it is also possible to think that to be modern no longer makes sense at this time in that the philosophies of postmodernity disqualify the cultural movements that promise utopias and foster progress.

It is not enough to explain these discrepancies as resulting from different conceptions of modernity in the economy, politics, and culture. Along with the theoretical question, political dilemmas enter into play. Is it worth it to promote crafts, restore or reuse historical patrimony, to continue to accept massive numbers of students into the humanities or disciplines tied to obsolete activities of elitist art or to popular culture? Does it make sense—personally and collectively—to invest in extended studies in order to end up in low-paying jobs, repeating tired old techniques and knowledge instead of dedicating oneself to microelectronics or telecommunication?

It is also not sufficient for understanding the difference between the views of modernity to resort to that principle of modern thought according to which ideological differences result from the unequal access that citizens and politicians, workers and entrepreneurs, and artisans and artists have to goods. The first hypothesis of this book is that the *uncertainty* about the meaning and value of modernity derives not only from what separates nations, ethnic groups, and classes, but also from the sociocultural hybrids in which the traditional and the modern are mixed.

How can we understand the presence of indigenous crafts and vanguard art catalogs on the same coffee table? What are painters looking for when, in the same painting, they cite pre-Columbian and colonial images along with those of the culture industry, and then reelaborate them using computers and lasers? The electronic media, which seemed to be dedicated to replacing high art and folklore, now are broadcasting them on a massive scale. Rock and "erudite" music are renewing themselves, even in metropolitan cities, with popular Asian and African American melodies.

This is not a question only of strategies of hegemonic sectors and institutions. We find them also in the economic and symbolic "reconversion" with which migrant farmworkers adapt their knowledge to live in the city, and their crafts to interest urban consumers; when workers reformulate their work culture in the face of new productive technologies without abandoning old beliefs, and popular movements announce their demands on radio and television. Any number of us have records and cassettes that combine classical music and jazz, folklore, tango and salsa, including composers like Piazzola, Caetano Veloso, and Rubén Blades who fused those genres, crossing cultivated and popular traditions in their works.

Just as the abrupt opposition between the traditional and the modern does not work, so the cultured, the popular, and the mass-based are not where we are used to finding them. It is necessary to deconstruct that division into three levels—that layered conception of the world of culture—and verify if its *hybridization*[1] can be understood using the tools of disciplines that are studied separately: art history and literature, which are concerned with the "cultured"; folklore and anthropology, which consecrate the popular; works on communication, which specialize in mass culture. We need nomad social sciences capable of circulating through the staircases that connect those floors—or better yet, social sciences that redesign the floor plans and horizontally connect the levels.

The second hypothesis is that the joint work of these disciplines can generate another way of conceiving of Latin American modernization: rather than like a foreign and dominant force that would operate by substituting the traditional and what is one's own, it would be like the attempts at reno-vation whereby diverse sectors take responsibility for the *multitemporal heterogeneity* of each nation.

A third hypothesis suggests that this transdisciplinary look at hybrid circuits has consequences that overflow the boundaries of cultural research. The explanation of why ethnic cultures and new technologies, and artisanal and industrial forms of production, coexist can illuminate political processes—for example, the reasons why popular as well as elite social layers combine modern democracy with archaic power relations. We find in the study of cultural heterogeneity one of the means to explain the oblique powers that intermingle liberal institutions and authoritarian habits, social democratic movements with paternalistic regimes, and the transactions of some with others.

We have, then, three questions at issue. How to study the hybrid cultures that constitute modernity and give it its specific profile in Latin America. Next, to reunite the partial knowledges of the disciplines that are concerned with culture in order to see if it is possible to develop a more plausible interpretation of the contradictions and the failures of our modernization. And third, what to do—when modernity has become a polemical or suspect project—with this mixture of heterogeneous memory and truncated innovations.

Neither Cultured, nor Popular, nor Massified

In order to analyze the comings and goings of modernity—the crossings of the indigenous and colonial legacies with contemporary art and electronic cultures—perhaps it would be better not to do a book. Nor a movie, nor a soap opera, nor anything that has chapters or proceeds from a beginning to an end. Maybe this text can be used like a city, which one enters via the path of the cultured, of the popular, or of the massified. On the inside, everything gets mixed together; every chapter refers to all the others and thus it is not important to know the approach by which one arrived.

But how do we speak about the modern city, which sometimes is ceasing to be modern and to be a city? What was once a collection of neighborhoods spills beyond what we can relate to since no one can include all the itineraries or all the loosely connected material and symbolic offerings that present themselves. The migrants cross the city in many directions and, precisely at the intersections, install their baroque stands of regional candies and contraband radios, medicinal herbs and videocassettes. How do we study the cleverness with which the city attempts to reconcile everything that arrives and proliferates, and tries to contain all the disorder— the peasant's exchange with the transnational corporation, the traffic jams in front of protest demonstrations, the expansion of consumption together with the demands of the unemployed, the duels between commodities and behaviors from all sides?

The social sciences contribute to this difficulty with their different levels of observation. The anthropologist arrives in the city by foot, the sociologist by car and via the main highway, the communications specialist by plane. Each registers what he or she can and constructs a distinct and, therefore, partial vision. There is a fourth perspective, that of the historian, which is acquired not by entering but rather by leaving the city, moving from its old center toward the contemporary margins. But the current center of the city is no longer in the past.

Art history, literature, and scientific knowledge have identified repertoires of contents that we must be familiar with in order to be *cultured* in the modern world. On the other hand, anthropology and folklore, as well as political populisms, by vindicating traditional knowledge and practices, constituted the universe of the *popular*. The cultural industries engendered a third system of *massified* messages that was attended to by new specialists: students of communications and semioticians.[2]

Both traditionalists and modernizers tried to construct pure objects. The former imagined "authentic" national and popular cultures, and sought to preserve them in the face of industrialization, urban massification, and foreign influences. The modernizers conceived of an art for art's sake, knowledge for knowledge's sake, without territorial boundaries, and entrusted their fantasies of progress to autonomous experimentation and innovation. The differences between these camps served to organize goods and institutions. Handicrafts went to fairs and popular competitions, works of art to museums and biennial expositions.

From nineteenth-century liberalism to developmentalism, modernizing ideologies accentuated this Manichaean compartmentalization by imagining that modernization would end with traditional forms of production, beliefs, and goods. Myths would be replaced by scientific knowledge, handicrafts by the expansion of industry, books by audiovisual means of communication.

Today there exists a more complex view of the relations between tradition and modernity. The cultured, in the traditional sense, is not eliminated by the industrialization of symbolic goods. More books and larger editions are published now than in any previous period. There are works that are erudite and massified at the same time, such as *The Name of the Rose,* a topic of hermeneutic debates at conferences and also a best-seller: by the end of 1986, before the release of the film based on this novel, it had sold five million copies in twenty-five languages. The stories of García Márquez and Vargas Llosa reach a greater audience than the film versions of their works.

From the popular side, we should be less concerned about its becoming extinct than about its being transformed. Never have there been so many artisans, or popular musicians, or such a distribution of folklore, because their products maintain traditional functions (provide work for indigenous people and peasants) and develop other modern ones: they attract tourists and urban consumers who find signs of distinction in folkloric goods and personalized references that industrialized goods do not offer.

Modernization diminishes the role of the cultured and the popular, in the traditional sense, in the symbolic market as a whole, but it does not suppress them. It relocates art and folklore, academic knowledge and industrialized culture, under relatively similar conditions. The work of the artist and that of the artisan approximate each other when each one feels that the specific symbolic order in which it is nourished is redefined by the logic of the market. Less and less can they remove themselves from modern information and iconography, from the disenchantment of their self-centered worlds and from the reenchantment that is favored by the spectacularization of the media. What disappears is not so much the goods formerly known as cultured or popular, but rather the claim of some to be self-sufficient universes and that the works produced in each field are uniquely the "expression" of their creators.

It is logical that there would also be a confluence among the disciplines that studied those universes. The art historian who used to write the catalog of an exposition would situate the artist or the tendency in an articulated succession of searches, a certain "advance" with respect to what had been done in that field. The folklorist and the anthropologist would place the handicrafts within an autonomous mythic matrix or sociocultural system that gave those objects precise meanings. Today those operations almost always present themselves to us as cultural constructions multiply conditioned by actors who transcend the artistic and the symbolic.

What is art is not only an aesthetic question; we have to take into account how it responds at the intersection of what is done by journalists and critics, historians and museum writers, art dealers, collectors and speculators. In similar fashion, the popular is not defined by an a priori essence but by unstable, diverse strategies with which the subaltern sectors themselves construct their positions, and also by the way the folklorist and the anthropologist stage popular culture for the museum or the academy, the sociologists and the politicians for the political parties, the communications specialists for the media.

Modernity after Postmodernity

These changes in the symbolic markets in part radicalize the modern project and in a certain way lead to a postmodern situation, understood as a rupture with what came before. The recent bibliography on this double movement helps in rethinking various Latin American debates—above all, the thesis that the disagreements between cultural modernism and social modernization make a defective version of the modernity canonized by the metropolis.[3] Or the inverse: that for being the land of pastiche and bricolage, where many periods and aesthetics are cited, we have had the pride of being postmodern for centuries, and in a unique way. Neither the "paradigm" of imitation, nor that of originality, nor the "theory" that attributes everything to dependency, nor the one that lazily wants to explain us by the "marvelously real" or a Latin American surrealism, are able to account for our hybrid cultures.

It is a question of seeing how, within the crisis of Western modernity—of which Latin America is a part—the relations among tradition, cultural modernism, and socioeconomic modernization are transformed. For that it is necessary to go beyond the philosophical speculation and aesthetic intuitionism that dominate the postmodern bibliography. The scarcity of empirical studies on the place of culture in so-called postmodern processes has resulted in a relapse into distortions of premodern thought: constructing ideal positions without any real difference.

A primary task is to take into account the contrasting conceptions of modernity. While postmodern currents are hegemonic in many countries in art, architecture, and philosophy, in Latin American economics and politics modernizing objectives prevail. The latest electoral campaigns and the political messages that accompany adjustment and reconversion plans consider it a priority for our countries to incorporate technological advances, modernize the economy, and overcome informal alliances in the structures of power, corruption, and other premodern defects.

The daily weight of these "deficiencies" makes the most frequent attitude toward postmodern debates in Latin America one of ironic underestimation. Why should we go around worrying about postmodernity if, on our continent, all modern advances have neither arrived nor reached everyone? We have not had a solid industrialization, nor an extended technologizing of agricultural production, nor a sociopolitical ordering based on the formal and material rationality that—as we read in thinkers ranging from Kant to Weber—has become the common sense of the West, the model of public space in which citizens would live together democratically and participate in the evolution of society. Neither evolutionist progressivism nor democratic rationalism has been a popular cause with us.

"How do you talk about postmodernity in the country of the Shining Path insurgency, which has so much of the premodern?" the Peruvian sociologist and presidential candidate, Henry Pease García, recently asked (166). The contradictions may be different in other countries, but the general opinion exists that although liberalism and its regime of parliamentary representativeness reached our constitutions, we lack a modern social cohesion and political culture sufficiently established to allow our societies to be governable. The political bosses continue to handle political decisions on the basis of informal alliances and wild relations of force. The positivist philosophers, and later the social scientists, modernized university life, as Octavio Paz says, but political bossism, religiosity, and media manipulation guide the thinking of the masses. The elites cultivate vanguard poetry and art, while most of the population is illiterate (1979, 64).

Modernity, then, is seen as a mask. A simulacrum conjured up by the elites and the state apparatuses, above all those concerned with art and culture, but which for that very reason makes them unrepresentative and unrealistic. The liberal oligarchies of the late nineteenth and early twentieth centuries acted as if they constituted states, but they only ordered some areas of society in order to promote a subordinate and inconsistent development; they acted as if they formed national cultures, and they barely constructed elite cultures, leaving out enormous indigenous and peasant populations, who manifest their exclusion in a thousand revolts and in the migration that is bringing "upheaval" to the cities. Populisms acted as though they were incorporating those excluded sectors, but their distributionist policies in the economy and culture, made without structural changes, were reversed a few years later or were diluted into demagogic clientelisms.

Why continue acting as if we have a state, asks the writer José Ignacio Cabrujas when the Presidential Commission for the Reform of the Venezuelan State consults him, if the state "is a scheme of dissimulations"? Venezuela, he explains, went on creating itself like an encampment, inhabited first by wandering tribes and later by Spaniards who used it as a stopover in the search for promised gold, on the way to Potosí or El Dorado. With progress, the encampment was converted into a gigantic hotel in which the residents feel like guests and the state a manager "in permanent failure when it comes to guaranteeing the comfort of the guests":

> To live, that is to say, to assume life, to pretend that my actions are translated into something, to move in a historical time toward an objective, is something that clashes with the rules of the hotel, given that when I stay in a hotel I don't try to transform its accommodations, nor to improve them, nor to adapt them to my wishes. I simply use them.

At some moment it was thought necessary to have a state capable of administrating it, a set of institutions and laws to guarantee a minimum of order, "certain elegant principles, more handsome than elegant, through which we were going to belong to the civilized world":

> It would have been more just to invent those rules that we always read upon entering a hotel room, almost always found on the door. "How you should live here," "at what time should you check out," "please do not eat in the rooms," "dogs are expressly forbidden entry into the rooms," etc., etc., that is, a pragmatic set of rules without any princely pretension. "This is your hotel; enjoy it and try to cause as little trouble as possible" could be the most sincere form of wording for the first paragraph of the National Constitution. (Cabrujas 1987)[4]

Can these disagreements between Latin American states, their corresponding societies, and their political culture be overcome? Before responding, we have to ask if the question is well stated. For these authors, and for the greater part of the Latin American bibliography, modernity continues to have necessary connections—in the way Max Weber thought about it—with the disenchantment of the world, with the experimental sciences and, above all, with a rationalist organization of society that culminates in efficient productive enterprises and well-organized state apparatuses. These characteristics are not the only ones that define modernity, neither in postmodern authors like Lyotard or Deleuze nor in the reinterpretations of those who continue to adhere to the modern project: among others, Habermas in the text cited earlier, Perry Anderson (1984), and Fredric Jameson (1989).

Our book seeks to connect this revision of the theory of modernity with the transformations that have occurred since the eighties in Latin America—for example, the changes in what was understood as economic and political modernization. Now the proposals for industrialization, import substitution, and the strengthening of independent national states are scorned as antiquated ideas, blamed for having delayed the access of Latin American societies to modernity. Although the requirement that production be efficient and resources be distributed where they yield the most remains part of a modern policy, it has become a "premodern ingenuousness" that a state protect its own country's production or, worse, reflect popular interests that tend to be viewed as contradictory to technological progress. Certainly the debate is open and we have reasons to doubt that the chronic inefficiency of our states and their developmentalist and protectionist policies will be resolved by opening up everything to international competition.[5]

What was understood by modernity also changed in society and culture. We abandoned the evolutionism that expected the solution of social problems through the simple secularization of practices: we have to pass, it was said in the sixties and seventies, from prescriptive to elective behaviors, from the inertia of rural or inherited customs to conduct proper to urban societies, where the objectives and collective organization are set according to scientific and technological rationality. Today we conceive of Latin America as a more complex articulation of traditions and modernities (diverse and unequal), a heterogeneous continent consisting of countries in each of which coexist multiple logics of development. In order to rethink this heterogeneity, the antievolutionist reflection of postmodernism is useful, and more radical than anything that preceded it. Its critique of the all-encompassing accounts of history can serve to detect the fundamentalist pretensions of traditionalism, ethnicism, and nationalism, and to understand the authoritarian derivations of liberalism and socialism.

Along this line, we conceive of postmodernity not as a stage or tendency that replaces the modern world, but rather as a way of problematizing the equivocal links that the latter has formed with the traditions it tried to exclude or overcome in constituting itself. The postmodern relativization of all fundamentalism or evolutionism facilitates revision of the separation between the cultured, the popular, and the mass-based, upon which modernity still attempts to base itself, and elaboration of a more open way of thinking that includes the interactions and integrations among levels, genres, and forms of collective sensibility.

It is inappropriate to treat these questions in the form of a book that progresses from a beginning to an end. I prefer the ductility of the essay, which allows one to move on various levels. As Clifford Geertz wrote, the essay makes it possible to explore in different directions, to correct the itinerary if something does not work, without the need to "defend oneself through a hundred pages of previous exposition, as in a monograph or a treatise."[6] But the scientific essay differs from the literary or philosophical essay in that it

bases itself, as in this case, on empirical investigations, in subjecting interpretations to a controlled handling of the data as much as possible.

I also tried to avoid the simple accumulation of separate essays that would
reproduce the compartmentalization and parallelism that exists among disciplines and territories. In searching for a structure for the book, in any case,
I intend to rework the conceptualization of modernity in various disciplines
through multifocal and complementary approaches.

The first chapter and, in part, the last two take up reflections on modernity and postmodernity in the metropolitan countries with the goal of examining the contradictions between the utopias of autonomous creation in
culture and the industrialization of the symbolic markets. In the second
chapter, a reinterpretation of the links between modernism and modernization is proposed based on recent historical and sociological research on
Latin American cultures. The third chapter analyzes how artists, middlemen, and the public behave in the face of two basic options of modernity:
innovate or democratize. The fourth, fifth, and sixth chapters study some
strategies of modern institutions and actors in utilizing historical patrimony
and popular traditions: how they are presented by museums and schools, by
folkloric and anthropological studies, by the sociology of culture, and by political populisms. Finally, we examine the hybrid cultures generated or promoted by the new communications technologies, by the reordering of the
public and the private in the urban space, and by the deterritorialization of
symbolic processes.

Bringing together such heterogeneous spaces allows us to see what can
happen to disciplines that conventionally engage only themselves if they accept the challenges of their neighbors. Is it possible to know something more
or different about the strategies of modern culture when anthropology
studies the rituals whereby art separates itself from other practices and economic analysis shows the limits under which the market erodes that pretension? Historical patrimony and traditional cultures reveal their contemporary functions when, from the perspective of political sociology, an inquiry
is made into how a dubious or wounded power dramatizes and celebrates
the past in order to reaffirm itself in the present. The transnationalization of
culture brought about by communications technologies, their reach, and
their efficacy are better appreciated as part of the recomposition of urban
cultures, along with the migrations and tourism that soften national borders
and redefine the concepts of nation, people, and identity.

Is it necessary to clarify that this gaze which is multiplied in so many fragments and hybrids does not follow the plot of a unique order that discipli-

nary separations would have covered up? Convinced that the Romantic integrations of nationalisms are as precarious and dangerous as the neoclassical integrations of Hegelian rationalism or of closed Marxisms, we refuse to admit nevertheless that the concern for social totality lacks meaning. One may forget about totality when one is interested only in the differences among people, not when one is also concerned with inequality.

We are aware that in this time of postmodern dissemination and democratizing decentralization the most concentrated forms of the accumulation of power and transnational centralization of culture that humanity has ever known are also growing. The study of the heterogeneous and hybrid cultural bases of that power can bring us to a somewhat better understanding of the oblique pathways, full of transactions, in which those forces come into play. It allows us to study the diverse meanings of modernity not only as simple divergencies among currents but also as a manifestation of unresolved conflicts.

Notes

1. Occasional mention will be made of the terms *syncretism, mestizaje,* and others used to designate processes of *hybridization.* I prefer this last term because it includes diverse intercultural mixtures—not only the racial ones to which *mestizaje* tends to be limited—and because it permits the inclusion of the modern forms of hybridization better than does "syncretism," a term that almost always refers to religious fusions or traditional symbolic movements.

2. The notions of *cultured, popular,* and *massified* will be discussed conceptually and historically in various chapters. The most uncomfortable is the first: Is it preferable to speak of cultured, elitist, erudite, or hegemonic? These terms overlap each other to some extent and none is satisfactory. Erudite is the most vulnerable because it defines this modality of organizing culture by the vastness of the accumulated knowledge while it obscures that which has to do with a type of knowledge: are not the healer and the artisan also erudite? We will use the notions of elite and hegemony to indicate the social position that confers upon the cultured its privileges, but we will employ the latter term more frequently because it is more commonly used in Spanish.

3. We adopt with a certain flexibility the distinction made by various authors, from Jürgen Habermas to Marshall Berman, between *modernity* as historical stage, *modernization* as socioeconomic process that tries to construct modernity, and *modernisms,* or the cultural projects that renew symbolic practices with an experimental or critical sense (Habermas 1987, Berman).

4. English translations of all citations are the translators' own, unless otherwise credited. Existing translations have been used when available.—*Trans.*

5. For a development of this critique, see Casar 1988.

6. See the argumentation in favor of the essay for the exposition of social knowledge in the Introduction to Geertz 1983.

1 | From Utopias to the Market

What does it mean to be modern? It is possible to condense the current interpretations by saying that four basic movements constitute modernity: an emancipating project, an expansive project, a renovating project, and a democratizing project.

By the *emancipating* project we understand the secularization of cultural fields, the self-expressive and self-regulated production of symbolic practices, and their development in autonomous markets. The rationalization of social life and increasing individualism form part of this emancipating project, especially in big cities.

We call the *expansive* project the tendency of modernity that seeks to extend the knowledge and possession of nature, and the production, circulation, and consumption of goods. In capitalism, this expansion is motivated chiefly by the increasing of profits; but in a broader sense it is manifested in the promotion of scientific discoveries and industrial development.

The *renovating* project is comprised of two aspects, which are frequently complementary: on the one hand, the pursuit of constant improvement and innovation proper to a relation to nature and society that is liberated from all sacred prescription over how the world must be; on the other hand, the need to continually reformulate the signs of distinction that mass consumption wears away.

We call the *democratizing* project that movement of modernity that trusts in education, the diffusion of art, and specialized knowledge to achieve rational and moral evolution. This extends from the Enlightenment to UNESCO, from positivism to education programs or the popularization of science and culture initiated by liberal and socialist governments and alternative and independent groups.

Emancipated Imagination?

As these four projects develop, they enter into conflict. As a first entry into this contradictory development, we will analyze one of the most potent and constant utopias in modern culture, from Galileo to contemporary universities, from the artists of the Renaissance period to the vanguards: to construct spaces in which knowledge and creation can unfold autonomously. However, economic, political, and technological modernization—born as part of that process of secularization and independence—proceeded to form an all-encompassing social fabric, which subordinates the renovating and experimental forces of symbolic production.

To capture the meaning of this contradiction, I see no more favorable place than the disjuncture between modern aesthetics and the socioeconomic dynamic of artistic development. While theorists and historians exalt the autonomy of art, the practices of the market and of mass communication—sometimes including museums—foment the dependence of artistic goods upon non-aesthetic processes.

Let us begin with three authors—Jürgen Habermas, Pierre Bourdieu, and Howard S. Becker—who have studied cultural autonomy as a defining component of modernity in their respective countries: Germany, France, and the United States. Despite diverse national histories and theoretical differences, they develop complementary analyses of the secularizing meaning of the formation of fields (Bourdieu) or worlds (Becker) of art. They find the distinctive indicator of the modern development of art to be the self-expressive and self-regulated production of symbolic practices.

Habermas takes up Max Weber's affirmation that the modern is constituted when culture becomes independent of substantive reason consecrated by religion and metaphysics, and consists of three autonomous spheres: science, morality, and art. Each one is organized in a regime structured by its specific problem—knowledge, justice, taste—and governed by appropriate instances of valorization, that is, truth, normative rectitude, authenticity, and beauty. The autonomy of each dominion is gradually institutionalized, and generates specialized professionals who become expert authorities in their area. This specialization accentuates the distance between the culture of the professional and that of the public, between scientific or artistic fields and everyday life. Nevertheless, Enlightenment philosophers, the protagonists of this enterprise, proposed at the same time to extend specialized knowledge in order to enrich daily life and rationally organize society. The growth of science and art, liberated from religious tutelage, would help to control natural forces, broaden the understanding of the world, progress morally, and make social institutions and relations more just.

The extreme contemporaneous differentiation between hegemonic morality, science, and art, and the disconnection of all three from everyday life, discredited the Enlightenment utopia. There has never been a lack of attempts to join scientific knowledge with ordinary practices, art with life, the great ethical doctrines with common conduct, but the results of these movements have been poor, according to Habermas. Is modernity, then, a lost cause or an inconclusive project? With respect to art, he maintains that we must take up and deepen the modern project of autonomous experimentation so that its renovating power does not dry up. At the same time, he suggests that we find other ways of inserting specialized culture into everyday praxis so that the latter does not become impoverished through the repetition of traditions. Perhaps it is possible to achieve this with new policies of reception and appropriation of professional knowledge, democratizing social initiative in such a way that people become "capable of developing institutions of their own that can set limits on the internal dynamic and the imperatives of an almost autonomous economic system and its administrative complements" (1983, 13).

The Habermasian defense of the modern project has received criticism, such as that of Andreas Huyssen, who objects that it facilely purifies modernity of its nihilistic and anarchistic impulses. He attributes this omission to the philosopher's aim of rescuing the emancipatory potential of the Enlightenment in the face of the cynical tendency that confuses reason with domination in France and Germany at the beginning of the 1980s, when Habermas read the lecture just cited (1983) in accepting the Adorno Prize (Huyssen 1987). In both countries, artists abandoned the political commitments of the previous decade, replacing documentary experiments in narrative and theater with autobiographies, and political theory and the social sciences with mythical and esoteric revelations. While for the French modernity would be more than anything an aesthetic question, whose source would be Nietzsche and Mallarmé, and for many young Germans getting rid of rationalism was equivalent to liberating themselves from

domination, Habermas attempts to recover the liberating version of rationalism that promoted the Enlightenment.

His Enlightenment reading of modernity would seem to be conditioned,
we would add, by two risks Habermas detected in modern oscillations. In
examining Marcuse and Benjamin, he noted that overcoming the autonomy
of art for political purposes could be harmful, as happened in the fascist critique of modern art and its reorganization in the service of a repressive mass
aesthetic (1985, 131ff.); in his recent critique of the postmodernists he shows
that the apparently depoliticized aestheticism of recent generations has
tacit, and sometimes explicit, alliances with neoconservative regression.[1] To
refute them, Habermas digs deeply into that selective reading of modernity
that he began in *Knowledge and Human Interest* with the goal of restricting
the Enlightenment legacy to its emancipating vocation. Thus he places outside of the modern project what it has of the oppressor and makes it difficult
to think what it means to say that modernity brings with it both rationality
and what threatens rationality.

Habermas's trajectory exemplifies how thought about modernity is constructed in dialogue with premodern and postmodern authors, according to
the positions those interpreters adopt in the artistic and intellectual field.
Would it not be consistent with the recognition Habermas himself makes
about the insertion of theory into social and intellectual *practices* to continue the philosophical reflection with empirical investigations?

Two sociologists, Bourdieu and Becker, reveal that modern culture is distinguished from all previous periods in that it constitutes itself in an autonomous space within the social structure. Neither one deals extensively
with the question of modernity, but in fact their studies seek to explain the
dynamic of culture in secularized societies in which an advanced technical
and social division of labor exists and institutions are organized according
to a liberal model.

For Bourdieu, in the sixteenth and seventeenth centuries a distinct period
in the history of culture was initiated as it integrated itself with relative independence into the artistic and scientific fields. As museums and galleries
are being created, works of art are valued without the coercion previously
imposed by religious powers in commissioning them for churches or by political powers in commissioning them for palaces. In those "specific instances of selection and consecration," artists no longer compete for theological approval or the complicity of the courtesans, but rather for "cultural
legitimacy" (1967, 135).[2] The literary salons and the publishing houses will reorganize literary practice in the same sense, beginning in the nineteenth

century. Each artistic field—the same as scientists with the development of lay universities—becomes a space formed by intrinsic symbolic capitals.

The independence won by the artistic field justifies the methodological autonomy of its study. Unlike most of the sociology of art and literature, which deduces the meaning of works from the mode of production or from the author's class origin, Bourdieu considers each cultural field to be guided by its own laws. What the author does is conditioned not so much by the global structure of society as by the system of relations established by the agents linked to the production and circulation of the works. The sociological investigation of art must examine how the cultural capital of each respective field has been constituted and how the struggle for its appropriation is carried out. Those who possess capital and those who aspire to possess it unleash battles that are essential for understanding the meaning of what is produced; but that competition involves a lot of complicity, and through it the belief in the autonomy of the field is also affirmed. In modern societies, when some power outside the field—the church or the government—wants to intervene in the internal dynamics of artistic work by means of censorship, artists suspend their confrontations in order to form an alliance in defense of "freedom of expression."

How can the capitalist tendency to expand the market by increasing the number of consumers be reconciled with this tendency to form specialized audiences in restricted spheres? Is not the multiplication of products for the purpose of increasing profits contradictory to the promotion of unique works in modern aesthetics? Bourdieu gives a partial answer to this question. He observes that the formation of specific fields of taste and knowledge, in which certain goods are valued for their scarcity and limited to exclusive consumers, serves to construct and renew the distinction of the elites. In modern democratic societies, where there is no blood superiority or titles of nobility, consumption becomes a fundamental area for establishing and communicating differences. In the face of the relative democratization produced by mass access to products, the bourgeoisie needs spheres that are separated from the urgencies of practical life in which objects are ordered—as in museums—for their stylistic affinities and not for their utility.

To appreciate a work of modern art one has to know the history of the field in which the work was produced, have sufficient competence to distinguish, by its formal characteristics, a Renaissance landscape from an Impressionist or a hyperrealist one. This "aesthetic disposition," which is acquired through belonging to a social class—that is, by possessing economic and educational resources that are also scarce—appears as a "gift," not as something one has but rather as something that one is. In this way, the separation of the field of art serves the bourgeoisie by pretending that its privileges are justified by something more than just economic accumulation. The difference between form and function—indispensable for modern art to be able to advance in the experimentation of language and the renewal of taste—is duplicated in social life in a difference between goods (efficient for material reproduction) and signs (useful for organizing symbolic distinction). Modern societies simultaneously need *exposure*—to broaden the market and the consumption of goods in order to increase the rate of profit—and *distinction*—which, in order to confront the massifying effects of exposure, recreates the signs that differentiate the hegemonic sectors.

Bourdieu's work, little attracted by the culture industry, does not help us to understand what happens when even the signs and spaces of the elites are massified and mixed with those of the popular. We have to start with Bourdieu but go beyond him in order to explain how the dialectic between exposure and distinction is reorganized when museums receive millions of visitors and classic or vanguard literary works are sold in supermarkets, or made into videos.

But first let us complete the analysis of the autonomy of the artistic field by looking at Howard S. Becker. As a musician, as well as a social scientist, he is particularly sensitive to the collective and cooperative character of artistic production. For that reason his sociology of art combines an affirmation of the creative autonomy of art with a subtle recognition of the social ties that condition it. Unlike literature and the visual arts, in which it was easier to construct the illusion of the creator as a solitary genius whose work owed nothing to anyone beyond himself or herself, a concert performance by an orchestra requires the collaboration of a large number of people. It also implies that the instruments have been made and maintained, that the musicians learned to play them in schools, that the concert was publicized, and that there is an audience educated by a musical history and with the available assets and time to attend and understand. In truth, all art presumes the manufacture of the necessary physical artifacts, the creation of a shared conventional language, the training of specialists and spectators in the use of that language, and the creation, experimentation, or mix of those elements to construct particular works.

It could be argued that in this constellation of tasks there are some exceptional ones that can only be carried out by especially gifted individuals. But the history of art is full of examples in which it is difficult to establish such a demarcation: sculptors and muralists who have part of their work done by students or assistants; almost all jazz, in which composition is less important than interpretation and improvisation; works like those of John Cage and Stockhausen, which leave parts for the person who plays the work to create; Duchamp when he puts a mustache on the *Mona Lisa* and makes Leonardo da Vinci into "support personnel." Since the most advanced technologies intervene creatively in the inspection and reproduction of art, the line between producers and collaborators becomes less clear: a sound technician creates montages of instruments recorded in different places, manipulates and electronically hierarchizes sounds produced by musicians of varying quality. Although Becker maintains that the artist can be defined as "the person who performs the central activity without which the work would not be art" (24-25), he dedicates most of his work to examining how the meaning of artistic acts is constructed in a relatively autonomous "art world"—not by the singularity of exceptional creators but rather by the agreements generated among many participants.

At times "support groups" (interpreters, actors, editors, photographers) develop their own interests and taste patterns such that they become protagonists in the creation and transmission of the works. As a result, what happens in the art world is a product of cooperation, but also of competition. Competition tends to have economic limits but is organized mainly within the "art world" according to the degree of adhesion to or transgression of the conventions that regulate the practice. These *conventions* (for example, the number of sounds that should be used as tonal resources, the appropriate instruments for playing them, and the ways they may be combined) are homologous to what sociology and anthropology have studied as norms or customs, and approximate what Bourdieu calls cultural capital.

Shared and respected by musicians, conventions make it possible for an orchestra to function coherently and to communicate with the public. The socioaesthetic system that guides the artistic world imposes heavy restrictions upon the "creators" and reduces to a minimum claims to be an individual without dependencies. However, two features exist that differentiate this conditioning in modern societies. One is that the restrictions agreed upon within the artistic world do not derive from theological or political prescriptions. The second is that in recent centuries there has been an increasing opening up of possibilities for choosing nonconventional ways of producing, interpreting, and communicating art, for which reason we find a greater diversity of trends now than in the past.

This opening and plurality is peculiar to the modern epoch, in which economic and political liberties and the greater diffusion of artistic techniques, according to Becker, allow many persons to act, jointly or separately, to produce a variety of recurring acts. Liberal social organization (although Becker does not call it that) gave the artistic world its autonomy and is the basis of the modern way of making art: with a conditioned autonomy. At the same time, the artistic world continues to have an interdependent relationship with society, as is seen when modification of artistic conventions has repercussions in social organization. Changing the rules of art is not only an aesthetic problem: it questions the structures with which the members of the artistic world are used to relating to one another, and also the customs and beliefs of the receivers. A sculptor who decides to make works out of earth, in the open air, works that are not collectible, is challenging those who work in museums, artists who aspire to display their work in them, and spectators who see those institutions as supreme realms of the spirit.

While they establish shared forms of cooperation and comprehension, the conventions that make it possible for art to be a social act also differentiate those who are operating in already consecrated modes of making art from those who find the artistic in breaking from what is agreed upon. In modern societies, this divergence produces two forms of integration and discrimination with respect to the audience. On the one hand, the artistic work forms a "world" of its own around the knowledge and conventions fixed by opposition to common knowledge, which is judged unworthy to serve as the basis of a work of art. The greater or lesser competition in the apprehension of those specialized meanings distinguishes the "assiduous and informed" from the "occasional" audience, and therefore the audience that can or cannot "fully collaborate" with the artists in the common enterprise of staging and reception that gives life to a work (71).

On the other hand, innovators erode this complicity between a certain development of art and certain audiences: at times, to create unexpected conventions that increase the distance between themselves and the untrained sectors of the audience; in other cases—Becker gives many examples, from Rabelais to Philip Glass—incorporating into the conventional language of the artistic world vulgar ways of representing the real. In the midst of these tensions are constituted the complex and not at all schematic relations between the hegemonic and the subaltern, the included and the excluded. This is one of the causes for which modernity implies processes of segregation as well as of hybridization between the various social sectors and their symbolic systems.

Becker's anthropological and relativist perspective, which defines the artistic not according to a priori aesthetic values but by identifying groups of persons who cooperate in producing goods that at least they call art, opens the way for nonethnocentric and nonsociocentric analyses of the fields in which these activities are practiced. Their dedication to the work and grouping processes, more than the works themselves, displaces the question of aesthetic definitions—which never agree upon the repertory of objects that merit the name of art—onto the social characterization of the modes of production and interaction of artistic groups. It also makes it possible to relate them comparatively among themselves and to other classes of producers. As Becker says, in modernity the art worlds are multiple and are not separated sharply among themselves nor from the rest of social life; each one shares with other fields the management of personnel, of economic and intellectual resources, and of mechanisms for distributing goods and audiences.

It is curious that his examination of the *internal* structures of the artistic world reveals centrifugal connections with society that are paid little attention by Bourdieu's *external* sociological analysis of the autonomy of cultural fields. On the contrary, Becker's work is less solid when it deals with the conflicts between members of the art world and between distinct worlds, since for him the disputes—between artists and support personnel, for example—are easily resolved through cooperation and the desire to bring artistic labor to culmination in the work, or they remain a secondary tension with respect to the mechanisms of collaboration that create solidarity among members of the artistic world. For Bourdieu, each cultural field is essentially a space of struggle for the appropriation of symbolic capital, and the trends (conservative or heretical) are organized as a function of the positions they have with respect to that capital (as either possessors or pretenders). The place that cultural capital and competition for its appropriation occupy in Bourdieu is filled in Becker's work by the conventions and accords that permit the contenders to continue their work: "Conventions represent the continuous adjustment of the parts that cooperate with respect to the changing conditions in which they are put into practice" (58).

The placement of artistic practices in the processes of social production and reproduction, of legitimation and distinction, made it possible for Bourdieu to interpret diverse practices as part of a symbolic struggle between classes and class fractions. He also studied the artistic manifestations that Becker calls "naive" and "popular" as an expression of the middle and dominated sectors that are less integrated into the "legitimate," autonomous culture of the elites.

In discussing the popular sectors, Bourdieu maintains that they are guided by "a pragmatic and functionalist aesthetic" imposed "by an economic necessity that condemns 'simple' and 'modest' people to 'simple' and 'modest' tastes" (1979, 441); popular taste is opposed to the bourgeois and modern by its incapacity to free certain activities of their practical meaning and give them a different autonomous aesthetic meaning. For that reason, popular practices are still defined, and devalued, by the same subaltern sectors, by always referring to them in terms of the dominant aesthetic, which is that of those who supposedly know what true art is, namely, that which can be admired in accord with the freedom and disinterestedness of "sublime tastes."

Bourdieu relates diverse aesthetic and artistic practices in a scheme stratified by the unequal appropriations of cultural capital. Although this gives an explanatory power in relation to the global society that Becker does not achieve, it is possible to wonder if the acts happen in this way today. Bourdieu ignores the development of popular art itself, its capacity to manifest autonomous nonutilitarian forms of beauty, as we will see in a later chapter analyzing popular crafts and fiestas. He also does not examine the restructuring of the classic forms of the cultured (the fine arts) and of popular goods upon being relocated within the media logic established by the culture industry.

The Vanguards Are Gone, the Rituals of Innovation Remain

The vanguards took the search for autonomy in art to extremes, sometimes trying to combine it with other movements of modernity—especially renovation and democratization. Its ruptures, its conflictive relations with social and political movements, its collective and personal failures can be read as exasperated manifestations of the contradictions among modern projects.

Although today they are seen as the paradigmatic form of modernity, some vanguards were born as attempts to stop being cultured and modern. Various artists and writers of the nineteenth and twentieth centuries rejected the cultural patrimony of the West and what modernity was doing with it. They were little interested in the advances of bourgeois rationality and well-being; industrial and urban development seemed dehumanizing to them. The most radical of them converted this rejection into exile. Rimbaud went to Africa and Gauguin to Tahiti to escape from their "criminal" society "governed by gold"; Nolde went to the South Seas and Japan; Segall to Brazil. Those who stayed, like Baudelaire, attacked the "mechanical degradation" of urban life.

There were, of course, those who enjoyed the autonomy of art and were excited by individual and experimental freedom. For some, the lack of social commitment became the symptom of an aesthetic life. Théophile Gautier used to say that "any artist who proposes something other than the beautiful is not, in our eyes, an artist," and "Nothing is more beautiful than that which has no use at all."

But in many trends aesthetic freedom is joined with ethical responsibility. Beyond Dadaist nihilism arose surrealism's hope of uniting artistic and social revolution. The Bauhaus school tried to overturn formal experimentation in favor of a new industrial and urban design, and the advances of the vanguards in everyday culture; it sought to create a "community of artifices without class differentiation that raises an arrogant barrier between the artisan and the artist," in which the opposition between the cold rationalism of technological development and the creativity of art would be transcended. The constructivists pursued all this, but with better opportunities for inserting themselves into the transformations of postrevolutionary Russia: Tatlin and Malevitch were put in charge of applying their innovations in monuments, posters, and other forms of public art; Arvatov, Rodchenko, and many other artists went into industries in order to reformulate design, promoted substantial changes in art schools with the goal of developing in the students "an industrial attitude toward form" and making them "design engineers" that would be useful in socialist planning (Arvatov). Everyone thought that it was possible to deepen the autonomy of art and at the same time reinscribe it in life, to generalize cultured experiences and convert them into collective acts.

We all know how things ended up. Surrealism was dispersed and diluted in a dizzying fit of internal struggles and excommunications. Bauhaus was repressed by Nazism, but before the catastrophe it was already beginning to manifest its naive fusion of technological rationalism and artistic intuition, structural difficulties that existed for inserting its functional renovation of urban production in the midst of capitalist property relations and of the real estate speculation left intact by the Weimar Republic. Constructivism was able to influence the modernization and socialization promoted in the first decade of the Soviet Revolution, but it finally collapsed beneath the repressive bureaucratization of Stalinism and was replaced by realist painters who restored the iconographic traditions of premodern Russia and adapted them to official portraiture.

The frustration of these vanguards was produced in part by the collapse of the social conditions that encouraged their birth. We also know that their experiences were prolonged in the history of art and in social history as a utopian reserve in which later movements, especially in the 1960s, found a stimulus for taking up the emancipating, renovating, and democratic projects of modernity. But the current situation of art and its social insertion exhibit a languid legacy of those attempts of the twenties and the sixties to convert the innovations of the vanguards into a source of collective creativity.

There is an unending bibliography of works that examine the social and aesthetic reasons for this persistent frustration. We want to propose here an anthropological approach, constructed from the starting point of the knowledge that this discipline developed around ritual, in order to rethink—since the failure of vanguard art—the decline of the modern project.

There is a moment when artists' *gestures* of rupture, which are not able to become *acts* (effective interventions in social processes), become *rituals*. The original impulse of the vanguards brought them into association with the secularizing project of modernity; their incursions sought to disenchant the world and desacralize the conventional, beautiful, complacent ways in which bourgeois culture represented it. But the progressive incorporation of their insolence into museums, their reasoned digestion in the catalogs and in the official teaching of art, made the ruptures into a convention. They established, says Octavio Paz, "the tradition of the rupture" (1987, 19). It is not strange, then, that the artistic production of the vanguards should be subjected to the most frivolous forms of ritualism: vernissages, the presenting of awards and academic consecrations.

But vanguard art was also converted into ritual in a different sense. To explain it, we must introduce a change in the generalized theory about ritual. It tends to study them as practices of social reproduction. It is assumed that they are places where society reaffirms what it is, defends its order and its homogeneity. In part, this is true. But rituals can also be movements toward a different order, which society still resists or proscribes. There are rituals for confirming social relations and giving them continuity (celebrations attached to "natural" acts: birth, marriage, death), and others are designed to effect, in symbolic and occasional scenarios, impracticable transgressions in real or permanent form.

In his anthropological studies of the Kabyle, Bourdieu (1990a) notes that many rituals do not have the sole function of establishing the correct ways of acting, and therefore of separating what is permitted from what is prohibited, but rather also of incorporating certain transgressions while limiting them. The ritual, "cultural act par excellence" (210), which seeks to impose order in the world, fixes which conditions are legitimate "necessary and inevitable transgressions of limits" (211). Historical changes that threaten the natural and social order generate oppositions and confrontations that can dissolve a community. Ritual is capable of operating, then, not as a simple conservative and authoritarian reaction in defense of the old order (as will be seen later with regard to traditionalist ceremonialism), but rather as a movement through which society controls the risk of change. Basic ritual actions are de facto *denied transgressions*. Ritual, through a socially approved and collectively assumed operation, must resolve the contradiction that is established "by constructing, as separate and antagonistic, principles that have to be reunited to ensure the reproduction of the group" (212).

In light of this analysis we can look at the peculiar type of rituals the vanguards establish. The literature on ritualism is concerned chiefly with *rites of entry or of passage*: who, and with what requirements, may enter a house or a church; what steps must be fulfilled in order to pass from one civil status to another or to assume an office or an honor. The anthropological contributions to these processes have been used to understand the discriminatory operations in cultural institutions. The ritualization that museum architecture imposes on the public is described: rigid itineraries, codes of action to be strictly represented and performed. Museums are like lay temples that, like religious ones, convert objects of history and art into ceremonial monuments.

When Carol Duncan and Alan Wallach study the Louvre Museum, they observe that the majestic building, the monumental corridors and staircases, the ornamentation of the roofs, the accumulation of works from diverse epochs and cultures, subordinated to the history of France, form an iconographic program that ritually dramatizes the triumph of French civilization, consecrating it as the heir to humanity's values. In contrast, the Museum of Modern Art in New York is housed in a cold building of iron and glass with few windows, as if the separation from the external world and the plurality of ways to go through the museum gave the feeling of being able to go where one wants, of individual free choice—as if the visitor were able to corroborate the creative liberty that distinguishes contemporary artists: "You are 'nowhere,' in an original nothing, a womb, a tomb, white but without sun, which seems to be situated outside of time and history." As one advances from Cubism to surrealism to abstract expressionism, the forms become more and more dematerialized, "just as the accent on such themes as light and air proclaim the superiority of the spiritual and the transcendental" over everyday and earthly needs (cf. Duncan and Wallach 1980, 1978). In short, the ritualism of the historical museum on the one hand, and that of the museum of modern art on the other, in sacralizing the space and the objects and imposing an order of understanding, also organize the differences between social groups: those that enter and those that remain outside; those capable of understanding the ceremony and those who are not able to perform significantly.

The postmodern trends in the visual arts, from the happening to performances and body art, as well as in theater and dance, accentuate this ritual and hermetic sense. They reduce what they consider rational communication (verbalizations, precise visual references) and pursue new subjective forms to express primary emotions smothered by dominant conventions (force, eroticism, fright). They cut the codified allusions to the daily world in search of the original manifestation of each subject and of magical encounters with lost energies. The cool form of this self-centered communication that art proposes, in reinstalling ritual as the nucleus of aesthetic experience, is the performances shown on video: to the absorption of the body itself in the ceremony, with the intimate code, is added the semihypnotic and passive relationship with the screen. Contemplation returns and suggests that the maximum emancipation of artistic language is motionless ecstasy—antimodern emancipation, that is, given that it eliminates the secularization of the practice and the image.

One of the most severe crises of the modern is produced by this return of ritual without myths. Germano Celant comments on a "happening" that John Cage presented, together with Rauschenberg, Tudor, Richards, and Olsen, at Black Mountain College:

> Given that the first idea of action does not exist, this accumulation of materials tends to liberate the different languages from their reciprocal condition of dependency, and also tends to show a possible "dialogue" between them as autonomous and self-significant entities. (32)

In lacking totalizing accounts to organize history, the succession of bodies, actions, and gestures becomes a different ritualism than that of any other ancient or modern society. This new type of ceremonialism does not represent a myth that integrates a community, nor the autonomous narration of the history of art. It does not represent anything except the "organic narcissism" of each participant.

"We are on our way to living each moment for its unique quality. Improvisation is not historical," declares Paxton, one of the most significant practitioners of performances. But then how do we go from each intimate and instantaneous explosion to the spectacle, which presupposes some kind of ordered duration of images and dialogue with the viewers? How do we go from loose pronouncements to discourse, from solitary pronouncements to communication? From the artist's perspective, performances dissolve the search for autonomy of the artistic field into the search for expressive emancipation of the subjects and, as the subjects generally want to share their experiences, they fluctuate between creation for their own sake and the spectacle; often this tension is the basis for aesthetic seduction.

This narcissistic exacerbation of discontinuity generates a new type of ritual, which is in truth an extreme consequence of what the vanguards came to do. We will call them *rites of exit*. Given that the maximum aesthetic value is constant renovation, to belong to the art world one cannot repeat what has already been done—the legitimate, the shared. It is necessary to initiate noncodified forms of representation (from impressionism to surrealism), invent unforeseen structures (from fantastic to geometric art), and relate images that in reality belong to diverse semantic chains and that no one had previously associated (from collages to performances). No worse accusation can be made against a modern artist than to show repetitions in his or her work. According to this sense of permanent escape, to be in the history of art one has to be constantly leaving it.

On this point I see a *sociological* continuity between modern vanguards and the postmodern art that rejects them. Although postmodernists abandon the notion of rupture—key in modern aesthetics—and use artistic images from other epochs in their discourse, their method of fragmenting and dislocating them, the displaced or parodic readings of traditions, reestablish the insular and self-referential character of the art world. Modern culture was formed by negating traditions and territories. Its impulse is still guided by museums that look for new audiences, by itinerant experiences, and by artists who use urban spaces that are culturally dissimilar, produce outside of their countries, and decontextualize objects. Postmodern art continues to practice these operations without claiming to offer something radically innovative, incorporating the past—but in an unconventional way—with that which renews the capacity of the artistic field to represent the ultimate "legitimate" difference.

Such transcultural experimentation engendered renovations in language, design, urban forms, and youth practices. But the main fate of the vanguards and of the disenchanted rituals of the postmodernists has been the ritualization of museums and of the market. Despite the desacralization of art and the artistic world, and the new open channels to other audiences, the experimentalists accentuate their insularity. The primacy of form over function, of the form of saying over what is said, requires from the spectator a more and more cultivated disposition in order to understand the meaning. Artists who inscribe in the work itself the questioning about what the work should be, who not only eliminate the naturalist illusion of the real and perceptive hedonism but who rather make the destruction of conventions, even those of last year, their method of visual enunciation, are assured, on the one hand, Bourdieu says, of dominion in their field, but on the other hand, they exclude the spectator who is not disposed to make of his or her participation in art an equally innovative experience. Modern and postmodern art propose a "paradoxical reading," since they presuppose "the dominion of the code of a communication that tends to question the code of communication" (1971, 1352).

Are artists really assured of dominion in their field? Who remains as proprietor of their transgressions? By having accepted the artistic market and the museums, the rites of exit, and incessant flight as the modern way of making legitimate art, do they not subject the changes to a framework that limits and controls them? What, then, is the social function of artistic practices? Have they not been assigned—with success—the task of representing social transformations, of being the symbolic scenario in which the transgressions will be carried out, but within the institutions that demarcate their action and efficacy so that they do not disturb the general order of society?

It is necessary to rethink the efficacy of artistic innovations and irreverences, the limits of their sacrilegious rituals. Attempts to break the illusion in the superiority and the sublime of art (insolence, destruction of one's own works, the artist's shit inside the museum) are, in the final analysis, according to Bourdieu, sacralizing desacralizations "that scandalize no one but the believers." Nothing demonstrates better the tendency toward the self-absorbed functioning of the artistic field than the fate of these apparently radical attempts at subversion, which "the most heterodox guardians of artistic orthodoxy" finally devour (1977, 8).

Is it possible to continue to affirm with Habermas that modernity is an inconclusive but realizable project, or should we admit—along with disenchanted artists and theorists—that autonomous experimentation and democratizing insertion in the social fabric are irreconcilable tasks?

If we want to understand the contradictions between these modern projects, it is necessary to analyze how the links between autonomy and dependency of art are reformulated in the current conditions of cultural production and circulation. We will take four interactions of modern and "autonomous" cultured practices with "different" spheres, such as premodern art, naive and/or popular art, the international art market, and the culture industries.

Fascinated by the Primitive and the Popular

Why do the promoters of modernity, who announce it as an advance over the ancient and the traditional, feel more and more attraction for references to the past? It is not possible to answer this question in this chapter alone. It will be necessary to explore the *cultural* need to confer a denser meaning on the present and the *political* need to legitimize the current hegemony by means of the prestige of the historical patrimony. We will have to investigate, for example, why folklore finds an echo in the musical tastes of young people and in the electronic media.

Here we will be interested in the increasing importance critics and contemporary composers give to premodern art and the popular. The high point that Latin American painters find at the end of the eighties and the beginning of the nineties in the markets of the United States and Europe can only be understood as part of the opening to the nonmodern initiated some years before.[3]

One way to verify what it is that the protagonists of contemporary art are looking for in the primitive and the popular is to examine how they stage it in museums and what they say to justify it in the catalogs. A symptomatic exposition was the one presented in 1984 by the Museum of Modern Art in New York entitled "'Primitivism' in 20th century art." The institution, which in the last two decades was the main instance for legitimating and consecrating new trends, proposed a reading of modern artists that emphasized the formal similarities of their works with ancient pieces rather than their autonomy and innovation. A woman by Picasso found her mirror in a Kwakiutl mask; the elongated figures of Giacometti in others from Tanzania; the *Mask of Fear* by Klee in a Zuni war god; a bird's head by Max Ernst in a Tusyan mask. The exhibit revealed that the dependencies of the modernists on the archaic encompass everyone from the Fauvists to the Expressionists, from Brancusi to earth artists and those who develop performances inspired by "primitive" rituals.

It is lamentable that the explanatory preoccupations of the catalog concentrated on detectivelike interpretations: establishing whether Picasso bought masks from the Congo in the Paris flea market, or whether Klee used to visit the ethnological museums of Berlin and Basel. The decentering of

Western and modern art remains halfway between being concerned only with reconstructing the ways objects from Africa, Asia, and Oceania arrived in Europe and the United States and with how Western artists assumed them, without comparing their original uses and meanings with those modernity gave them. But what interests us above all is to note that this type of collection of great resonance relativizes the autonomy of the cultural field of modernity.

"PRIMITIVISM" IN 20TH CENTURY ART
THE MUSEUM OF MODERN ART, NEW YORK

Another notable case was the 1978 exposition in the Museum of Modern Art in Paris, which brought together so-called naive or popular artists: landscape painters, builders of personal chapels and castles, baroque decorators of their everyday rooms, self-taught painters and sculptors, and makers of unusual dolls and useless machines. Some, like Ferdinand Cheval, were known through the efforts of historians and artists who knew how to value works that were foreign to the art world. But the majority lacked any training or institutional recognition. They produced works of originality or novelty, without any publicity, monetary, or aesthetic concerns—in the sense of the fine arts or the vanguards. They applied unconventional treatments to materials, forms, and colors, which the specialists who organized this exposition judged presentable for a museum. The catalog prepared for the collection has five prologues, as if the museum had felt a greater need to explain and forewarn than with other exhibits. Four of the prologues seek to understand the works by relating them to trends in modern art rather than by looking for anything specific to the artists being exhibited. They remind Michael Ragon of the Expressionists and surrealists by their "delirious imagination," and of Van Gogh by their "abnormality"; he declares them artists because they are "solitary or maladjusted individuals"—"two characteristics of all true artists." The most delightful prologue is that of the director of the museum, Suzanne Page, who explains her having entitled the exhibit "Les singuliers de l'art" because the participants are "individuals who freely own their desires and their extravagances, who impose upon the world the vital seal of their irreducible uniqueness." She assures the reader that the museum is not mounting the exhibition in order to look for an alternative to a "tired vanguard," but rather to "renovate the look and reencounter what there is of the savage in this cultural art."

To what is owed this insistence on uniqueness, the pure, the innocent, the savage, at the same time that they acknowledge that these men and women produce by mixing what they learned from the pink pages of the *Petit Larousse, Paris Match, La Tour Eiffel,* religious iconography, and the newspapers and magazines of their time? Why does the museum that is trying to free itself from the now untenable partialities of "the modern" need to classify that which escapes it not only in relation to legitimized art trends but also to the boxes created for naming the heterodox? Raymonde Moulin's prologue provides several keys. After pointing out that since the beginning of the twentieth century the social definition of art has been extending itself incessantly and that the uncertainty thus generated results in the also incessant labeling of strange manifestations, she proposes to consider these works as "unclassifiable," and wonders about the reasons why they were selected. Above all because, for the cultured gaze, these naive artists "achieve their artistic salvation" while "partially transgressing the norms of their class"; next, because

> they rediscover in the creative use of free time—that of leisure or, frequently, of retirement—the lost knowledge of individual work. Isolated, protected from all contact and from all commitment with cultural or commercial circuits, they are not suspected of having obeyed any other need than an interior one: neither

magnificent nor damned, but rather innocent. . . . In their works the cultivated gaze of a disenchanted society believes it perceives the reconciliation of the pleasure principle and the reality principle.

High Art Is No Longer a Retail Trade

The autonomy of the artistic field, based on aesthetic criteria set by artists and critics, is diminished by the new determinations that art suffers from a rapidly expanding market in which extracultural forces are decisive. Although the influence in the aesthetic judgment of demands outside of the field is visible throughout modernity, since the middle of this century the agents in charge of administrating the determination of what is artistic—museums, biennial expositions, journals, big international awards—have been reorganized in relation to the new technologies of commercial promotion and consumption.

The extension of the artistic market from a small circle of "amateurs" and collectors to a wide audience that is often more interested in the economic value of the investment than in aesthetic values changes the ways art is appraised. The journals that indicate the prices of works present their information together with the advertising of airlines, automakers, antique dealers, real estate companies, and manufacturers of luxury products. A study by Annie Verger of the changes in the processes of artistic consecration, following the indexes published by *Connaissance des arts*, observes that for the first of these, published in 1955, the journal consulted a hundred personalities selected from among artists, critics, art historians, gallery directors, and museum conservators. For the subsequent lists, which are compiled every five years, the group of informants changes; it includes non-French individuals (taking into account the growing internationalization of aesthetic judgment), and artists are disappearing (25 percent in 1955 compared with 9.25 percent in 1961, and none in 1971); more collectors, museum conservators, and dealers are included. The changes in the list of those consulted, which express modifications in the struggle for artistic consecration, generate other selection criteria. The percentage of vanguard artists is reduced while there is a resurgence of the "great ancestors," given that modernity and innovation cease to be the supreme values (Verger 1987).

The most aggressive manifestations of these extra-aesthetic conditions on the artistic field can be found in Germany, the United States, and Japan. Willi Bongard, journalist with a financial magazine, published *Kunst und Kommerz* in 1967, in which he criticizes the "badly administered retail trade" tactics of galleries that lack display windows, are located on a building's upper floor and seek confidential relations with their clientele, display the products for only two or three weeks, and consider advertising to be a luxury. He advises using advanced techniques of distribution and commercialization, which were in fact adopted beginning in 1970 with the establishment of lists of the most prestigious artists in the economic journal *Kapital*, and the publication by the art world of its own journal, *Art aktuel*, which communicates the latest trends in the artistic market and suggests the best way to administer the collection itself.

"What a pleasure," says the company or uncultured millionaire eager for prestige. "The pleasure is mine," responds the critic or museum conservator. Is that how the conversation goes? "Definitely not," concludes the historian Juan Antonio Ramírez in verifying that the highest prices paid at auctions do not correspond to the works experts judge to be the best or the most significant (1989). In no country is the power of impresarios, and thus of "art administrators," so evident as in the United States, where this is a prosperous career that can be studied at various universities. Graduates are instructed in art and investment strategies and occupy special positions, along with the artistic director, in big North American museums. When they plan their annual programming, they make it known that the type of art that is promoted influences the financial policies and the number of employees not only of cultural institutions but of commerce, hotels, and restaurants. These multiple repercussions of exhibits attract corporations, which are interested in financing prestigious collections and using them as publicity. With the artistic field subjected to these games between commerce, advertising, and tourism, where did its autonomy, the intrinsic renewal of the aesthetic searches, and the "spiritual" communication with the audience stop? If the self-portrait *I, Picasso* can earn an annual profit of 19.6 percent—as it did for Wendell Cherry, President of Humana, Inc., who bought it for $5.83 million in 1981 and sold it for $47.85 million in 1989—art becomes more than anything else a privileged area of investment. Or, as Robert Hughes says in the article from which this information is taken, "a full-management art industry."

In a society like that of the United States, in which tax evasion and publicity are euphemized as part of the national traditions of philanthropy and charity, it continues to be possible that donations to museums "preserve" the spirituality of art.[4] But even these simulacra begin to fall: in 1986 the Reagan administration modified legislation that permitted tax deductions of donations, a key resource for the spectacular growth of museums in that country. If works by Picasso and van Gogh are worth forty to fifty million dollars, as

The end of the separation between the cultured and the mass-based? Picasso and Umberto
Eco on the covers of international magazines. The artist who always breaks records at art
auctions,

SPOTLIGHT ON THE CIA
Its Part in the Iran Deal

Newsweek

THE INTERNATIONAL NEWSMAGAZINE

December 22, 1986

The
Code
Breaker

'Name of the Rose'
Author Umberto Eco
Has Won Fame
and Fortune
Interpreting
the Signs
We Live By

Number 51

and the scholar who is able to sell more than five million copies of his "semiotic" novel in twenty-five languages. Destruction of the codes of cultured knowledge or the aestheticization of the market?

they were sold for by Sotheby's at the end of 1989, then museums in the United States—whose highest annual budgets range from two to five million dollars—should transfer the most expensive pieces to private collectors. As this skyrocketing of prices raises insurance costs to the point that a van Gogh exhibit planned by the Metropolitan Museum in 1981 would now cost five billion dollars just to insure the works, not even that museum is able to move these paintings from personal collections into public display. A few of the utopias of modernity that were part of the foundation of these institutions—expand and democratize the great cultural creations, valued as common property of humanity—have become, in the most pernicious sense, museum pieces.

If this is the situation in the metropolis, what remains of art and its modern utopias in Latin America? Mari-Carmen Ramírez, curator of Latin American art at the Huntington Gallery of the University of Texas, explained to me how difficult it is for museums in the United States to expand their collections by incorporating classic works and new trends from Latin America (interview 1989) when paintings by Tarsila, Botero, and Tamayo are worth between $300,000 and $750,000.[5] Even more remote, obviously, is any kind of program to update museums in Latin American countries that have been abandoned by "austere" official budgets and bourgeoisies little accustomed to making art donations. The result is that in the next few years the best, or at least the most expensive, Latin American art will not be seen in our countries; museums will become poorer and more ordinary because they will not be able to pay even the insurance for private collectors to loan works by the most important artists of their own country.

Annie Verger talks of a reorganization of the artistic field and of the patterns of legitimation and consecration due to the advances in new agents in the competition for monopoly of aesthetic estimation. In our view, we are also confronted by a new system of connections between cultural institutions and strategies of investment and appraisal of the commercial and financial world. The strongest evidence for this is the way in which museums, critics, biennial exhibitions, and even international art fairs lost importance in the eighties as universal authorities of artistic innovations and became followers of the leading galleries in the United States, Germany, Japan, and France, which are united in a commercial network "that presents the same artistic movements in all the Western countries and in the same order of appearance," using both the resources of symbolic legitimation of those cultural institutions and the techniques of marketing and mass advertising (Moulin, 315). The internationalization of the art market is more and more associated with the transnationalization and general concentration of capital. The autonomy of the cultural fields is not dissolved in the global laws of capitalism, but it *is* subordinated to them with unprecedented ties.

In centering our analysis on visual culture, especially on the visual arts, we want to demonstrate the loss of symbolic autonomy of the elites in a field that, together with literature, constitutes the nucleus that is most resistant to contemporary transformations. But, since the beginning of this century, modern high culture includes a good part of the products that circulate in the culture industry, as well as the mass distribution and reelaboration that the new media make of literary, musical, and visual works that heretofore belonged exclusively to the elites. The interaction of high culture with popular tastes, with the industrial structure of the production and circulation of almost all symbolic goods, and with business patterns of costs and effectiveness, is rapidly changing the organizing devices of what is now understood as "high culture" in modernity.

In the movies, records, radio, television, and video the relations between artists, middlemen, and the public imply an aesthetic far removed from the one that sustained the fine arts: artists do not know the public, nor can they directly receive its appraisals of their works; businesspeople acquire a more decisive role than any other aesthetically specialized mediator (critic, art historian) and make key decisions on what should or should not be produced and communicated; the positions of these privileged middlemen are adopted, giving the greatest weight to economic gain and subordinating aesthetic values to what they interpret as market trends; the information for making these decisions is obtained less and less through personalized relations (of the type that exist between the gallery owner and his or her clients) and more and more through electronic techniques of market research and ratings calculations; the "standardization" of the formats and the changes permitted are made according to the commercial dynamic of the system, based on what ends up being manageable or profitable and not on the independent choices of the artists.

One can wonder what Leonardo, Mozart, or Baudelaire would do today within this system. The answer was given by a critic: "Nothing, unless they played by the rules" (Ratcliff).

The Modern Aesthetic as Ideology for Consumers

Since these changes are still little known or assumed by the majority of the public, the ideology of modern high culture—autonomy and practical disinterest of art, singular and tormented creativity of isolated individuals—subsists more among mass audiences than among the elites who originated these beliefs.

This is a paradoxical situation: at the moment when artists and "cultured" spectators abandon the aesthetic of the fine arts and of the vanguards because they know that reality works differently, the very culture industry that broke down those illusions in artistic production is rehabilitating them in a parallel system of advertising and dissemination. Through biographical interviews with artists, inventions about their personal life or about the "anguished" work involved in making a film or a theatrical work, it keeps alive Romantic arguments about the lonely and misunderstood artist and of work that exalts the values of the spirit in opposition to generalized materialism. This has occurred to such an extent that aesthetic discourse has ceased to be a representation of the creative process and instead has become a complementary resource destined to "guarantee" the verisimilitude of artistic experience at the moment of consumption.

The overview presented in this chapter demonstrates another paradoxical disjuncture, between the sociology of modern culture and the artistic practices of the last twenty years. While philosophers and sociologists like Habermas, Bourdieu, and Becker see in the autonomous development of the artistic and scientific fields the explanatory key to its contemporary structure, and influence research with this methodological approach, practitioners of art base reflection on their work on the decentering of the fields, on the inevitable dependencies of the market and the culture industry. This appears not only in the works themselves but also in the work of museologists, organizers of international and biennial expositions, and journal editors, who find in the interactions of the artistic and the nonartistic the fundamental nucleus of what has to be thought and exhibited.

What is the cause of this discrepancy? In addition to the obvious differences in focus between one discipline and another, we see a key in the decrease of creativity and innovative force of art at the end of the century. That works of the visual arts, theater, and cinema are increasingly collages of citations of past works cannot be explained solely by certain postmodern principles. If museum directors make use of retrospectives as a frequent resource in assembling exhibits, if museums seek to seduce the public through architectural renovation and staging techniques, it is also because contemporary arts no longer generate trends, great figures, or stylistic surprises as they did in the first half of the century. We do not wish to leave this observation with the simple critical flavor it has as we have presented it. We think that the innovative and expansive impulse of modernity is reaching its limit, but perhaps this allows us to think about other forms of innovation that are not an unceasing evolution toward the unknown. We agree with Huyssen when he says that the culture that comes out of the seventies is "more amorphous and diffuse, more rich in diversity and variety than that of the sixties in that the trends and movements evolved in a more or less ordered sequence" (1988, 154).

Finally, we have to say that the four openings of the high artistic field described here show how they relativize their autonomy, their confidence in cultural evolutionism, and the agents of modernity. But it is necessary to distinguish between the forms in which modern arts interact with the other in the first two cases and in the last two.

With respect to ancient and primitive art, and with respect to naive or popular art, when the historian or the museum takes possession of them the subject of enunciation and appropriation is the cultured and modern subject. William Rubin, director of the exhibit on primitivism in twentieth-century art, says, in his extensive introduction to the collection, that he is not concerned with understanding the original function and meaning of each of the tribal or ethnic objects, but rather "in terms of the Western context in which 'modern' artists discovered them." We saw in the exhibit "Les singuliers de l'art" the same difficulty historians and critics had to stop talking in an elitist way about modern culture when they encounter the difference between it and the naive or the popular.

In contrast, the art of the West, confronted by the forces of the market and of the culture industry, is not able to sustain its independence. The other of the same system is more powerful than the otherness of far-off cultures, already economically and politically subject to the West, and also stronger than the difference of the subalterns or marginalized groups in their own society.

Notes

1. See also the prologue by the French translators of *The Philosophical Discourse of Modernity*, Christian Bouchindhomme and Rainer Rochlitz, who show how the Habermasian work of the last decade was formed in a polemic with the German uses of the critiques of the modern world made by Derrida, Foucault, and Bataille (1988).

2. Other texts on Bourdieu's theory of fields are *Le marché des biens symboliques* and "Quelques propriétés des champs." The Spanish version of the latter work, titled *Sociología y cultura*, includes an introduction in which we expand the analysis of Bourdieu we make here.

3. Various critics also attribute this effervescence of Latin American art to the expansion of the "Hispanic" clientele in the United States, to the greater availability of investments in the art market, and the proximity of the Quincentennial. See Sullivan, "Mito y realidad," and Goldman, "El espíritu latinoamericano."

4. It is understandable that the eighty billion dollars "donated" annually by people of the United States to religious activities (47.2 percent), educational activities (13.8 percent), and the arts and humanities (6.4 percent) help them to believe that disinterest and gratuity continue to be leading ideological centers of art. See the excellent issue 116 of *Daedalus,* dedicated to "Philanthropy, Patronage, Politics"—especially the articles by Stephen R. Graubard and Alan Pifer, from which these data are taken.

5. For more data, see Seggerman 1989; 164-65.

2 | Latin American Contradictions: Modernism without Modernization?

The most-reiterated hypothesis in the literature on Latin American modernity may be summarized as follows: we have had an exuberant modernism with a deficient modernization. We have already seen this position in the citations from Paz and Cabrujas. It also circulates in other essays and in historical and sociological studies. Given the fact that we were colonized by the most backward European nations, subjected to the Counter-Reformation and other antimodern movements, only with independence could we begin to bring our countries up-to-date. From then on there have been waves of modernization.

At the end of the nineteenth century and beginning of the twentieth, it was driven by the progressive oligarchy, alphabetization, and Europeanized intellectuals; between the 1920s and 1930s by the expansion of capitalism, the democratizing ascent of the middle classes and liberalism, the contribution of immigrants, and the massive spread of schools, the press, and radio; since the 1940s by industrialization, urban growth, greater access to intermediate and higher education, and the new cultural industries.

But these movements could not fulfill the operations of European modernity. They did not form autonomous markets for each artistic field, nor did they achieve an extensive professionalization of artists and writers, or an economic development capable of sustaining efforts at experimental renewal and cultural democratization.

Some comparisons are illustrative, as Renato Ortiz demonstrates. In

literacy rate rose from 30 percent in the ancien régime to 90 per-
o. The 500 periodicals published in Paris in 1860 grew to 2,000 in
and at the beginning of the twentieth century had a 97 percent literacy ra...; the *Daily Telegraph* doubled its circulation between 1860 and
1890, reaching 300,000; *Alice in Wonderland* sold 150,000 copies between
1865 and 1898. A double cultural space is created in this way. On the one
hand, that of restricted circulation, with occasional high sales, as with Lewis
Carroll's novel, in which literature and the arts are developed; on the other
hand, the wide distribution network, led by daily papers in the first decades
of the twentieth century, which begin the training of mass audiences in the
consumption of texts (Ortiz 1988, 23-28).

The case of Brazil is very different. How could writers and artists have a
specific audience if 84 percent of the population was illiterate in 1890, 75 percent in 1920, and 57 percent as late as 1940? The average print run for a novel
was only a thousand copies as late as 1930. For several more decades, writers
would not be able to live from literature and had to work as docents, civil
servants, or journalists, a situation that made literary development dependent upon the state bureaucracy and the mass information market. For that
reason, Ortiz concludes, no clear distinction was created in Brazil between
artistic culture and the mass market, nor did their contradictions take on as
antagonistic a form, as in European societies (29).

Works on other Latin American countries show a similar or worse picture. Since modernization and democratization include only a small minority, it is impossible to form symbolic markets in which autonomous cultural
fields can grow. If being cultured in the modern sense is above all to be let-
tered, that was impossible for more than half the population in our continent in 1920. That restriction was especially acute at the higher levels of the
educational system—those that truly give access to modern high culture. In
the 1930s fewer than 10 percent of secondary school students were admitted
into the university. A "traditional constellation of elites," Brunner says, referring to the Chile of that era, is required to belong to the leading class in order
to participate in literary salons and write in cultural journals and newspapers. Oligarchic hegemony is based on divisions in society that limit its
modern expansion; "against the organic development of the state, it opposes
its own constitutive limitations (the narrowness of the symbolic market and
the Hobbesian fractionalization of the leading class)" (1985, 32).

Modernization with restricted expansion of the market, democratization
for minorities, renewal of ideas but with low effectiveness in social
processes—the disparities between modernism and modernization are use-

ful to the dominant classes in preserving their hegemony, and at times in not having to worry about justifying it, in order simply to be dominant classes. In written culture, they achieved this by limiting schooling and the consumption of books and magazines; in visual culture, through three operations that made it possible for the elites, against every modernizing change, to reestablish over and over their aristocratic conception: *(a)* spiritualize cultural production under the guise of artistic "creation," with the consequent division between art and crafts; *(b)* freeze the circulation of symbolic goods in collections, concentrating them in museums, palaces, and other exclusive centers; *(c)* propose as the only legitimate form of consumption of these goods the also spiritualized, hieratic method of reception that consists in contemplating them.

If this was the visual culture that the schools and museums reproduced, what could the vanguards do? How could they represent in another way—in the double sense of converting reality into images and being representative of reality—heterogeneous societies with cultural traditions that coexist and contradict each other all the time, with distinct rationalities unevenly acquired by different sectors? Is it possible to impel cultural modernity when socioeconomic modernization is so unequal? Some art historians conclude that innovative movements were "transplants," "grafts," disconnected from our reality. In Europe

Cubism and futurism correspond to the admiring enthusiasm of the first vanguard against the physical and mental transformations provoked by the first mechanization boom; surrealism is a rebellion against the alienations of the technological era; the concrete movement arose together with functional architecture and industrial design with the intention of programmatically and integrally creating a new human habitat; informalism is another reaction against the rationalist rigor, asceticism, and assembly-line production of the functional era, and corresponds to an acute crisis of values and to the existential vacuum provoked by the Second World War. . . . We have practiced all these trends in the same sequence as in Europe but without having entered the "mechanical kingdom" of the futurists, without having reached any industrial peak, without having entered fully into consumer society, without being invaded by assembly-line production or restrained by an excess of functionalism; we have had existential anguish without Warsaw or Hiroshima.
(Yurkievich, 179)

Before questioning this comparison, I want to say that I too cited—and extended—it in a book published in 1977. Among other disagreements I now have with that text (which is why it is not being reprinted) are those deriving from a more complex view of Latin American modernity.

Why do our countries fulfill badly and late the metropolitan model of modernization? Is it only because of the structural dependency to which we are condemned by the deterioration of the terms of economic exchange, because of the petty interests of leading classes that resist social modernization and dress themselves up with modernism in order to lend elegance to their privileges? In part, the error of these interpretations issues from measuring our modernity with optimized images of how that process happened in the countries of the center. It is necessary to examine, first, whether so many differences exist between European and Latin American modernization. Then we will determine whether the view of a repressed and postponed Latin American modernity, complete with mechanical dependency on the metropolis, is as certain and as dysfunctional as the studies of our "backwardness" are accustomed to saying.

How to Interpret a Hybrid History

A good path for rethinking these questions begins with an article by Perry Anderson that, in speaking about Latin America, nevertheless repeats the tendency to view our modernity as a belated and deficient echo of the countries of the center ("Modernity and Revolution"). He maintains that European literary and artistic modernism reached its highest moment in the first three decades of the twentieth century, and then persisted as a "cult" of that aesthetic ideology, without either works or artists of the same vigor. The subsequent transfer of the creative vitality to our continent could be explained because

> For in the Third World generally, a kind of shadow configuration of what once prevailed in the First World does exist today. Pre-capitalist oligarchies of various kinds, mostly of a landowning character, abound; capitalist development is typically far more rapid and dynamic, where it does occur, in these regions than in the metropolitan zones, but on the other hand is infinitely less stabilized or consolidated; social revolution haunts these societies as a permanent possibility, one indeed already realized in countries close to home—Cuba or Nicaragua, Angola or Vietnam. These are the conditions that have produced the genuine masterpieces of recent years that conform to Berman's categories: novels like Gabriel García Márquez's *One Hundred Years of Solitude*, or Salman Rushdie's *Midnight's Children*, from Colombia or India, or films like Yilmiz Güney's *Yol* from Turkey. (109)

This long quote is useful because it exhibits the mix of accurate observations with mechanical and hasty distortions that frequently are used to interpret us in the metropolis, and that too often we repeat as shadows. Nevertheless, Anderson's analysis of the relations between modernism and modernity is so stimulating that what interests us least is to critique it.

It is necessary to question above all that mania that has almost fallen out of use in Third World countries: to speak of the Third World and include in the same package Colombia, India, and Turkey. The second annoyance lies in his attributing to *One Hundred Years of Solitude*—dazzling coquetry with our supposed magical realism—the status of symptom of our modernism. The third is to reencounter in Anderson—one of the most intelligent writers to enter the debate on modernity—the crude determinism according to which certain socioeconomic conditions "produced" the masterpieces of art and literature.

Although this residue contaminates and infects several parts of Anderson's article, there are more subtle exegeses in it as well. One is that cultural modernism does not express economic modernization; he demonstrates that his own country, England, the precursor to capitalist industrialization, which dominated the world market for a hundred years, "didn't produce any native movement of the modernist type of any significance in the first decades of this century." The modernist movements arose in continental Europe, not where *structural* modernizing changes occur, Anderson says, but rather where complex conjunctures exist, "the intersection of different historical temporalities" (104). That type of conjuncture presented itself in Europe as a cultural force field triangulated by three decisive coordinates: *(a)* the codification of a highly formalized academicism in the visual and other arts, institutionalized by states and societies in which aristocratic or landowning classes dominated, overcome by economic development but that still set the political and cultural tone before the First World War; *(b)* the emergence in those same societies of technologies generated by the second industrial revolution (telephone, radio, automobile, etc.); *(c)* the imaginative proximity of the social revolution, which began to manifest itself in the Russian Revolution and in other social movements of Western Europe (104):

> The persistence of the '*anciens régimes*' and the academicism that accompanied them provided a critical set of cultural values against which the insurgent forces of art could be measured, but also in terms of which they could partially articulate themselves to themselves. (105)

The old order, precisely with what it still possessed of the aristocratic, offered a set of codes and resources from which intellectuals and artists, even the innovators, saw it possible to resist the devastations of the market as the organizing principle of culture and society.

Although the energies of mechanization were a potent stimulus for the imagination of Parisian Cubism and Italian futurism, these currents neutralized the material sense of technological modernization by abstracting the techniques and artifacts of the social relations of production. When the entirety of European modernism is observed, says Anderson, we are warned that it flourished in the first decades of the century in a space in which were combined "a classic past still usable, a technical present still undetermined and a political future still unforeseeable. . . . In the intersection of a dominant semi-aristocratic order there arose a semi-industrialized capitalist economy and a semi-emergent or semi-insurgent workers' movement" (ibid.).

If modernism is not the expression of socioeconomic modernization but *the means by which the elites take charge of the intersection of different historical temporalities and try to elaborate a global project with them,* what are those temporalities in Latin America and what contradictions does their crossing generate? In what sense do these contradictions obstruct the realization of the emancipating, expansive, renovating, and democratizing projects of modernity?

Latin American countries are currently the result of the sedimentation, juxtaposition, and interweaving of indigenous traditions (above all in the Mesoamerican and Andean areas), of Catholic colonial hispanism, and of modern political, educational, and communicational actions. Despite attempts to give elite culture a modern profile, isolating the indigenous and the colonial in the popular sectors, an interclass mixing has generated hybrid formations in all social strata. The secularizing and renovating impulses of modernity were more effective in the "cultured" groups, but certain elites preserve their roots in Hispanic-Catholic traditions, and also in indigenous traditions in agrarian zones, as resources for justifying privileges of the old order challenged by the expansion of mass culture.

In houses of the bourgeoisie and of middle classes with a high educational level in Santiago, Lima, Bogotá, Mexico City, and many other cities, there coexist multilingual libraries and indigenous crafts, cable TV and parabolic antennas with colonial furniture, and magazines that tell how to carry out better financial speculation this week with centuries-old family and religious rituals. Being cultured—including being cultured in the modern era—implies not so much associating oneself with a repertory of exclusively modern objects and messages, but rather knowing how to incorporate the art and literature of the vanguard, as well as technological advances, into traditional matrices of social privilege and symbolic distinction.

This *multitemporal heterogeneity* of modern culture is a consequence of a history in which modernization rarely operated through the substitution of the traditional and the ancient. There were ruptures provoked by industrial development and urbanization that, although they occurred after those of Europe, were more accelerated. An artistic and literary market was created through educational expansion, which permitted the professionalization of some artists and writers. The struggles of the liberals of the end of the nineteenth century and the positivists of the beginning of the twentieth—which culminated in the university reform of 1918, initiated in Argentina and soon extended to other countries—achieved a lay and democratically organized university before many European societies did. But the constitution of those autonomous scientific and humanistic fields was confronted with the illiteracy of half of the population and with premodern economic structures and political habits.

These contradictions between the cultured and the popular have received greater importance in the artistic and literary works themselves than in the histories of art and literature, which are almost always limited to recording what those works mean for the elites. The explanation of the disparities between cultural modernism and social modernization, taking into account only the dependency of intellectuals on the metropolis, disregards the strong preoccupations of writers and artists with the internal conflicts of their societies and with the obstacles they face in communicating with their audiences.

From Sarmiento to Sábato and Piglia, from Vasconcelos to Fuentes and Monsiváis, literary practices are conditioned by questions about what it means to make literature in societies that lack a sufficiently developed market for an autonomous cultural field to exist. In the dialogues of many works, or in a more indirect way in the preoccupation with how to narrate, there is an investigation of the meaning of literary work in countries with a precarious development of liberal democracy, scarce state investment in cultural and scientific production, and in which the formation of modern nations overcomes neither ethnic divisions nor the unequal appropriation of an apparently shared patrimony. These questions appear not only in essays, in polemics between "formalists" and "populists," and if they do appear it is because they are constitutive of the works that differentiate Borges from Arlt and Paz from García Márquez. It is a plausible hypothesis for the sociology of reading that someday in Latin America it will be thought that these questions contribute to organizing relations between these writers and their audiences.

To Import, Translate, and Construct One's Own

To analyze how these contradictions between modernism and moderniza-tion condition the works and the sociocultural function of artists, what is necessary is a theory freed from the ideology of reflection and from any sup-position about a direct mechanical correspondence between the material base and symbolic representations. I see an inaugural text for this rupture in Roberto Schwarz's introduction to his book on Machado de Assis, *Ao Vence-dor as Batatas*, the splendid article "As idéias fora do lugar."

How was it possible that the Declaration of the Rights of Man was written into part of the Brazilian Constitution of 1824 while slavery still existed there? The dependency of the *latifundista* agrarian economy on the external market brought to Brazil bourgeois economic rationality with its require-ment that work be done in a minimum amount of time, but the ruling class—which based its domination on the complete disciplining of the life of the slaves—preferred to extend work to a maximum amount of time, and thus to control the entire day of the subjugated. If we want to understand why those contradictions were "unessential" and could coexist with a suc-cessful intellectual diffusion of liberalism, says Schwarz, we have to take into account the institutionalization of the *favor*.

Colonization produced three social sectors: the *latifundista*, the slave, and the "free man." Between the first two the relation was clear. But the multi-tude of members of the third sector, who were neither property owners nor workers, depended materially on the favor of the powerful. Through that mechanism a wide sector of free men was reproduced; in addition, the favor was extended to other areas of social life and involved the other two groups in administration and politics, commerce and industry. Even the liberal pro-fessions such as medicine, which in the European conception did not owe anything to anyone, were governed in Brazil by this process, which becomes "our almost universal mediation."

The favor is as antimodern as slavery, but "more pleasant" and susceptible to being joined to liberalism because of its element of compromise and the fluid play of esteem and self-esteem to which material interest is subjected. It is true that while European modernization is based on the autonomy of the person, the universality of the law, disinterested culture, objective remuner-ation, and the work ethic, the favor practices personal dependency, the exception to the rule, interested culture, and the remuneration of personal services. But given the difficulties of surviving, "no one in Brazil would have the idea or, more important, the power to be, let us say, a Kant of the favor," battling against the contradictions that implied.

The same thing happened, Schwarz adds, when the desire arose to create a modern bourgeois state without breaking with clientelist relations; when European decorative papers were posted or Greco-Roman architectural motifs were painted on adobe walls; and even the lyrics to the hymn of the republic, written in 1890, full of progressive sentiments but unconcerned about whether they corresponded to reality: "Nos nem creemos que escravos outrora/Tenha havido en tão nobre país" ("We don't believe that in a person's time, slaves could have existed in such a noble land") (*outrora* was two years earlier, since abolition occurred in 1888).

We advance little if we accuse liberal ideas of being false. Perhaps they could have been discarded? It is more interesting to go along with their simultaneous playing with truth and falsity. Liberal principles are not asked to describe reality but to give prestigious justifications for the adjudication exercised in the exchange of favors and for the "stable coexistence" that the latter permits. Referring to "dependence as independence, caprice as utility, exceptions as universality, kinship as merit, privilege as equality" might seem incongruous to someone who believes that liberal ideology has a cognitive value, but not for those who are constantly living moments of "loaning and borrowing—particularly in the key instant of reciprocal recognition" because neither of the two sides is disposed to denounce the other in the name of abstract principles, even though they might have the elements for doing so.

This manner of adopting foreign ideas with an inappropriate meaning is at the basis of the majority of our literature and our art, in Machado de Assis as analyzed by Schwarz; in Arlt and Borges, as Piglia reveals in his examination to which we will refer later; in the theater of Cabrujas, for example, *El día que me quieras* (The day you love me), when he presents a conversation in a typical Caracas house of the 1930s between a couple obsessed with going to live in a Soviet kolkhoz in front of a visitor who is as much admired as the Russian Revolution: Carlos Gardel.

Are these contradictory relations between the culture of the elite and their society a simple result of their dependency on the metropolises? In reality, says Schwarz, this dislocated and discordant liberalism is "an internal and active element of [national] culture," a mode of intellectual experience destined to assume jointly the conflictive structure of society itself, its dependency on foreign models, and the projects to change it. What artistic works do with this triple conditioning—internal conflicts, external dependency, and transforming utopias—using specific material and symbolic procedures, cannot be explained by means of irrationalist interpretations of art and literature. Far from any "magical realism" that imagines there to be a formless and confusing material at the base of symbolic production, socioanthropological study demonstrates that the works can be understood if we include at the same time the explanation of the social processes that nourish the methods that the artists rework.

If we move to the visual arts we find evidence that this inadequacy between principles conceived in the metropolises and local reality is not always an ornamental resource of exploitation. The first phase of Latin American modernism was promoted by artists and writers who were returning to their countries after a period of time in Europe. It was not so much the direct—transplanted—influence of the European vanguards that gave rise to the modernizing vein in the visual arts on the continent, but rather the questions of the Latin Americans themselves about how to make their international experience compatible with the tasks presented to them by developing societies, and in one case—Mexico—a society in full revolution.

Aracy Amaral notes that the Russian painter Lazar Segall did not find an echo in the overly provincial artistic world of São Paulo when he arrived in 1913, but Oswald de Andrade had a great reception among the Italian immigrants living in São Paulo upon returning that same year from Europe with Marinetti's futurist manifesto and confronting the industrialization that was beginning to take off. Together with Mario de Andrade, Anita Malfatti, who became a Fauvist after her stay in Berlin, and other writers and artists, they organized the Week of Modern Art in 1922, the same year the centennial of independence was celebrated.

Here is a suggestive coincidence: to be cultured it is no longer indispensable, as it was in the nineteenth century, to imitate European behaviors and reject "neurotically our own characteristics," Amaral says; the modern is joined with the interest in knowing and defining the Brazilian. The modernists drank from double and facing fountains: on the one hand, international information, above all French; on the other, "a nativism that would be evidenced in the inspiration and search for our roots (research into our folklore also began in the twenties)." That confluence is seen in the *Muchachas de Guarantinguetá* of Di Cavalcanti, in which Cubism provides the vocabulary for painting mulattas; also in the works of Tarsila, which modify what he learned from Lhote and Léger, imprinting upon the constructivist aesthetic a color and atmosphere representative of Brazil.

In Peru, the break with academicism is made in 1929 by young artists concerned as much with formal liberty as with commenting artistically on the national questions of the moment and painting human types that corresponded to the "Andean man." For that reason they were called "indigenists," although they went beyond the identification with folklore. They wanted to establish a new art and represent the national by locating it within modern aesthetic development (Lauer 1976).

The agreement of social historians of art is significant when they relate the rise of cultural modernization in various Latin American countries. It is not a question of a transplant, above all in the main artists and writers, but rather of reelaborations eager to contribute to social change. Their efforts at constructing autonomous artistic fields, secularizing their image, and professionalizing their work do not imply that they encapsulated themselves in an aestheticist world, as some European vanguards did who opposed social modernization. But in all the histories, individual creative projects run into the rigidity of the bourgeoisie, the lack of an independent art market, the provincialism (even in large cities like Buenos Aires, São Paulo, Lima, and Mexico City), the arduous competition with academics, the harmful colonial legacy, and ingenuous Indianism and regionalism. Faced with the difficulties of taking on at once the indigenous traditions, the colonial traditions and the new trends, many feel what Mario de Andrade synthesizes at the end of the decade of the twenties: he said that the modernists were a group "isolated and shielded in their own convictions,"

> the only sector of the nation that makes the national artistic problem a case of almost exclusive preoccupation. In spite of this, it does not represent anything of Brazilian reality. It is outside of our social rhythm, outside of our economic inconstancy, outside of Brazilian preoccupation. If this minority is acclimatized within Brazilian reality and lives intimately with Brazil, Brazilian reality, in contrast, did not get used to living intimately with this minority. (Quoted in Amaral, 274)

Complementary information allows us to be less harsh today in our evaluation of those vanguards. Even in countries where ethnic history and many ethnic traditions were wiped out, as in Argentina, artists "addicted" to European models are not mere imitators of imported aesthetics; nor can they be accused of denationalizing their own culture. Nor, in the long run, do these minorities always end up being insignificant, as they were assumed to be in their texts. A movement as cosmopolitan as that of the journal *Martín Fierro* in Buenos Aires, nourished by Spanish extremism and the French and Italian vanguards, redefines those influences in the midst of its country's social and cultural conflicts: emigration and urbanization (so in evidence in the early Borges), the polemic with previous literary authorities (Lugones and the *criollista* tradition), and the social realism of the Boedo group. If we attempt to continue to use

> the metaphor of translation as the image of the typical intellectual operation of the literary elites of capitalist countries that are peripheral with respect to the cultural centers, say Altamirano and Sarlo, it is necessary to observe that it is the *entire* field that generally operates as the matrix of translation. (Altamirano and Sarlo 1983, 88-89)

However precarious the existence of this field might be, it functions as a scene of reelaboration and as a reorganizing structure of external models.

In several cases, cultural modernism, instead of being denationalizing, has given impulse to, and the repertory of symbols for, the construction of national identity. The most intense preoccupation with "Brazilianness" begins with the vanguards of the 1920s. "We will be modern only if we are national," seems to be its slogan, says Renato Ortiz. From Oswald de Andrade to the construction of Brasília, the struggle for modernization was a movement for critically raising a nation opposed to what the oligarchic or conservative forces and the external dominators wanted. "Modernism is an out-of-place idea that is expressed as a project" (Ortiz 1988, 34-36).

After the Mexican Revolution, various cultural movements simultaneously carry out a work of modernization and autonomous national development. They take up again the project of the literary forum begun, with sometimes disjointed efforts during the Porfiriate—for example, when Vasconcelos tries to use the popularization of classical culture to "redeem the Indians" and liberate them from their "backwardness." But the confrontation with the Academy of San Carlos and the insertion in the postrevolutionary changes has, for many artists, the aim of reestablishing key divisions of unequal and dependent development: those that oppose high and popular culture, culture and work, vanguard experimentation, and social consciousness. In Mexico, the attempt to overcome these critical divisions of capitalist modernization was linked to the formation of the national society. Together with the educational and cultural diffusion of Western knowledge among the popular classes, an effort was made to incorporate art and Mexican handicrafts into a patrimony that would, was hoped, be shared. Rivera, Siqueiros, and Orozco proposed iconographic syntheses of the national identity simultaneously inspired by Maya and

Aztec works, church altarpieces, the decorations in cantinas, the designs and colors of Pueblan pottery, Michoacán lacquers, and the experimental advances of European vanguards.

This hybrid reorganization of the language of visual art was aided by changes in the professional relations between artists, the state, and the popular classes. Murals on public buildings, calendars, and widely distributed posters and magazines were the result of a powerful affirmation of the new aesthetic trends within the incipient cultural field and of the novel links that artists were creating with the administrators of official education, unions, and movements from below.

Mexican cultural history of the 1930s through the 1950s demonstrates the fragility of that utopia and the attrition it was suffering as a result of intra-artistic and sociopolitical conditions. The visual arts field, hegemonized by dogmatic realism, the dominance of content, and the subordination of art to politics, loses its former vitality and produces few innovations. In addition, it was difficult to promote the social action of art when the revolutionary impulse was being "institutionalized" or barely survived in marginal opposition movements.

Despite the singular formation of the modern cultural fields in Mexico and the exceptional opportunities to participate in the transformative process with monumental and massive works, when the new modernizing phase erupts in the 1950s and 1960s, the Mexican cultural situation was not radically different from that of other countries in Latin America. The legacy of nationalist realism remains, although it produces almost no important works. A richer and more stable state than the average one on the continent continues to have resources for building museums and cultural centers, and giving scholarships and subsidies to intellectuals, writers, and artists. But these aids are constantly becoming diversified to foster new trends. The main polemics are organized around axes similar to those in other Latin American societies: how to articulate the local and the cosmopolitan, the promises of modernity and the inertia of tradition; how cultural fields can achieve greater autonomy and at the same time make that will for independence compatible with the precarious development of the artistic and literary market; and in what ways the industrial reordering of culture re-creates inequalities.

We must conclude that in none of these societies has modernism been the mimetic adoption of imported models, or the search for merely formal solutions. Even the names of the movements, Jean Franco observes, show that the vanguards had a social rooting; whereas in Europe the renovators chose names that indicated their rupture with the history of art—Impressionism, symbolism, Cubism—in Latin America they prefer to refer to themselves with words that suggest responses to factors external to art: modernism, New Worldism, indigenism (1986, 15).

It is true that these projects of social insertion were diluted partially in academicisms, variants of official culture or market games, as occurred to different degrees with Peruvian indigenism, Mexican muralism, and Portinari in Brazil. But their frustrations are not due to a fatal destiny of art, nor to the disorder of socioeconomic modernization. Their internal contradictions and discrepancies express sociocultural heterogeneity and the difficulty of being realized in the midst of conflicts between different historical temporalities that coexist in the same present. It would seem, then, that unlike stubborn readings in taking the side of traditional culture or of the vanguards, it is necessary to understand the sinuous Latin American modernity by rethinking modernisms as attempts to intervene in the intersection of a semi-oligarchic dominant order, a semi-industrialized capitalist economy, and semitransformative social movements. The problem lies not in our countries having badly and belatedly fulfilled a model of modernization that was impeccably achieved in Europe; nor does it consist in reactively seeking how to invent some alternative and independent paradigm with traditions that have already been transformed by the worldwide expansion of capitalism. Especially in the most recent period, when the transnationalization of the economy and culture makes us "contemporaries of all people" (Paz), and nevertheless does not eliminate national traditions, choosing exclusively between dependency or nationalism, between modernization or local traditionalism, is an untenable simplification.

The Expansion of Consumption and Cultural Voluntarism

In the 1930s a more autonomous system of cultural production begins to be organized in Latin American countries. The middle classes that arose in Mexico after the revolution, those that gain access to political expression with Argentine radicalism, or in similar social processes in Brazil and Chile, constitute a cultural market with its own dynamic. Sergio Miceli, who studied the Brazilian process, speaks of the beginning of "import substitution" in the publishing sector (1972, 72). In all these countries, immigrants with experience in the area and emergent national producers begin to generate a culture industry with commercialization networks in the urban centers. Together with the expansion of cultural circuits produced by growing literacy, writers, businesspeople, and political parties stimulate a considerable national production.

In Argentina, the workers' libraries, popular study centers and literary forums started by anarchists and socialists at the beginning of the century, expand in the 1920s and 1930s. The publishing house Claridad, which publishes editions of ten to twenty-five thousand copies during those years, responds to a rapidly growing readership and contributes to the formation of a political culture, as do the newspapers and magazines that intellectually elaborate national processes in relation to renovating tendencies of international thought (Romero 1986; Corbiere).

But it is at the beginning of the second half of this century that the elites in the social sciences, art, and literature encounter signs of solid socioeconomic modernization in Latin America. Between the 1950s and the 1970s, at least five classes of events indicate structural changes:

a) the takeoff of a more sustainable and diversified economic development, based on the growth of advanced technology industries and the increase in industrial imports and salaried employment;

b) the consolidation and expansion of urban growth begun in the 1940s;

c) the expansion of the market for cultural goods, in part due to the greater urban concentrations but especially to the rapid increase in school attendance at all levels: illiteracy is reduced to 10 or 15 percent in most countries and the university population in the region increases from 250,000 students in 1950 to 5,380,000 at the end of the 1970s;

d) the introduction of new communications technologies, especially television, which contribute to the massification and internationalization of cultural relations and support the dizzying sale of "modern" products now made in Latin America: cars, electrical home appliances, and so on;

e) the advance of radical political movements, which trust in a modernization that can include profound changes in social relations and a more just distribution of basic goods.

Although the articulation of these five processes was not easy, as we know, today it is clear that they transformed the relations between cultural modernism and social modernization, and between the autonomy and dependencies of symbolic practices. There was a secularization perceptible in everyday culture and political culture; careers in social science were created that replaced essayistic and often irrationalist interpretations with empirical studies and explanations more consistent with Latin America societies. Sociology, psychology, and studies of mass media contributed to modernizing social relations and planning. In alliance with industrial firms, and with the new social movements, they converted the structural-functionalist version of the opposition between tradition and modernity into a core of common sense among the educated. Confronted with rural societies governed by subsistence economies and archaic values, they preached the benefits of urban, competitive relations in which individual free choice thrived. Developmentalist policy promoted this ideological and scientific turn and used it to create a consensus among new generations of politicians, professionals, and students for their modernizing project.

The growth in higher education and the artistic and literary market contributed to professionalizing cultural functions. Even writers and artists who were not able to live from their books and paintings—the majority—began to get into teaching or specialized journalistic activities in which the autonomy of their trade was acknowledged. In various capitals the first museums of modern art and numerous galleries were created that established specific spaces for the selection and valorization of symbolic goods. Museums of modern art were born in 1948 in São Paulo and Rio de Janeiro, in 1956 in Buenos Aires, in 1962 in Bogotá, and in 1964 in Mexico City.

The expansion of the cultural market favors specialization, experimental cultivation of artistic languages, and a greater synchrony with the international vanguards. As high art becomes absorbed in formal searches, a more abrupt separation is produced between the tastes of the elites and those of the popular and middle classes controlled by the culture industry. Although this is the dynamic of the expansion and segmentation of the market, the cultural and political movements of the left generate opposing actions destined to socialize art, communicate the innovations of thought to larger audiences, and make them participate in some way in the hegemonic culture.

A confrontation occurs between the socioeconomic logic of the growth of the market and the voluntaristic logic of political culturalism, which was particularly dramatic when it was produced inside a particular movement or even within the same persons. Those who were carrying out the expansive and renovating rationality of the sociocultural system were the same ones who wanted to democratize artistic production. At the same time that they were taking to extremes the practices of symbolic differentiation—formal experimentation, the rupture with common knowledges—they were seeking to fuse with the masses. At night, artists would go to the vernissages at vanguard galleries in São Paulo and Rio de Janeiro, to the happenings at the Instituto di Tella en Buenos Aires; the next morning they would take part in the distributing and "consciousness-raising" actions of the Popular Centers of Culture or of militant unions. This was one of the schisms of the 1960s. The other—complementary—one was the growing opposition between the public and private sectors, with the resulting need of many artists to divide their loyalties between the state and private enterprise, or between private enterprise and social movements.

The frustration of political voluntarism has been examined in many works, but that is not the case with cultural voluntarism. Its decline is attributed to the suffocation or crisis of the insurgent forces in which it was inserted—which is partly true but which fails to analyze the cultural causes of the failure of this new attempt to link modernism with modernization.

A first key is the overestimation of the transformative movements without considering the logic of development of the cultural fields. Almost the only social dynamic that attempts to understand this in the critical literature on art and culture in the 1960s and the beginning of the 1970s is that of dependency. But this ignored the reorganization that was being produced beginning two or three decades earlier in the cultural fields, as well as in their relations with society. This failure becomes clear when one rereads now the manifestos, political, and aesthetic analyses and polemics of that era.

The new perspective on the communication of culture that has been constructed in the last few years derives from two basic trends in social logic: on the one hand, the specialization and stratification of cultural productions; on the other, the reorganization of relations between the public and private sectors, to the benefit of large companies and private foundations.

I see the initial symptom of the first trend in the changes in Mexican cultural policies during the 1940s. Taking Germanism as its starting point, the state that had promoted an integration of the traditional and the modern, the popular and the cultured, pushes a project in which popular utopia gives way to modernization, revolutionary utopia to the planning of industrial development. In this period, the state differentiates its cultural policies in relation to social classes: the National Institute of Fine Arts (NIFA) is created, which is dedicated to "erudite" culture, and almost in the same years the National Museum of Popular and Industrial Arts and the National Indigenist Institute are founded. The separate organization of bureaucratic apparatuses institutionally expresses a change in direction. However much the NIFA may have had periods in which it sought to de-elitize high art, and some organisms dedicated to popular cultures sometimes reactivate the revolutionary ideology of multiclass integration, the divided structure of its cultural policies reveals how the state conceives of social reproduction and the differential renovation of consensus.

In other countries, state policies collaborated in the same way with the segmentation of symbolic universes. But it was the increase in differentiated investments in the elite and mass markets that most accentuated the distance between both. Joined to the growing specialization of the producers and the audiences, this bifurcation changed the meaning of the split between the cultured and the popular. It was no longer based—as it had been until the first half of the twentieth century—on the separation of classes, between well-educated elites and illiterate or semiliterate majorities. High culture became an area cultivated by fractions of the bourgeoisie and the middle classes, while the majority of the upper and middle classes, and virtually all of the popular classes, were becoming attached to the mass programming of the culture industry.

The culture industry provides the visual arts, literature, and music with a more extensive scope than they would have achieved with the most successful campaigns of popular distribution originating in the goodwill of the artists. The multiplication of concerts in folk music get-togethers and political acts reaches a minimal audience compared to what is offered to the same musicians by discos, cassettes, and television. Cultural serials and fashion or decoration magazines sold at newsstands and supermarkets bring innovations in literature, the visual arts, and architecture to those who never visit bookstores or museums.

Along with this change in the relations between "high" culture and mass consumption comes a modification of the access different classes have to the innovations of the metropolises. It is not indispensable to belong to the family clans of the bourgeoisie or to receive a foreign scholarship to be aware of the variations in artistic or political taste. Cosmopolitanism is democratized. In an industrialized culture, which constantly needs to expand consumption, the possibility of reserving exclusive repertories for minorities is reduced.[1] Nevertheless, the differential mechanisms are renewed when diverse subjects appropriate the novelties.

The State Cares for the Patrimony, Companies Modernize It

The procedures of symbolic distinction move on to operate in a different way. This occurs by means of a double separation: on the one hand, between the traditional administered by the state and the modern supported by private corporations; on the other, the division between modern or experimental high culture for elites promoted by one type of corporation and mass culture organized by another type. The general tendency is that the modernization of culture for elites and for masses remains in the hands of private enterprise.

While traditional patrimony continues to be the responsibility of states, the promotion of modern culture is increasingly the task of private corporations and organizations. From this difference two styles of cultural action derive. While governments understand their policies in terms of protection and preservation of the historical patrimony, innovative initiatives remain in the hands of civil society, especially of those with the economic power to finance risk. Both seek two types of symbolic yield in art: states seek legitimacy and consensus in appearing as representatives of national history; corporations seek to obtain money and, through high, renovating culture, to construct a "disinterested" image of their economic expansion.

As we saw in our analysis of the metropolises in the last chapter, the modernization of visual culture, which historians of Latin American art tend to conceive of only as an effect of the artists' experimentation, has been heavily dependent on big corporations for the past thirty years. Above all this has been through the role these corporations play as patrons of producers in the artistic field or transmitters of these innovations to mass circuits through industrial and graphic design. A history of the contradictions of cultural modernity in Latin America would have to demonstrate to what degree this was the work of that policy that has so many premodern characteristics, which is patronage. It would have to begin with the subsidies with which the oligarchy of the late nineteenth century and the first half of the twentieth supported artists and writers, literary forums, literary and visual arts salons, concerts, and musical associations. But the decisive period is that of the 1960s. The industrial bourgeoisie accompanies the productive modernization and the introduction of new habits in consumption that it itself promotes with foundations and experimental centers destined to win for private initiative the leading role in the reordering of the cultural market. Some of these actions were promoted by transnational corporations and arrived as exports of aesthetic currents of the postwar period, born in the metropolises—especially in the United States. Thus the critiques of our dependency that multiplied in the 1960s were justified; among them, the studies of Shifra Goldman stand out in particular. Documented with North American sources, she was able to see the links between the large consortia (Esso, Standard Oil, Shell, General Motors) and museums, magazines, artists, and North and Latin American critics in order to disseminate on our continent a "depoliticized" formal experimentation that would replace social realism (*Contemporary Mexican Painting in a Time of Change*, especially chapters 2

and 3). But interpretations of history that place all the weight on the conspiratorial intentions and Machiavellian alliances of the dominant powers
impoverish the complexity and the conflicts of modernization.

In those years, the radical transformation of society, education, and culture summarized in the preceding pages was taking place in the countries of
Latin America. The adoption of new materials (acrylic, plastic, polyester)
and constructive procedures (lighting and electronic techniques, serial multiplication of works) in artistic production was not a simple imitation of the
art of the metropolises, since such materials and technologies were being incorporated into industrial production and therefore into daily life and taste
in Latin American countries. We can say the same about the new icons of the
visual arts of the vanguards: television sets, fashion clothing, mass communication personalities.

These material, formal, and iconographic changes were consolidated with
the appearance of new spaces for exhibiting and valuating symbolic production. In Argentina and Brazil, the representative institutions of the agro-
export oligarchy—the academies, magazines, and traditional newspapers—
were displaced and the di Tella Institute, the Matarazzo Foundation, and
sophisticated weeklies like *Primera Plana* gained ground. A new system of
circulation and appraisal was set up that, at the same time that it proclaimed
more autonomy for artistic experimentation, was displaying it as part of the
general process of modernization in industry, technology, and the daily environment, under the guidance of the businessmen who were managing
those institutes and foundations.[2]

In Mexico, the cultural action of the modernizing bourgeoisie and of the
vanguard artists did not arise in opposition to the traditional oligarchy,
which was marginalized by the revolution at the beginning of the century,
but rather by contradicting the nationalist realism of the Mexican school
backed by the postrevolutionary state. The polemic was bitter and long
among those who were taking over the hegemony of the visual arts field and
the new painters (Tamayo, Cuevas, Gironella, Vlady), who were struggling to
transform figurative representation.[3] But the quality of the latter and the
rigidity of the former resulted in the new currents being acknowledged in
galleries, in private cultural spaces, and by the state apparatus itself, which
began to include them in its policies. To the creation of the Museum of
Modern Art in 1964 were added other official instances of consecration: the
vanguards were receiving awards, national and foreign exhibits promoted by
the government, and commissions for public works.

Until the mid-1970s, state sponsorship and private sponsorship of art in

Mexico were in equilibrium. Despite the inadequacy of the patronage of both in relation to the demands of the producers, that equilibrium gave the artistic field a profile that was less dependent on the market than in countries like Colombia, Venezuela, Brazil, or Argentina. At the end of the seventies, but especially beginning with the economic crisis of 1982, the neoconservative trends that reduce the size of the state and end the developmentalist policies of modernization bring Mexico closer to the situation in the rest of the continent. As soon as broad sectors of production are transferred to private companies, sectors that were heretofore under the control of public power, one type of hegemony—based on subordinating different classes to the nationalist unification of the state—is replaced by another, in which private companies appear as promoters of the culture of all sectors of society.

The cultural competition between private enterprise and the state is concentrated in a large corporate complex: Televisa. This corporation manages four national television channels with many affiliated stations in Mexico and the United States, video producers and distributors, publishing houses, radio stations, and museums in which high and popular art are exhibited (until 1986, they included Rufino Tamayo Museum of Contemporary Art, and still include the Cultural Center of Contemporary Art). Such diversified activity, but under one monopolistic administration, structures the relations between cultural markets. We said that from the 1950s to the 1970s the split between elite and mass culture was deepened by the investments of different types of capital and the growing specialization of producers and audiences. In the 1980s, large corporations appropriated at once cultural programming for elites and for the mass market. Something similar happened in Brazil with the Rede Globo—owner of television networks, radio stations, soap operas for national audiences and for export, and creator of a new business mentality toward culture that establishes highly professional relations between artists, technicians, producers, and the public.

These corporations' simultaneous ownership of large exposition halls, advertising and critical spaces afforded by TV and radio chains, magazines, and other institutions allows them to program cultural activities that have an enormous impact and are very expensive, to control the networks over which they will be broadcast, the critiques, and even to a certain extent the decodification that different audiences will make.

What does this change mean for elite culture? If modern culture is achieved by making autonomous the field formed by the specific agents of each practice—in art, artists, galleries, museums, critics, and the public—

the all-encompassing sponsoring foundations attack something central to that project. In subordinating the interaction between the agents of the artistic field to a single corporate will, they tend to neutralize the autonomous development of the field. As for the question of cultural dependency, although the imperial influence of the metropolitan corporations does not disappear, the enormous power of Televisa, Rede Globo, and other Latin American organisms is changing the structure of our symbolic markets and their interaction with those of the countries of the center.

A notable case of this evolution of sponsoring monopolies is that of the almost one-man institution run by Jorge Glusberg—the Center of Art and Communication (CAYC) in Buenos Aires. Owner of one of the largest light-fixture companies in Argentina—Modulor—he has at his disposal resources for financing the activities of the center, of the artists he brings together (first the Group of Thirteen, later the CAYC Group), and of others who exhibit their works in this institution or who are sent abroad by the center. Glusberg pays for the catalogs, the publicity, the shipping of the works, and sometimes the materials if the artists lack the means. Thus he establishes a dense network of professional and paraprofessional loyalties with artists, architects, city planners, and critics.

In addition, CAYC acts as an interdisciplinary center that combines these specialists with communications researchers, semiologists, sociologists, technologists, and politicians, which gives Glusberg great versatility in playing a role in different fields of Argentine cultural and scientific production, as well as in connecting him to institutes on the international cutting edge (his catalogs tend to be published in Spanish and English). For the past two decades he has been organizing annual exhibits of Argentine artists in Europe and the United States. He also organizes exhibitions of foreign artists and colloquiums in Buenos Aires, with the participation of prominent critics (Umberto Eco, Giulio Carlo Argan, Pierre Restany, etc.). At the same time, Glusberg has deployed a many-faceted critical activity, which includes almost all of CAYC's catalogues, the management of art and architecture pages in the main newspapers (*La Opinión*, later *Clarín*), and articles in international magazines of both specialties, which publicize the work of the center and suggest readings of art in keeping with the proposals of the expositions. A key resource for maintaining this multimedia activity has been the permanent control that Glusberg has had as president of the Argentine Association of Art Critics and as vice president of the International Association of Critics.

Through this management of several cultural fields (art, architecture, the press, professional associations) and their links with economic and political forces, in twenty years CAYC has achieved an astonishing continuity in a country where only one constitutional government was able to complete its mandate during the last four decades. It also seems to be a consequence of his control over so many instances of artistic production and circulation that the center has received nothing but confidential critiques, none of which has questioned it seriously enough to diminish its recognition in the country, despite its having passed through at least three contradictory phases.

In the first, from 1971 to 1974, it carried out a combined action with artists and critics of diverse orientations. Its work contributed to autonomous aesthetic innovation in sponsoring experiments that still lacked value in the artistic market, such as the conceptualists. In some cases it sought a wider audience—for example, with the planned expositions in Buenos Aires plazas, of which only one took place in 1972, and which was repressed by the police. Beginning in 1976, Glusberg changed his approach. He had excellent relations with the military government established that year until 1983, as is proven, for example, by the official promotion his exhibitions received, and the telegram from the president, General Videla, which congratulated him on his having won the award of the Fourteenth Bienal of São Paulo in 1977, to which he replied by committing himself, in front of the general, to "represent the humanism of Argentine art abroad." The third phase opens in December of 1983, the week following the end of the dictatorship and the assumption of power by Alfonsín, when Glusberg organized the Workdays for Democracy in CAYC and other Buenos Aires galleries.[4]

In the 1960s, the growing importance of gallery owners and art sellers brought about talk in Argentina of "distributors' art" to refer to the intervention of these agents in the social process whereby aesthetic meanings are constituted (Slemenson and Kratochwill). The recent foundations include much more since they not only deal with the circulation of the works but also reformulate the relations between artists, middlemen, and the public. To achieve this they subordinate to one or a few powerful figures the interactions and conflicts between agents who occupy diverse positions in the cultural field. It thus passes from a structure in which the horizontal links, the struggles for legitimacy and renovation, were effected with predominantly artistic criteria and constituted the autonomous dynamic of the cultural fields, to a pyramidal system in which the lines of power are obliged to converge under the will of private patrons or corporations. Aesthetic innovation is converted into a game within the international symbolic market, where the national profiles that were the concern of some vanguards until the middle of this century are diluted, just as they are in the arts that are most dependent upon advanced and "universal" technologies (cinema, television, video). Although the internationalizing trend has been characteristic of the vanguards, we note that some united their experimental search in materials and languages with an interest in critically redefining the cultural traditions from which they were being expressed. This interest is now giving way to a more mimetic relation with hegemonic trends in the international market.

In a series of interviews we did with Argentine and Mexican visual artists about what an artist should do to sell and gain recognition, what we heard more than anything were insistent references to the depression of the Latin American market of the 1980s and the "instability" to which artists are subjected, as much by the continuous obsolescence of aesthetic currents as by the economic variability of demand. In these conditions, the pressure is very strong to be in tune with the uncritical and playful style of art at the end of this century, without social concerns or aesthetic daring, "without too much stridency, elegant, not very passionate." The most successful artists point out that a work of significance must be based both on visual discoveries or skill and on journalistic resources, publicity people, clothing, trips, huge telephone bills, and following international journals and catalogs. There are those who resist having extra-aesthetic implications occupy the main place, but even so they say that these complementary resources are indispensable.

Being an artist or a writer, producing significant works in the midst of this reorganization of global society and of the symbolic markets, and communicating with broad audiences have become much more complicated. In the same way that artisans or popular producers of culture—as we shall see later—can no longer refer only to their traditional universe, artists too cannot carry out socially acknowledged projects if they enclose themselves in their field. The popular and the cultured, mediated by an industrial, commercial, and spectacular reorganization of symbolic processes, require new strategies.

Arriving at the 1990s, it is undeniable that Latin America has modernized, as a society and as a culture: symbolic modernism and socioeconomic modernization are no longer so divorced. The problem lies in modernization's having been produced in a different way from what we expected in earlier decades. In this second half of the century, modernization was not made so much by states as by private enterprise. The "socialization" or democratization of culture has been achieved by the culture industry—almost always in the hands of private corporations—more than by the cultural or political goodwill of the producers. There continues to be inequality in the appropriation of symbolic goods and in access to cultural innovation, but that inequality no longer takes the simple and polarized form we thought we would encounter when we were dividing every country into dominant or dominated, or the world into empires and dependent nations. Having examined structural changes, it is necessary to ascertain how various cultural actors—producers, middlemen, and audiences—relocate their practices in the face of such contradictions of modernity, or how they imagine they could do so.

Notes

1. Almost no work has been done on these transformations, but Durand is a pathbreaking text on this topic.

2. We extensively study this process in Argentina in *La producción simbólica*, especially the chapter "Estrategias simbólicas del desarrollismo económico."

3. Outstanding in the literature on this period is the documentation and analysis presented in Rita Eder's book, *Gironella*, especially chapters 1 and 2.

4. Judgments of CAYC and of Glusberg are divided between artists and critics, as can be seen in the research of Luz M. García, M. Elena Crespo, and M. Cristina López.

3 | Artists, Middlemen, and the Public: To Innovate or to Democratize?

It is not easy to examine the reorientation of the main actors in the face of changes in the symbolic markets. In Latin America there are few empirical studies designed to find out how artists seek out their audience and clients, how middlemen operate, and how audiences respond. It is also difficult too because the discourses by which some judge the transformations of modernity do not always coincide with the adaptations or resistances that can be detected in their practices. We shall take some examples that might be representative of a crisis that is not only a personal one for intellectuals and artists but one also of their role as mediators and interpreters of social change.

First we choose two writers—Jorge Luis Borges and Octavio Paz—whose innovative achievements at once secured the autonomy of the literary field and made them protagonists of mass communication. Next we will follow some movements in the visual arts that seek to unite experimentation with the premodern heritage and with popular symbols. Analyzing the difficulties encountered in trying to locate contemporary art in these two traditions leads us to rethink the debates over the communication and democratization of symbolic innovations, the role of critics and functionaries of cultural institutions; but what interests us above all is to know what happens to the audience and what it means—from the perspective of museum visitors, readers, and spectators—to be modernity's public.

From Paz to Borges: Behaviors in front of the Television Set

The artists and writers who contributed most to the independence and professionalizing of the cultural field have made the critique of the state and of the market the axes of their argumentation. But for different reasons the rejection of state power tends to be more virulent and consistent than the rejection of the market. Cabrujas's text, which we cited in the "Entrance" to this book, exacerbates one of the most often-heard theses: you cannot take into account Latin American states because you cannot take them seriously; but this playwright, who produced works for cultured theater and who is at the same time the most successful scriptwriter of Venezuelan soap operas, does not formulate an equally critical reflection with respect to the culture industry. The explanation of why he makes soap operas of two hundred hours' duration, adapting his dramatic work to the requirements of television production, is a premodern one: he wants Latin Americans "to identify with the great myths about themselves" and "to acknowledge them as beautiful and sublime myths" (Gabaldón and Fuentes, 8).

We will linger with Octavio Paz's position, which is more worked out and influential. Beginning with his early texts, he states that the liberty the artist needs is obtained by distancing oneself from the "prince" and the market. But in fact he has expressed a growing indignation in his work toward state power, while he seeks a productive relation in his links to the market, and resorts to the mass media in order to expand his discourse. Paz's antistatist emphasis is joined with the defense of a conception at once traditional and modern, ambivalent, toward the autonomy of the artistic field.

Paz is a prototype of the cultured writer; not only because of the demands his formal experimentation imposes upon the reader, the implicit knowledge that lends density to his poetry and his essays, and the complicity of those with whom he shares the same literary and aesthetic sources, but also because in his interpretations of culture, history, and politics he is mainly interested in elites and ideas. Occasionally he mentions social movements, technological changes, and the material vicissitudes of capitalism and socialism, but he never systematically examines any one of these processes; his references to the socioeconomic structure are scenographic signs that he immediately slights in order to move on to what really concerns him: artistic and literary movements, and especially individual creators and their reactions in the face of the "threats" of technique and of state bureaucracies.

He is a magnificent example of how a militant adherence to aesthetic modernism can be combined with an energetic rejection of socioeconomic modernization. The material aspect of modernity, of which states would be the bureaucratic and perverse expression, suffocates living reality, and the myths and rituals that preserve it, with "rational geometries." The paradoxical mission of intellectuals and artists is to shed light on neglected traditional values with the brilliance of aesthetic innovations: in the USSR, the primitivism of the Russian people; in Western Europe, the many poetic traditions that have disintegrated since Romanticism, but whose common impulse Paz would like to recover by following authors as different as Baudelaire, Mallarmé, Eliot, Pound, and the surrealists, and, in Mexico, a mix of the pre-Columbian cultural heritage, colonial New Spain, and a Zapatism interpreted as premodern utopia.[1]

The historian Aguilar Camín notes the inconsistency of these regressions. How can the attacker of the Stalinist concentration camp system celebrate the architectural magnificence and political stability of the sixteenth and seventeenth centuries in New Spain, which were constructed with the harshness of swords and the extermination of two-thirds of the indigenous inhabitants? The vindication of Zapatism as the genuine core of the Mexican Revolution—which other authors base on that movement's radical and intransigent struggle for redistribution of the land—matters to Paz as an "attempt to return to origins," to "a community in which the hierarchies were not of a socioeconomic, but rather of a traditional or spiritual order" (1979, 27). Dematerialized in this way, Zapatism

> ceases to be a social struggle to become the conscience of a magical sect subordinated to the myth of the return of the golden age; its struggle for survival is a "revelation," not a struggle; its religiosity is a fortress against the ecclesiastical bureaucracy, not an expression of the colonial dominion and penetration of that bureaucracy and of that church; its lack of perception and national sense (of *a neighboring country,* the United States) is a value that can be redeemed in the future and not the profound limitation of its movement, the secret of its defeat—like that of so many other peasant movements—at the hands of factions for which "the cruel abstractions" of the State and the Nation were the concrete political horizon—and they are still there—that it was necessary to manage and construct. (Aguilar Camín 1982, 226-27)

We want to understand why one of the most subtle promoters of modernity in Latin American literature and art is fascinated with returning to the premodern. We see a symptom in the interpretation of the Zapatist utopia as the return to "a community in which the hierarchies were not of a socioeconomic, but rather of a traditional or spiritual order." Who could represent those spiritual hierarchies today? It cannot be the priests, given the fact that secularization diminished their influence and Paz himself abhors ecclesiastical hierarchy as much as he does that of the state. What remains, then, are writers and artists. Thus the simultaneous exaltation of aesthetic modernism and social premodernity are shown to be compatible: the priests of the modern art world, feeling that their autonomy and symbolic power are fragile because of the advance of state powers, the industrialization of creativity, and the massification of audiences, see an alternative in sheltering themselves in an idealized antiquity.

Is it possible from this simultaneous repudiation of modernization and exaltation of modernism to confront the contradictions between our cultural and social modernity, the reorganization of high culture in societies where even the traditional elite sanctuaries—for example, the museums—are placed under the industrial laws of communication? There is a text of Paz's that dramatizes these contradictions, one he wrote for the catalog for the Picasso exposition put on by the Tamayo Museum of Mexico City.

If at the end of 1982 there was some spectator who had not yet done a thesis on Picasso, nor even read an article about him, nor seen reproductions, the Televisa corporation, which acquired the museum in that period, daily showed paintings of his from different periods on its channels and recounted not only how much it cost the artist to make his work but also the efforts of those who brought it to the Tamayo Museum. For the half-million people who visited the exhibit it became evident that it was more and more difficult to find an event that was not converted into a news item, a pleasure without prior publicity. The art of the last century tried to be the refuge of the unforeseen, of the ephemeral and incipient delight, to be always in a place different from where one went looking for it. Nevertheless, museums arrange those searches and transgressions, the mass media prepare us to arrive at them without surprises, and locate them within a classificatory system that is also an interpretation, a digestion.

Precisely for having participated in almost all the irreverences and inaugurations of this century, Picasso has become an author who is difficult to see in an original way, little able to offer up unexpected encounters. Television organized massive visits for him, although the Tamayo Museum tried to maintain the contemplative rules of elite art: it only allowed twenty-five people at a time to go in. As a result there were gigantic lines. Television filmed them, presented them as a form of advertising, and thus encouraged others to join the lines. Thanks to this coming and going, we in Mexico were able to enjoy—besides the work of Picasso—one of those seductive games of contradiction and complicity between art for the elites and art for the masses that are common in institutions like the Pompidou Center or the Metropolitan Museum.

After hearing in the publicity almost everything there is to know about the creative sacrifices of the artist and of those who succeeded in bringing the exhibition, it can seem normal that one has to wait in tiring lines to reach the sanctuary where the end result is displayed: the museum line as procession. Nevertheless, just as happens in many indigenous religious fiestas, the line at the Tamayo Museum was converted into a fair. Hot dog and soft-drink stands, posters and informal clothes as souvenirs, and flags signed by the artist accompanied the ritual.

The catalog counteracted this massified image of Picasso by presenting him as an exceptional individual. "Wild individualist and rebel artist," Octavio Paz says in his text. And the spectators can resemble him if they adopt an adequate contemplative attitude and if they know how to abandon themselves, with "innocent eyes," to the liberating message of the work and share its innovative force. But the visitor discovered that his or her own innova-

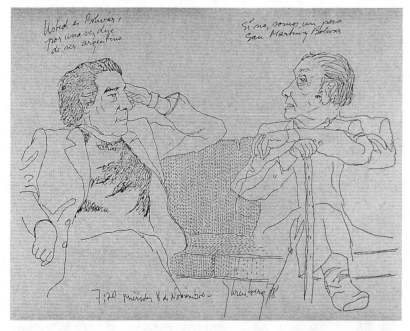

When Borges came to Mexico in November 1978, invited by Channel 13 to have several conversations for television with Juan José Arreola, Octavio Paz visited him in the Camino Real Hotel. Since Paz was under contract to Televisa, neither it nor Channel 13—the official channel—allowed the meeting to be filmed. But Felipe Ehrenberg was permitted to sketch the meetings.

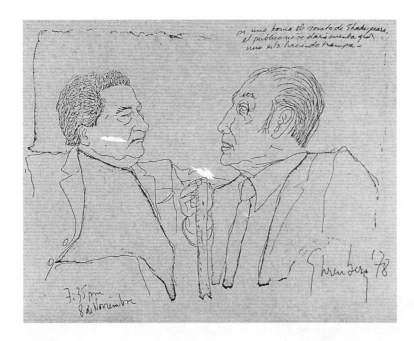

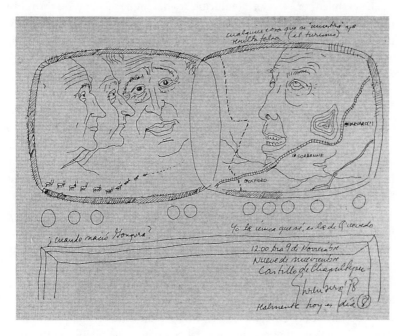

tion was prohibited. It was not possible to return to paintings in an earlier room or to make up one's own itinerary. The guards prevented one from breaking the sequence and order imposed by the museum staff. The line continued inside the building, more as penance than as procession.

What is Picasso, finally—art for the elites or art for the masses? The Picassos shown by Televisa reveal how certain "opposites" can complement, interpenetrate, and confuse each other. The most well known television news anchor dedicated more than ten minutes to broadcasting the opening of the Picassos and recommended the latest issue of *Vuelta* with Octavio Paz's article on the painter. Great painting, great literature, and a magazine that communicates them to the few can also be television spectacles. And the inverse is possible as well: Televisa appears in the museum—financing, putting its logo at the entrance to the exhibit, suggesting how the audience should view it. The differences between cultures and between classes are "reconciled" in the encounter between high art and popular spectators. But this simulacrum of democratization needs a neutralizing operation: the prologue of the Writer, the discourse that depoliticizes one of the most critical artists of the century and dissolves his revolutionary attachments into rebelliousness, politics into morality, morality into Art.

The grandeur of Picasso, Paz affirms, resides in the fact that "in the midst of the anonymous racket of publicity, he was preserved." "Especially now that we see so many artists and writers running with their tongues hanging out after fame, success, and money," just when the culture industry brings him to Mexico and explains him, it is necessary to say that Picasso has nothing to do with that racket. Paz's text acknowledges at the outset the effort of the museum, personalized in its founders, Rufino and Olga Tamayo: an institution devoted to Culture is not anonymous like publicity; it has persons and artists at its origins. He says nothing about the participation of Televisa, and when he analyzes Picasso's rebelliousness against social anonymity, he refers to the party, best-sellerism, and galleries. He remembers that Picasso "chose to join the Communist Party precisely at the moment of Stalin's apogee," but he leaves the question with an ellipsis. No explanation is given for this fact or for the relation to his work in the anti-Nazi resistance and to other political struggles that would prevent a reduction of his work to an "aesthetic of rupture" with society.

The text suggests that political authoritarianism and the market were jointly his enemies, that both are comparable threats, at least for the artist. Of those who really brought Picasso, who are showing how to view him by means of publicity, there is not a word. Does it help to understand Picasso's complex—and contradictory—relations with the art market and the party to speak about them in the abstract?

But more than lingering on that history of distant conflicts, today we are interested in asking what happens to modern literature and art, which are almost always made for intimate relations with their audiences, when their mass distribution brings them to us along with television messages, hot dogs, soft drinks, and, for the most demanding, "Tamayo sandwiches" *(sic)* on the ground floor of the museum. The basic question, which goes beyond this exhibit, is how this aggregate of symbolic traditions, formal procedures, and mechanisms of distinction that is called high art is reconverted when it interacts with the majority population under the rules of those who tend to be its most effective communicators: the culture industry.

It is here that the confrontation with Borges may be useful. Like Paz, he too opposed the writer to the politician, the writer as the highest expression of the individual and the politician as the manifestation of collectivist threats. His anarchist statements are well known, as is his desire that there be "a minimum of government" and that the state not be noticed, as in Switzerland, "where they do not know the president's name" (a position that wavered when his admiration for conservatives led him to praise authoritarian governments).

He also knew the discomfort of being Borges, the shocks one has to suffer in order to sustain a cultured cultural project in the midst of cultural massification. In his final years, Borges was, more than a work to be read, a biography to be divulged. His paradoxical political statements, his relationship with his mother, his marriage to María Kodama, and the news accounts of his death demonstrated to the point of exasperation the way mass culture tends to treat high art: by substituting anecdotes for the work, by inducing a delight that consists less in the enjoyment of texts than in the consumption of the public image.

What becomes instructive in the case of Borges is that in his last decades he converted that obligatory interaction with mass communication into a source of critical elaboration, a place where the representative of elite literature tries out what can be done with the challenge of the media.

The first reaction is that the cultured artist cannot avoid intervening in the symbolic mass market and at the same time feeling this to be intolerable. Let us listen to him evoking his membership in the group around the journal *Martín Fierro,* many years later: he said he was disgusted to have been in the group because it represented the French idea that literature is constantly being renewed. "Since Paris had literary groups that wallowed in publicity and idle discussion, we had to keep up with the times and do the same."

One of the most idle discussions carried out in the presence of mass distribution is the one that developed around that central idea of cultured modernity—originality. Being a famous writer means having to suffer imitators. And the imitators, says Borges,

> are always superior to the masters. They do it better, in a more intelligent way, with more tranquillity. So much so that I, now, when I write, try not to resemble Borges because there are already many people who do it better than I.

Imitation is only one of the tactics for being competitive in the literary market. What can the famous writer do with the prestigious careers in which editors involve him?

> They tell me that in Italy Sábato's books are sold with a label that says, "Sábato, the rival of Borges." This is strange since mine do not carry a label that says, "Borges, the rival of Sábato."

Faced with imitations and competition, the reader is left with the ritual of dedications and autographs that give "authenticity" to the book. In the midst of proliferating sales that make any reader anonymous, that "personal" relation with the writer attempts to restore the originality and unrepeatability of the work and of the cultured reader. Borges discovers: "I have signed so many copies of my books that the day I die one without it will be worth a lot. I am convinced that some will erase it so that the book will not be sold so cheaply." In a Buenos Aires bookstore where there was a signing ceremony for a new book of his, a reader told him, knowing that he was blind, that what he was putting in front of him was the German translation. The writer asked him: "Do I have to sign in Gothic?"

We have to take seriously these occasional interviews and statements by Borges,[2] which, in an oblique way, are part of his work. Just as he was sensitive from his earliest years—which also were the first years of the culture industry—to the narrative matrices and the tactics of semantic reelaboration of the film (remember his articles on the western and detective movies, and his bedazzlement by Hollywood), he understood that critical fortune, the network of readings that are made of a writer, is constructed as much in relation to the work as in those other public relations that propitiate the mass media. Then he incorporates into his activity as writer a specific genre of that apparently extraliterary space: statements to journalists.

In order to defend himself against enslavement to publicity and the perverse revelations that subordinate the autonomy worked by the writer to a massive textuality, it is necessary to carry "the production of discourse as spectacle to its ultimate possibilities," notes José Sazbón (24). Borges parodies the procedures of mass communication, but also the consumption habits that infect the universities, including literature specialists:

> In the universities of the United States, students are obliged to memorize trivialities and not to read at home. Reading is done in libraries, and only the books assigned by the professor. I spoke to a student about *The Arabian Nights* and he told me that he did not know it because he had not continued his Arabic course. "Me neither," I told him. "I read it in night school."

It used to please him to point out the basic operations in the construction of mass discourse: the conversion of immediate history into spectacle, the textualization of social life, the ground zero where the media converts every affirmation into a "show of the statement," says Sazbón. But he also transgresses and erodes those proceedings by constantly changing his statements and the place from which he is speaking: "It bores me to repeat myself, so I say something different every time."

These statements continue his work because he made them into another genre, and also because his aesthetic is coherent with that of his narrative and his poetry. Autonomous and innovative but at the same time able to admit its dependencies, Borges's literature incorporated into his texts the quotes and translations as proof that to write, especially in peripheral countries, is to occupy a space that is already occupied. Many critics read in this cosmopolitan erudition the proof of what it means to be cultured in a dependent society, and thus it was commonplace to attack Borges as a European writer who was unrepresentative of our reality. The accusation falls apart as soon as we notice that there is no European writer like Borges. There are many French, English, Irish, and German writers that Borges has read, quoted, studied, and translated, but none of them would know all the others because they belong to provincial traditions that are unaware of each other. It is characteristic of a peripheral writer, trained in the conviction that great literature is in other countries, to be anxious to know—in addition to its own—so many others; only a writer who believes that everything has already been written devotes his work to reflecting upon the quotes of others, upon reading, translation, and plagiarism, and creates characters whose lives are used up in deciphering distant texts that reveal their meaning to him.

It is true that he seeks to justify his stories by resorting to models of universal history, but, as Ricardo Piglia explains, a great part of his literary game consists of falsifying data, mixing the real with the apocryphal, parodying others and himself. Borges laughs at those who believe that secondhand culture is culture, but not because he laments not being native to one of the great "true" cultures or believes that we should found one of our own—as he makes fun of the universalist pretensions of the literatures of the center in his forged encyclopedic texts, in which he takes up the gaucho and popular urban thematic of Argentina and ridicules the illusion of finding essences of "local color."[3]

All the supports of modern art—novelty, individual celebrity, signatures that seem to confer authenticity, cosmopolitanism, and nationalism—are fragile fictions. According to Borges, rather than becoming indignant at the disrespectful demolition that "mass society" inflicts upon them, it is better to assume, by means of this skeptical work, the impossible autonomy and originality of literature. Perhaps the task of the writer at a time when the literary is formed in the interaction of diverse societies and different classes and traditions is to reflect upon this posthumous situation of modernity. Borges's paradoxical narratives and statements place him at the center of the postmodern scene, in this vertigo generated by the rituals of cultures that are losing their borders, in this perpetual simulacrum that is the world.

The Ironic Laboratory

Borges's behavior toward the culture industry is a proposal about the functions the high arts, or what is left of them, should abandon and about those they could perform. It is not about competition with the media, as if it were possible to fight the media on an equal basis; nor is it about the messianic voluntarism of those who aspire to rescue the people from mass manipulation. It is also not about the melancholic, apocalyptic complaint because autonomous and innovative projects have become hopeless tasks.

If we accept as irreversible trends the massification of society, urban expansion, and the expansion of the culture industry, if we see them—even in their contradictions—with humor, it is possible to think about the function of artists in a different way. Paz examines irony, along with analogy, as the two key ingredients of modern literature. In the beautiful pages he dedicates to them in *Los hijos del limo,* he understands analogy as the Neoplatonic vision, picked up by the Romantics, that imagines the universe as a system of correspondences and thinks of language as the double of the universe. But in the modern world, which lost the belief in linear time and in the myths that responded to its contradictions, and which lives history as change and the sum of exceptions, irony accompanies analogy. Any attempt to look for the originary spring, the source of the correspondences, is eroded by modernity's changes without fixed rules. Secularization leads to the poverty of conscience, says Paz, to the grotesque, the bizarre, the destruction of order. Ironic thought that relativizes analogy only sends it to tragedy: its last station can be nothing other than death (Paz 1987, chapter 6).

Borges, in contrast, exercises irony with humor, that wise detachment that allows him to depart from habitual paths, to be able to think and say "something different every time." Constant displacement, continuous will to experiment: in spite of the theoretical and practical crisis of originality, innovation has not ceased. Although some might often respond to the demands of the market, or might be expropriated by it, there are those who are made uncomfortable with the knowledge and existence brought about by the cunning of mockery.

The cultural field may still be a laboratory, a place to play and try things out. Faced with productivist "efficiency," it reclaims the playful; against the obsession with money, the freedom to rework, without interest, the inheritances that remain in memory, the uncapitalizable experiences that can free us from monotony and inertia. Sometimes this conception of art as a laboratory is compatible with socially recognized efficacy. Just as history knows scientific discoveries that are converted into technological solutions, so there are artistic experiments that lead to renovations in industrial design and the mass media (we cite Bauhaus and constructivism; we must add op and pop, Expressionism and hyperrealism, and a long list of unexpected applications at the beginning of the searches).

But another list may be made of artistic experiences with no material efficacy, and of games that offer nothing more than pleasure, sometimes only for the few. This trend almost no longer has to struggle against its opposite: the modern puritanism that wanted to evaluate all innovations according to their mass applicability. The contemporary aesthetic learned from anthropology and history that in all societies there were "gratuitous" and "ineffective" practices, such as painting one's body or having feasts in which a community spends the surplus of an entire year and much time working on ornaments that will be destroyed in one day. Human beings have always made art out of concern for something more than its pragmatic value—for example, for the pleasure it gives us or because it seduces or communicates something of ourselves. If many popular practices lack "utility," if they seek only the affective expression and ritual renovation of identity, why accuse high art of being purely sensitive and formal experimentation?

If we leave aside the puritan or productive requirements, the question of symbolic efficacy arises. Against the triumphant modalities in the organization of culture—*the market,* the media—Borges's mockery seems fruitful. It is not the only possible response; but in every laboratory, keeping certain questions alive, or experimenting with different ways of asking them, can at least have the value of maintaining them. Because they do not achieve spectacular and immediate repercussions, because at times they do not even have repercussions, irony and self-irony are at the center of those experiences.

Irony, critical distance, and playful reelaboration are three fruitful characteristics of modern cultural practices in relation to premodern challenges and the industrialization of the symbolic fields. We are particularly interested in how this question is worked out in some of the visual arts. To organize the exposition, we will present it as a response to three questions: (1) What do we do with our origins? (2) How to continue to paint in the era of radical industrialization and commercialization of visual culture? (3) What would be the paths for generating a contemporary Latin American art? We ask the question in the plural form because there is no single route, nor anyone that clearly predominates. It is also clear that the examples are only that, and that they could be multiplied.

What can we do with our origins? The euphoric era of modernity had underestimated the question. For many vanguards, only the future was valued and the only possible task linked to the past was to get rid of it. In any case, mercantile and political expansion has continued to utilize history. Large museums, antiquities and souvenir circuits, and retro fashions in the media and in industrial and graphic design all prove it. The past has not stopped eroding modernity's claims of an absolute break.

Some artists offer more discreet forms of talking about origins or about history. I know of none more modest than that of geometric painters and sculptors. It is a line that begins with Torres García, but we will concentrate on the geometrism that has unfolded since the 1960s. It is curious that the visual artists who preferred functional, ascetic structures and who adapted art to the constructive requirements of technological development are the ones who evoke the American past in such a rich way.

Why does César Paternosto, a painter concerned in the sixties with the pure expressivity of matter, and in the seventies with the stripping away of the surface to the point of leaving it entirely blank and painting only the borders, now dedicate himself to reworking pre-Columbian designs?

Paternosto asks: Is it not possible that such concerns were constructive in the formal searches of the Incas when they carved and polished stone?

Therefore, great modern sculptors visited Peru and Mexico, from Josef Albers to Henry Moore. Paternosto incorporates into his geometric work textures in movement, vibrations that paraphrase the *t'oqapus* (embroideries), Quechua pyramid-shaped signs. There are no literal references to pyramids; their triangular forms and scaled lines are alluded to with a discreet treatment. Far from any kind of nostalgia or facile mimetism, his work springs from a comparative reflection on the resources with which different epochs treated the relations between sculpture and architecture, the location of art in the scheme of nature, and the ways of signifying and ritualizing what we construct.[4]

In the same way as Paternosto, another Argentine who takes up the pre-Hispanic heritage in a way that is neither repetitive nor folklorist, Alejandro Puente, made his initial approach to Inca art while living in New York. The discovery of his distance from Anglo-Saxon culture and the difficulty of integrating himself led him to investigate the abstract discoveries, the development of flat surfaces, and the fractured lines of pre-Columbian visual art, with which a geometric art can address contemporary questions. Unlike the Renaissance artists who established as the nucleus of the modern vision a centripetal organization of space, the Inca past provides—more than a repertory of signs for emblematically using the mode of the "Tellurian realisms"—"an open conception of vision" (Puente 1988). This is a return to premodern origins as a resource for decentering and disseminating a contemporary gaze.

Whoever knows the trajectory of these painters and sculptors discards any suspicion of anachronism in their devotion to the remote past. They are not fleeing from an inhospitable present; they want to incorporate the fullness of history into the modern gaze. As with the productivists who worked after the Russian Revolution and the Bauhausians during the Weimar Republic, in our continent the constructive impulse was associated with the emergence of social transformations. It was anticipated in the Americanist geometricism of Torres García cited earlier, in the Concrete Art-Invention Group and the Madí Movement in Argentina in the 1940s, in the Argentine and Venezuelan kineticists of the 1960s and 1970s (Le Parc, Sobrino, Soto, Cruz Diez), and also in Oscar Niemeyer and Lúcio Costa, whose entire architecture, not only in Brasilia, joins functionalist rationalism with the cultural sensuality of his people and with the projection toward the future of the nation.

If visual and architectonic constructivism was manifested in these countries even before it was part of productive development, it was because that trend, more than a reflection of technological prosperity, sought to provide a modernizing impulse. We have a constructive vocation, says Federico Morais, exaggerating a bit, because we inhabit an uncodified space in which everything remains to be done. It is "a geometry that goes beyond geometry"; it adopts organic forms, becomes lyrical, "hot," as Tores Agüero called it, participative as in Le Parc. Morais sees a parallelism (not causal, of course) between the expansion of constructive ideas, urban-industrial development, and the efforts at economic and political unification of Latin American countries (78–94). More than a manifestation of advanced societies, the constructive utopia is a symptom of the takeoff in Brazil and Venezuela, and, in Mexico, the struggle against the orthopedic view of the art field and the tired language of muralism. This "sensitive geometry" of which Roberto Pontual speaks is a "healthy corrective" to our mystic and irrational excesses, affirms Juan Acha. It is neither an alienated transplant nor a misfit with its own reality, but an attempt to order the modern world without abdicating history.

The utopian will of constructivism culminates in the Sculptural Space, constructed on the university campus in Mexico City. It is a circular area 120 meters in diameter, made of black lava, and demarcated by a circle of sixty-four polyhedral modules, each one three by nine meters at the base and four meters high. Vegetation having been cleaned off the volcanic rock, its immobile waves concentrate one's admiration. But that dry force erupts thanks to the modular structure that crowns it. The style of construction and its monumentality evoke pre-Columbian pyramidal forms. At the same time, they are coherent with the earlier work of the team of sculptors that conceived it: Helen Escobedo, Manuel Felguérez, Mathías Goeritz, Hersúa, and Sebastián and Federico Silva. Yet although it was born as a group project, it does not resemble the style of any one of the six artists.

It was an interdisciplinary work that included engineers, mathematicians, botanists, and chemists. It is used as a stage for theatrical and dance works, concerts, and performances. The strict ritualization of the naked rock generates an open work, a place where are fused sciences and the arts, history and the present. In the inauguration ceremony, which coincided with the university's fiftieth anniversary, it was said that this work sharpens the communitarian and disinterested sense of modern art, that it "cannot be converted into a object of personal monetary profit, nor hidden for the benefit of a privileged few," and that it "is born under the sign of the unity of opposites, of the love of a transformation that, precisely for being that, is nourished by the best traditions."

After this work, the artists, under the auspices of the university, continued to make individual works, of lesser interest, in areas near the Sculptural

Space. Except for Goeritz, Escobedo, and a few other sculptors with large public works, such as González Cortázar, in Mexican visual arts the prevailing objective of the geometric movement has been to replace muralism, with similar pretentions of dominating the artistic field and similar descents into rhetorical decorativism. Something equivalent happened with the Venezuelan kineticists, who blocked the rise of other aesthetic approaches in their country. Absorbed by the market, and with less support for producing works of collective reverberation, today geometrism seems to share with other lifeless currents the doubt that it is possible to construct something with art.

A path that is to some extent opposed to this is explored in Argentina by artists like Luis Felipe Noé and in Brazil by Rubens Gerchman. For them a properly Latin American visuality would be to display the expressionist brutalism of nature, to exasperate color, and to make images equivalent to the historic scenes of America explode on the canvas or in installations or in performances.

Noé says that rather than dedicating themselves to the nostalgic "search for nonexistent tradition," Latin American artists should adopt a type of perception that engenders "a stuffed space, a vibrant coloring." Perhaps the importance of the baroque in our history and in contemporary painters derives from "an incapacity to make a synthesis in the face of the excess of objects" (1982; see also 1988). Their expressionist force derives, as he says, from feeling like a primitive against the world, but exceeded not so much by nature as by the variety and dispersion of cultures. He expresses it in paintings that escape from the frame, continuing along to the roof and the floor, in tempestuous landscapes that "rediscover" the Amazon, historic battles, the perspective of the first conquistador. In this dialogue between nature and myths, the painter does not start from scratch—with the result that one of his works is entitled *Fleeing like Gauguin or Dreaming like Rousseau*.

The expressionism of Gerchman, like the conceptual neo-pop of Felipe Ehrenberg—which I will discuss shortly—also springs from the crowd, but of the urban universe. Painting does not want to be art, in the sense of aestheticized representation; it competes with the news of the newspapers, anecdotes, and cityscapes, applies irony to its "bad taste" as much as to the consecrated taste of the art market. Related to this is its vocation for the stereotype: young women posing in line, soccer players, crowds in buses, photos of police lineups. The critic Wilson Coutinho has shown what separates Gerchman from Mexican muralism—which is admired, nevertheless, by the painter—and from other utopian movements of modernity:

(a) "there is no ideology of the national ... but rather immersion in a semi-identity that is national, strong, and transparent on the one hand, and, on the other, opaque, unrealizable, fleeting, and fickle"; *(b)* Gerchman seeks what is "identical in a barbarous polyphony"; *(c)* he shows "isolated people" and "anonymous people from the street."

How to continue to paint in the era of the radical industrialization and commercialization of visual culture? I asked Ehrenberg: what rituals must the artist carry out in order to work in impure arts, mixing images of art history, popular culture, and the mass media, and to be admitted into galleries?

> The first condition is ubiquity. To use images like an alphabet, together with signs that say one thing in one work, and something different in another. I entitled one of my articles "Disobedience as a method of work." Thus I run the risk of being marked as diffuse, scattered. The rite that challenges me most is that of creating the context for understanding the language that is being created. (Ehrenberg 1988)

In Mexico, he adds, there is a strong history of interactions between elite visual culture and popular visual culture:

> Covarrubias researched folklore at the same time that he reworked the images of folklore in his paintings and drawings; Diego Rivera painted popular scenes of different ethnic groups, collected their objects, and was capable of distinguishing their representatives in the street: "This is Mazatecan, that is Mazahuan."

But today it is more difficult to work in the midst of interactions that have multiplied and ideological certainties that have diminished:

> It is not easy to open a work in so many directions: toward the mass media, toward the soft technologies (the mimeograph, the photocopier), to use multimedia to create the context, and on the other hand toward the world of *amates* and popular art. That is why I encounter resistance from the Mexican artistic field. Sometimes one can be more of a Mexican artist in the United States than in Mexico.

Ehrenberg's work is a forerunner, along with that of Toledo—who prefers to root himself in indigenous visuality and myths—of a very fluid relationship between the Mexican and the cosmopolitan and between traditional rituals and current popular taste, which has become common among young painters: for example, Arturo Guerrero, Marisa Lara, Eloy Tarcisio, and Nahúm Zenil. Far from being concerned with indoctrinating, with defining *one* symbolic universe, as was the case in earlier generations, they are more freely linked to the ambiguities of the past and of immediate life. They accept naturally the coexistence of the Virgin of Guadalupe with the television set, the proliferation of artifacts and modern gadgets together with the "poor," the downtrodden, brilliant, boisterous taste of the popular sectors, which brings them close to the Chicano aesthetic. They do not make nationalism into a lay religion, nor do they have nostalgia for the primitive, observes Monsiváis; their declared and defended Mexicanism is not based on the dogmatic definition of an exclusive repertory, but rather on the "malicious use of ingenuity," on fragmentary experiences of the culture that reaches them from all over, unified—without pretentions of constructing compact totalities—by the ironic and sensual assimilation of the quotidian (Monsiváis 1989).

But how can these works gain recognition in the market? Ehrenberg says that he works his scale models for murals like any artisan, like a stonecutter or a jeweler, but in order to produce a work that aspires to enter "mainstream art, in other words to transgress without divorcing oneself completely." What needs to be done in order to differentiate oneself from the simply artisanal?

> There are different recourses. For example, leaving a little white border on a sheet of paper, not like the poster that bleeds to the border. Or the tactility of the surface: if I were to make it totally flat it would be too posterized and I could not treat it within the discourse of art. There is no reason to forget all the recourses accumulated by the history of art. But I also appropriate the techniques of *amate* painters—for example, the readings from right to left and the snail itineraries in the presentation of the figures.

What, then, would be the contemporary paths for generating a Latin American art? The responses may be, simultaneously, those we just gave: to reelaborate our origins and our hybrid present with a geometric, constructive, expressionist, multimedia, and parodic perspective. Therefore, they are liminal artists, who live at the limit or in the intersection of several trends, artists of ubiquity. They take images from the fine arts, Latin American history, handicrafts, the electronic media, and the chromatic variety of the city. They deprive themselves of nothing: they want to be popular and mass-based, to enter the art mainstream, to be in their own country and in others. This is the moment to say that they achieve very little of all this.

For the same reason, here the structure of our book ends up unbalanced. In the preceding chapter, we examined how modern and postmodern art of the metropolises leads to the impossibility of cultivating absolute autonomy and with what strategies—of museums, the market, the interaction with the culture industries—it is reinserted into broader social movements. In look-

TODAY, ART IS A PRISON.
OGGI, L'ARTE E' UN CARCERE.
HOY, EL ARTE ES UNA CARCEL.

I am preparing a book on this theme, if you would like to collaborate please send your reply on this page. Thanks.
Horacio Zabala

name: PAWEL PETASZ   date: 14.11.'78
                                  (.III.75)

TODAY, ART IS A PRISON.
OGGI, L´ARTE E´ UN CARCERE.
HOY, EL ARTE ES UNA CARCEL.

I am preparing a book on this theme, if you would like to collaborate please send your reply on this page. Thanks.
Horacio Zabala

name: HERNAN CASTELLANO GIRON (CHILENO)   date: JUNIO 1977

ing for equivalents of this process in Latin America, we described works, personal projects, and stylistic solutions. These experiments and reflections on how to articulate contemporary art with history, popular art, constructive preoccupations, and mass utopias are well valued by the critics, but the artists cited barely sell enough to survive and they do not come to shape cultural alternatives and appropriate collective projects in a lasting way for their societies. Occasionally they request from them a public sculpture, a mural, and, in extraordinary cases, they finance for them a work of wide impact like the Sculptural Space.

This is due in large part to the fact that these experiences lead to a tragic reflection. The constructive and democratizing impulse leads as much to the Sculptural Space, to the celebration of historical signs, and to the festive parody of the media as it does to the sad ironies of the Argentine architect and artist Horacio Zabala. In 1976, he sent two hundred poets, visual artists, critics, photographers, theorists, and designers a sheet of millimetered paper with the request that they comment on this phrase: "Today art is a prison." In the introductory text to the responses, Zabala affirms, with Foucault, that the prison is an "invention," a technique of identification and framing of individuals, of their gestures, their activity, and their energy. "It is the place of the intolerable accumulation of time; it is the place of useless and circular paths." That is why he associates art with it more than with the cemetery. Just as the death of God does not put an end to churches, the probable death of art does not generate "the death of the art world." Like the prison, that world is "a closed, isolated, and separate system," a totality that limits liberty by excluding and denying, where everything suffocates, and from which it is only possible to subtract by means of "the forced imagination itself."

He remembers that at the beginning of the 1970s he formed part of the CAYC Group with the intention of reconsidering art in relation to studies on communication and language. He warned then that the art world brings to life any renovation with the requirement that it immediately die, with a programmed obsolescence. He mounted an exhibit in CAYC in 1973 to display architectonic projects of prisons as a metaphor for the situation of artists. He also looked for raw material for his work in that survey, an ironic game of questions answered by members of the field. Now it can be seen what remains for the artist: "animation, participation, diffusion, simulation, reproduction, exposition, imitation." Today art is a prison: in choosing, more than a definition, a slogan, part of the assumption of what artists can do is "to introduce themselves into any continuing process and interrupt it for an instant" (Zabala).

Faced with the impossibility of constructing acts, to avoid falling into rituals art elects to be gesture.

The Modernity of the Receivers

Prison as the ultimate laboratory. Are there no other exits than submission to the market, transgressing irony, the marginal search of solitary works, and re-creation of the past? In the sixties, the high point of democratizing movements generated the expectation of an art that would overcome its isolation and inefficacy by linking itself in a different way with individual receivers and even with popular movements. The hardly encouraging balance sheet of those attempts brings us beyond a simple evaluation of their achievements. We want to verify if the sought-after ends made sense. A practical question: is it possible to abolish the distance between artists and spectators? And an aesthetic one: is there any value in efforts to reconvert artistic messages to functional ones for mass audiences?

We relied more on political proposals and voluntaristic essays than on theoretical and aesthetic elaborations of these questions. A first approach to these pragmatic responses is *pedagogical contextualization*. It is a question of ending the specialists' monopoly of knowledge and giving to neophytes, in accelerated treatments, what they lack to be artists or to be as informed as the specialists are. Museums were filled with instructive posters, traffic signs, and guided visits in various languages. Based on the much-heeded thesis that any artistic product is conditioned by a fabric of social relations, museology, catalogs, critiques, and audiovisual materials that come with exhibits should situate the paintings and sculptures in the midst of contextual references that would help them to be understood.

In the face of this communicational reformulation, there are two types of critique, one that we will call "cultured," the other democratic. According to the first, contextualizing the works impairs the disinterested contemplation that ought to characterize any relationship to art. Didactic efforts reduce the work to its context, the formal to the functional, the empathetic relation with a culture incorporated into the family and the school to a relation explained with information learned in disenchanted museums. So much pedagogy eliminates the complicity of the "educated" with their own cultural capital; the theatrical seduction and even the physical possibility of seeing the works are blocked by the multitudes. The sanctuary has been desacralized, says Gombrich; peregrination has been replaced by the tourist excursion, the object by the souvenir, the exposition by the show:

I have gloomy visions of a future museum in which the contents of Aladdin's cave will have been removed to the storeroom and all that will be left will be an authentic lamp from the period of the Arabian Nights with a large diagram at its side explaining how oil lamps worked, where the wick was inserted, and what was the average burning time. I grant that oil lamps are after all, human artefacts and tell us more about the lives of ordinary people than the precious tinsel of Aladdin's cave. But must I receive this improving instruction while I support myself on my tired feet rather than sitting snugly in a chair and reading about the history of domestic illumination? (196)

Although there is some sense to these objections, Gombrich leaves aside the central problem of how cultured institutions can coexist with massifying tendencies. Attempts at democratization that accept the risk of opening up exclusive enclaves, or that assume that the crossing is inevitable and try to verify that the distribution achieves the objectives it announces, seem to me to be more radical. Studies on European and Latin American audiences allow us to conclude that the contextualization of artistic works increases their legibility but obtains little as far as attracting more spectators and incorporating new perceptual patterns are concerned. Untrained spectators feel that the art-history summaries provided in an exposition do not eliminate the distance between everything modern works carry with them as implicit knowledge and what can be digested during a brief visit. What happens most often is that the public displaces its concentration on the work onto the artist's biography and replaces the struggle with forms with historical anecdote (see, for example, Bourdieu and Darbel, *L'amour de l'art;* Eder, "El público de arte en México").

A second way consists in *pulling works out of museums and galleries* and bringing them into desacralized spaces: squares, factories, and unions. Artists are tired of having to take turns in inaugurations as their only audience. Several have ridiculed this in their works—such as Hervé Fischer when, in 1971, he put on a "hygienic exhibit" in which the gallery was empty and the walls were covered with mirrors. What is resolved by missionary efforts to bring art to profane places? Sometimes it is useful. But artists and sociologists have discovered that works conceived by taking into account the modern autonomy of formal searches, and made for spaces where those insular languages can speak without interferences, tend to become mute when they are seen in the midst of urban noise by spectators who were not out walking in the street or bringing their children to the park with the idea of having aesthetic experiences. Artists noted that if they want to communicate with mass audiences in contemporary cities saturated with traffic, advertising, and political messages, it is better to act like graphic designers.

Some have produced valuable nonutilitarian experiences of resignification of the environment (ecological art, performances, public installations, etc.). But the practitioners of sociological art, who take these experiences to the extreme, also knew how to measure their limits. They sensitized rural zones against contamination by organizing, together with the inhabitants, foods colored with lead; they planted symbolic trees in parking lots; they published pages of local French information in German newspapers and vice versa, so that opposing national groups might begin to understand each other starting from their daily experiences. In tracing the balance sheet, Hervé Fischer says that there was something desperate in those efforts by artists to compete with mass communication and the ordering of urban space, for which they were "condemned to failure or to disappointed simulacra." They serve more as "polemical interrogation" within the artistic field, to "oblige art to tell the truth about art," than for changing society or the relationship between art and society (8, 101-2).

The third rupture, which is believed to be the most radical with respect to the autonomy and aristocratism of the artistic field, would be to promote *workshops of popular creativity*. It was a question of "returning action to the people," not of popularizing only the product but rather the means of production. Everyone would become painters, actors, filmmakers. In seeing murals of the Chilean brigades, participatory theatrical works directed by Boal in Brazil and Argentina, by Alicia Martínez in the Tabasco Peasant Theater in Mexico, the works of the Colombians Santiago García with La Candelaria and Enrique Buenaventura with the Experimental Theater of Cali, and the films of Sanjinés and Vallejo, we confirmed that amateurs can produce valuable works without going through ten years of artistic schooling. But after also having suffered through so much involuntary aesthetic terrorism by those who believe that the best creative method is participative goodwill, that quality is measured by ideological clarity, and that clarity by the uncritical adherence to an ideology, I wonder if the intervention of talented professionals like those just mentioned has not played a central role in these happy experiences. I am not exalting anything that resembles genius, but rather the capacity of artists well trained in their trade and in the autonomous rules that make the visual-arts, theatrical, or cinematographic fields function, and who are flexible enough to imagine openings in the autonomous codes in order to make them understandable to the untrained artist and audience.

It is symptomatic that after the proliferation of these experiments during two decades—the sixties and seventies—they have diminished in number and quality without, in any country, producing a dissolution of the artistic field into a generalized, deprofessionalized creativity that erases the distance between creators and receivers. In the 1980s, almost all these groups were dissolved and there is a tendency to restore the autonomy of the artistic field, and the professionalization and revalorization of individual (though not necessarily individualistic) work. Since this has also happened in Cuba and Nicaragua, it is not possible to blame the decline of utopia on the "hostile objective conditions of capitalist development" or the "artists' bourgeois contradictions." Rather, it would seem necessary to think about whether practicable socialization—instead of being the abolition of the artistic field and the transfer of creative initiative to an indiscriminate "everyone"— might not lie in the democratization of experiences together with a professional specialization made more accessible to all classes.

Perceiving the limitations of these movements served to end the treatment of spectators as artists who were repressed or discriminated against. It also served to not interpret the fact that spectators were not artists as a deficiency that could be resolved through a generous pedagogy or the self-sacrificing transference of the means of cultural production. If we link this conclusion with what the theories of literary reception propose about reading as *an act of meaning production* that is at the same time *asymmetric* with that of writing, it is possible to arrive at a more attractive vision of what happens in the relations between production and reception of art.

A methodological change may open up another perspective for us. Up to this point we have been examining the fate of modernity from the positions of those who emit, communicate, and reelaborate it. It is necessary to look at how it unfolds from the receivers' side. One way to determine this is to investigate cultural consumption. The other is the study and debate about the situation of popular cultures. This second path overlaps the first to some degree, although not entirely—because the popular classes are not the only receivers of culture and because, from a theoretical and methodological point of view, both investigative strategies have followed different directions. We will deal with the relations between modernity and popular cultures in a subsequent chapter. Here we are going to analyze the scope of the reception.

In order to not limit the question of cultural consumption to the empiricist listing of the public's tastes and opinions, it is necessary to analyze it in relation to a central problem of modernity: that of hegemony. How to construct unified and coherent societies in which continuity and changes are not imposed but are rather a product of consensus? In the perspective of this book, this means: how to combine the movements that are constitutive of modernity—the secular reorganization of society, the renovation of the vanguards, and economic and cultural expansion—with the democratization of social relations.

It is difficult to know of what use culture is to hegemony because of the scarce information available in Latin American countries on cultural consumption. We know the intentions of modernizing policies but there are very few studies on their reception. There are statistics on attendance at certain institutions and market surveys by the mass media. But neither institutions nor the media tend to verify from what patterns of perception and understanding their audiences are related to cultural goods, and even less so what effect their everyday conduct and their political culture generate.

To evaluate the efficacy of democratizing attempts requires investigating cultural consumption qualitatively. To what extent have educational campaigns and the spread of art and science permeated society? How does each sector interpret and use what schools, museums, and mass communication want to do with them? We will look for answers to these question through a study of museum audience.

There may be objections to our using museums as an example, given their deficient development in Latin America. We do not choose them because they played a notable role in the construction of cultural modernity in the metropolises. What interests us is the almost complete absence of museums in our countries, until three or four decades ago, as a symptom of our relationship with the past and of the context in which modernizing efforts are carried out. It reveals, of course, the neglect of memory, but also the lack of another more subtle function of museums: to construct a relation of hierarchized continuity with society's own precedents. The grouping of objects and images by rooms, one for each century or period, visually reconstructs historical scenes and makes them almost simultaneous. A rigorous study of museums distinguishes the decisive stages in the foundation or change of a society and proposes explanations and interpretative keys for the present.

Museums not only place societies in relation to their origin but also create in cultural production relations of filiation and replication with previous practices and images. The operation of rupture that went into constructing European artistic modernity was forged by reflecting upon its sources. If pictorial modernism is initiated in the works that Manet did in 1860, their novelty does not ignore the logic of previous visual arts. *Olympia*, for example, is a modification of Titian's *Venus of Urbino*. Foucault says, therefore, that that work and *Déjeuner sur l'herbe* were the first museum paintings in the sense that they were responding to what had been accumulated by Giorgione,

Raphael, and Velázquez, and they made themselves recognizable and legible because they spoke of a shared and saved imaginary. Like Flaubert with the library, Manet paints from the history in which he is inserted. Both "guide their art with the archive," Foucault adds, and renew the procedures of representation in the same act in which they affirm the continuity with a cultural field that they consecrate as autonomous without eliminating its social roots and its character of historical testimony (1977, 92–93). This is something similar to what we read in Perry Anderson when he says that the renovating forces of art are linked among themselves in relation to a set of previous values that they at once use as a frame of reference and criticize.

The weak rooting in its own history accentuates the impression in Latin America that modernization would be an imported demand and an absolute inauguration. In politics as much as in art, our modernity has been an insistent pursuit of a newness that could be imagined without conditions of renouncing memory. This relationship of estrangement with the past is more visible in the countries where the social project represented a self-denial of history—for example, in Argentina and Uruguay. There the question of the efficacy of the museum may do little more than prove the almost complete lack of that system of visual references to the past in the formation of modern culture. Two hypotheses could be useful for exploring the causes of this lack and its effects on the population. The first is the prevailing individualism in conceptions of culture and cultural politics. In several Latin American countries, being educated was understood by the governing liberal elites to be an individual task. Massive literacy and popular education campaigns existed, but the works of artists and writers were not easily inscribed in the collective patrimony because they often were formed in opposition to popular cultures.

The other track we should work is that of the predominance of written over visual culture in the countries that first reached a moderate level of literacy, or where the formation of modernity was in the hands of elites that overestimated writing. In Argentina, Brazil, Chile, and Uruguay, the initial documentation of cultural traditions was carried out more by writers—narrators and essayists—than by researchers of visual culture. Ricardo Rojas and Martínez Estrada, and Oswald and Mario de Andrade, opened the study of folkloric and historical patrimony, or they valued and conceptualized it for the first time within the context of national history. This literary gaze at patrimony, including visual culture, contributed to the divorce between the elites and the people. In societies with a high rate of illiteracy, documenting and organizing culture chiefly through written means is a way of reserving memory and the use of symbolic goods for the few. Even in countries that incorporated large sectors of the population into formal education in the first half of the twentieth century, such as those we named, the predominance of writing implies a more intellectualized mode of circulation and appropriation of cultural goods, foreign to the subaltern classes, who were accustomed to the visual elaboration and communication of their experiences. It is easy to understand what this means in a continent where even today barely 53 percent of children reach the fourth grade of primary school—the minimum necessary to acquire a lasting literacy.

Being cultured has implied repressing the visual dimension in our perceptive relationship with the world and inscribing its symbolic elaboration in a written record. In Latin America we have more histories of literature than of the visual and musical arts—and of course more on literature of the elites than on equivalent manifestations of the popular classes.

In Mexico, artists have contributed more than in other societies toward shaping a collective and public visuality. Even institutions specialized in "enclosing" art, like museums, give to the production of visual art a social space equivalent to that of Europe. Equivalent, but not identical. Their influence is more delayed since they begin to multiply in the 1940s, when visual culture had two decades under the influence of film and four centuries of being shaped by Catholic iconography and colonial urban space. They also differ, as we shall see, in their relationship with the audience.

In any case, it was the conviction of the important role museums played as cultural mediators that prompted us to investigate the spectators of four large exhibits held in Mexico City in 1982 and 1983. We chose that of Rodin presented in the Palace of Fine Arts, those of Henry Moore and Tapio Wirkkala in the Museum of Modern Art, and a joint exhibit of Frida Kahlo and Tina Modotti in the National Museum of Art. I will give the basic facts in order to be able to present some hypotheses on the relations between modernization and modernism, and to discuss the value of the democratizing slogan that culture should be for everyone. We are especially interested in understanding how meaning is produced from the side of the receivers and how they work out their asymmetrical relation with the hegemonic visuality.[5]

Despite massive attendance at the main Mexican museums, the surveys show that the vast majority come from middle- and upper-class layers of the population. Those who have completed or are working on university degrees predominate (61 percent); the proportion drops sharply in the case of those who have completed only secondary education (13 percent) and those who have completed only primary education (7.5 percent). The occupational information confirms the picture: 40 percent are students, 26 percent professionals, 9 percent administrative employees, 6 percent work at home, and 3 percent said they were technicians and specialized workers.

Could it be the intensive use of the mass media, especially television, in publicizing the exhibits that caused museum attendance to grow in the last decade? The surveys reveal that they play a significant role in the increase in visitors, though not as omnipotent a role as one might think. Visitors who said they learned of the exhibits through television, radio, and the press made up 52 percent; the other half found out about them through recommendations by friends, announcements placed in the streets by the museums, and through schools that brought them or sent them to the exhibits as an assignment. In other words, the influence of the mass media is almost identical in terms of percentage as that of microsocial or interpersonal forms of communication.

Moreover, if we take into account the fact that in all the exhibits the attendance of persons who only had a primary education was very low, and that 48 percent of the visitors said they were going to the museum for the first time (especially those with less schooling), it is evident that the impact of the media has limited success in the diffusion of art. Mass communication distributes the news extensively and can suggest the importance of attending and succeed in getting a certain number of people do so once, but its occasional action has little capacity to create lasting cultural habits.

The high proportion of the audience with a university education indicates that the interest in modern art museums grows in proportion to an increase in economic status, educational level, and prolonged familiarization with the elite culture. On this point our study coincides with one done by Pierre Bourdieu and Alan Darbel in European museums: the relationship to art is little fostered by timely stimuli such as those of mass communication. The media are useful for attracting people predisposed to enjoy cultured goods by the more systematic action of the school and the family.

We already mentioned that in Mexico the constitution of modernity, and within it the formation of an autonomous cultured field, was carried out in part through state action. We also said that the separation between the cultured and the popular was subordinated, in the postrevolutionary period, to the organization of a national culture that gave more space to popular traditions to develop themselves and more integration with the hegemonic than in other Latin American societies. Thus our results do not coincide with those obtained in studies of the metropolises and of other countries of the continent with respect to the correspondence between the conception of art expressed in museums and that of the attending public.

Bourdieu attributes the greater affinity of the dominant classes with the ideology of the museums to their greater disposition toward differentiating in artistic goods the formal values that modern art made independent. In Mexican art museums the exhibition criteria almost always reproduce that modern conception of the autonomy of the artistic object. This was particularly notable in the Moore exhibit and motivated complaints by the public in the responses to the survey. In those of Rodin, Wirkkala, and Kahlo-Modotti some historical and contextual explanations were given but the curating strategy (arrangement of the works, identification cards, catalogs) indicated that the value of what was presented resided primarily in formal discoveries.

The decodification of the public followed a different logic. Even the majority with a university education was not used to differentiating the formal from the functional, the beautiful from the useful. Instead of basing their judgments on the intrinsic aesthetic values of the works, they tried to relate them to the biography of each artist or to the facts of daily knowledge. In no exhibit did more than 10 percent of the audience allude to the internal structure of the works or use a specifically formal language to comment on them.

The opinions and behavior of the receivers showed them to be closer to the aesthetic that hegemonized Mexican visual art during the first half of the twentieth century. Their criteria proceeded from the nationalism of the muralist school, crafts, archeological and historical objects, and religious iconography. Armed with ingredients from various traditions, the responses of the public make up a mixed discourse in which also figure principles of what we can call modern humanism. In spite of the little attention that the public gives to the autonomy of artistic works, other aspects of modern visual thought are found very widely: "realism," the central place of the human body in artistic representation, the positive valorization of the relation of art to history, of the technical ability of the creators, and the use of that ability to express noble sentiments. These elements are articulated with a perceptive and evaluative syntax proper to diverse sectors.

Let us look at three examples of this heterodox appropriation of modern principles: the relation between affectivity and creative independence, the evaluation of the works more for the meaning of the materials than of the formal treatment, and the combination of the artistic with the decorative and the utilitarian.

a) Most of the public clings to the Romantic current of modernity that concedes greater legitimacy and value to art to the extent one can see in it a broad prolongation of its everyday affectivity. In asking visitors to the Rodin exhibit if they preferred a work that expressed a personal emotion (like *The Kiss*) or those that referred to historical personalities or events (like *The Burghers of Calais* or *Balzac)*, most opted for the former. This would not be surprising given that the latter works allude to an alien history. What does attract our attention is the argument that the works that manifest the subjective would be made by a free act of the artist, and would have a "purity" absent in the historical works, which were carried out on commission. Aside from the inaccuracy of these judgments (*The Kiss* was made on commission with government financing, and Rodin's economic success stemmed from pieces that had an amorous theme), what stands out is the fact that they attribute more value to artistic creation if it is liberated from economic determinations or authorities foreign to art, and that they exalt the artist as a representative hero of great emotions (Cimet and Gullco).

b) In all the exhibits analyzed, a part of the works did not come across to the receivers, at least not in the sense proposed by the museum staff, the catalog, and art criticism. The Henry Moore exhibit presented the greatest difficulties, although it had a very large flow of visitors—180,000—and was one of the most publicized because of the quality of the works on display and the size of the exhibit. The public did not share the praises of the publicity and the critical reviews, concerning what art historians consider the most valuable part of Moore's production: his sculptures. "They repeat a lot" and "He must have gotten bored doing all these works since they all look alike" were comments we heard over and over again. "The deformations become grotesque," "I don't understand modern art," and "It's too abstract" were the most frequent conclusions. Nevertheless, what stood out was the contrast between the visitors' rejection of Moore's formal games and the richness of their opinions upon being questioned about the materials of the sculptures that they preferred. Those who opted for bronze—most of those questioned—argued that "the texture is nicer" and noted that it was "soft," "warm," "polished," "emanates brilliance," "invites one to touch it," "projects tranquillity and passivity," transmits strength, is grandiose, delicate, sublime, suggests "elegance, dignity." The different treatments of the bronze generated different emotions in some of the visitors: "trying to feel the process of how they were done and how they turned out" (García Canclini 1987a). All references to the materials demonstrated more ease in expressing sensual and affective reactions and tactile or warm sensations. For a wide layer, the possibility of developing or mobilizing their sensibility is linked to the material presence of the works more than to the formal treatment or the conceptual meaning contained in them. The privilege conceded to this approximation is coherent with realist preferences, with the "empiricist" and immediate manner of perceiving art, but the variety and subtlety of many responses make one think that access to the works through their materials is not at all superficial.

c) The exhibit of the Finnish artist and designer Tapio Wirkkala, who occupied a third of the space with sculptures and the rest with objects of industrial design, was the one that provoked the most positive reaction from the public. This was mainly a result of the convergence between the beautiful utilitarian objects and the perceptive habits of the public. The sculptures and carvings had little place in preferences and almost no one spoke of their formal merits—for example, the use of the branching and spiraling of the wood, the occasional accentuation of color—about which information was given by the identification cards and the guided tours. There also was little mention made of Wirkkala's formal searches in opinions about the tableware, ceramics, and crystal; we found, however, frequent specifically aesthetic judgments with reference to the materials, and an evaluation attentive to the sensitive and affective effects achieved by the technical skill and by "the union of simplicity with refinement." In asking the public to classify which objects they considered *artistic,* which *decorative,* and which *utilitarian,* we observed that the dividing line between the first two categories ended up being unclear: they judged many pieces to be both artistic and decorative. With respect to the exhibition of practical objects in the museum, only 4 percent were opposed to it: the rest approved, sometimes emphatically, the fact that museums were not dedicated exclusively to what has only an aesthetic value: "exhibitions don't necessarily have to be of paintings"; "It's necessary to associate all artistic and decorative manifestations"; also the design of useful objects "awakens in one the sense of beauty."

In response to questions about the pieces they would like to own and what use they would put them to, there was a clear separation between the museum and the home, between symbolic use—or for distinction—and the utilitarian, between the aesthetic and the quotidian. But they also demanded that the museum be less estranged from daily life, that it link the artistic with the decorative and the utilitarian. The recognition of "modern values" was greater than in the exhibits in which only artistic works were presented. The union of aesthetic pursuits with industrial design showed the value of the museum in becoming "creative," "enriching expressive capacity," and "becoming acquainted with things that one cannot have at home" (García Canclini 1987c).

Culture for Everyone?

The study of artistic consumption in Mexico reveals enormous differences between the museums' offerings and the public's codes of reception. Beginning with this material it is possible to rethink several open problems raised in the preceding chapter and in this one: the disjunctures between social modernization and cultural modernism, between elite politics and mass consumption, and between experimental innovations and cultural democratization.

A first conclusion is that these disjunctures between emitters and receivers of art should not be seen as deviations or incomprehension of the latter with respect to a supposed true meaning of the works. If the meaning of the cultural goods is a construction of the field—that is, of the interactions between artists, the market, museums, and critics—the works do not contain fixed meanings established once and for all. Different structures in the artistic field, and sometimes in their links with society, engender diverse interpretations of the same works. The open character of modern artistic pieces and literary texts makes them particularly available to empty spaces, virtual places, being occupied by unforeseen elements in the process of communication. But this is a property of all cultural manifestations, only more evident in those designated as artistic. It also happens that objects to which only historical or anthropological value were attributed may be read aesthetically, and works judged as artistic lose that recognition through a reorganization of the field.

In the same way, the notion of the public is dangerous if we take it as a homogeneous set of constant behaviors. What is called public is really a sum of sectors that belong to diverse economic and educational strata, with different habits of cultural consumption and availability to relate to goods offered in the market. Especially in complex societies, where the cultural offering is very heterogeneous, there coexist various styles of reception and understanding, formed in unequal relations with goods deriving from cultured, popular, and mass cultural traditions. This heterogeneity is accentuated in Latin American societies by the coexistence of distinct historical temporalities.

On these bases, the aesthetics of reception questions the existence of unique or correct interpretations—as well as incorrect ones—of literary texts. All writing and all messages are plagued with blank, silent, interstitial spaces in which the reader is expected to produce new meanings. Works, according to Eco, are "lazy mechanisms" that demand the cooperation of the reader or the spectator to be complete (1981, 76; see also Jauss, Iser). Of course, the works tend to include more or less veiled instructions, rhetorical devices, to induce readings and delimit the productive activity of the receiver. A more sociological view, generally absent in the aesthetics of reception, will include in these strategies of conditioning editorial and curating operations, publicity, and criticism. But what is fundamental is that the asymmetry between emission and reception be acknowledged, and that in this asymmetry be seen the very possibility of reading and looking at art. There would properly be no literature and no art if there only existed sets of texts and works repeating themselves in an endless monologue.

There is a change in the object of study in contemporary aesthetics. To analyze art is no longer to analyze only works, but the textual and extratextual, aesthetic and social conditions in which the interaction between members of the field engenders and renews meaning. Although the aesthetics of reception works with literary texts, its paradigmatic course is applicable to other artistic fields. In the visual arts, historians who analyze "critical fortune," in other words the reelaborations experienced by a work or a style, also see art "as a relation: the relation between an object and all the gazes that have been cast upon it throughout history" and that have "incessantly transformed" it. This is how Nicos Hadjinicolaou presents it in the book where he demonstrates that *Liberty Leading the People* is the bearer not only of an intrinsic meaning—the one Delacroix wanted to imprint upon it— but of the meanings that built up in the uses made of this work by schoolbooks, advertising, other contemporary artists, readings by historians of different eras and ideologies, and the posters that have reproduced it for disparate political ends.

In listing this variety of often conflicting interpretations, it does not seem possible to conceive of links between members of the artistic field as a mere "interpretative cooperation" (see Eco 1981, chapters 3 and 4) as defined by specialists in the aesthetics of reception. We are presented with a problem equivalent to the one we encounter when Becker talks about cooperation among the members of the art world. Can we eliminate the dilemma of deciding between the degree of correction and the degree of aberration in the readings? Can a text be made to say anything, or are there ways of judging among multiple interpretations? And although it may be difficult to move from cultural relations to the social base, how are operations of definition and control of the interpretations related to the social positions and strategies of the agents?

The asymmetry that almost all the authors of the aesthetics of reception examine as if it only occurred between the text and the reader is an asymmetry between the members of the artistic field as well. Further, it is an asymmetry between the unequal powers of artists, distributors, and audiences, which give to each one different capacities to shape the interpretations that will be judged most legitimate. The conflict over the consecration of the legitimate reading must be included in the analysis. Hence the importance of studying—as do some literary specialists—the "reading agreements" that are established among producers, institutions, market, and public in order to make possible the functioning of literature. To the extent these agreements are achieved, the arbitrariness of the interpretations and the disjunctures between the offer and the reception are reduced. Agreements are reached about what we may call *the possible hermeneutic community* in a given society and time, permitting artists and writers to know what levels of variability and innovation they can manage in order to associate themselves with which audiences, institutions to define policies of communication, and receivers to better understand what their activity of producing meaning may consist of.

It is evident that these questions are related to the debate about how to articulate the innovations and democratization of culture. How could this debate be reformulated in the midst of the limited conditions of development of the autonomous cultural fields and of their democratization in Latin America?

In Mexico the encounters and disjunctures between hegemonic cultural politics and reception are explained by the history of the transformations and cultural agreements. Mass attendance at museums is the result of the programs of cultural diffusion undertaken over the course of decades, while the difficulties in their appropriating international contemporary art stem from the fact that that diffusion only partially resolved inequality. The public's eclectic taste, which mixes the principles of traditional Mexican visual art with an idealist and romantic conception of art, can be correlated with the state's wavering between promoting a culture that is popular-national rather than mercantile and, on the other hand, the conception of the system of museums and artistic education as scenarios of individual consecration in agreement with the aesthetic of the fine arts.

The place of sedimentation and crossing of diverse cultural currents, of unresolved fusion, artistic consumption testifies to the contradictions of social history. Instead of seeing in consumption the docile echo of what cultural politics or some perverse manipulation wants to do with the public, we have to analyze how its own conflictive dynamic accompanies and mimics the waverings of power. Is not hegemony made up of this type of coincidences and complicities between society and the state, more than of the impositions of the latter upon the former? Is not this complicity, attained from relatively different positions, the key to each acknowledging the other and feeling mutually represented? Is not this complicity—which will reappear in the following chapters on social uses of the historical patrimony and popular culture—one of the cultural secrets of the political regime's stability?

Now we are clarifying that this restatement of the relations between cultural policy and consumption, in opposition to the deductive model that analyzes policies as actions imposed by the state upon civil society, does not lead one to imagine a kind of harmony between the two. To acknowledge the relatively independent role of consumers and therefore their specificity as an object of study does not imply forgetting their subordinate position. To affirm that the culture of the receivers has a different history, parallel to the strategies of the hegemonic transmitters, does not mean that cultural policy in Mexico has not been a deliberate project by the rulers, exercised through conflicts and struggles, transactions, and sociocultural agreements.

In these unresolved vacillations and contradictions of consumption are manifested the ambiguities of modernization, the coexistence of diverse cultural traditions, and the unequal appropriation of the patrimony. In the opinions and tastes of the public appear the (relative) success and (relative) failure of social modernization and cultural modernism. What, then, is the efficacy of the innovating and democratizing project? Perhaps Mexico is the Latin American country in which the answer to this question is the most complex and the richest, because it had the *earliest* experience of modern revolution in a society that did not try to renounce its pre-Columbian and colonial traditions, an experience that could be more *radical* and *prolonged* because it manifested a continuous policy destined to popularize culture and develop its own symbolic sources, with changes in direction but without the abrupt alterations of coups d'état suffered by other countries. The conclusion is that modern culture has been shared by a minority (much broader, obviously, than if there had been no revolution) and that ethnic or local cultures were not fully joined to a national symbolic system, although they cannot be foreign to it either. Neither the modernizing nor the unifying projects triumphed completely. But their relative success cannot authorize traditional utopias either. Stated differently: we did not arrive at *one* modernity but rather at various unequal and combined processes of modernization. For that reason today, the most defined feature, the least indecisive adjective in the discourse of cultural functionaries, is not that of nationalist or indigenist or modern but the one that designates society as "pluralist." But what can this word mean today?

When we interviewed those vast numbers of people who were going to a museum for the first time, we found very diverse responses. In the exhibits more akin to their sensibilities—those of Rodin and Kahlo-Modotti—the majority expressed the aesthetic delight that the works aroused in them. But the bewilderment with respect to Moore, the laconic phrases with which they responded to our questions, and the rapid pace at which they moved through the exhibit were ways of saying that at times they did not know why they had been made to listen to the radio, the television, or the school. In seeing that in all the exhibits analyzed about half of the visitors were going to a museum for the first time, we inferred that a large proportion of those who visit do not return, or at least do not acquire the habit of going often. In view of these reactions, is it desirable that *everyone* attend art exhibits?

What purpose is served by a policy that tries to abolish cultural heterogeneity? To suppress some differences and to mark others. Massively spreading what some understand to be "culture" is not always the best way to encourage democratic participation and artistic sensitization; because at the same time that mass distribution of "select" art is a socializing action, it also is a procedure for securing the distinction of those who are familiar with it, those who are capable of separating form and function, those who know how to use the museum. The mechanisms of reinforcement of distinction tend to be resources for reproducing hegemony.

The utopia of socializing modern culture—attempted by Latin American revolutions from the Mexican to the Nicaraguan and by populist regimes—has reduced inequality in the appropriation of some goods considered to be of common interest. But those movements have arrived at points very far from the modern humanism that saw the abolition of divisions between scientists and workers, artists and the people, creators and consumers as an extension of the struggle against economic injustice. If we review the discourses of those movements of radical democratization, in many there appears a homogenizing conception of equality that resembles the projects of unlimited expansion of the communications market. We are not ignoring the ethical and political differences between the action of cultural promoters and the commercial proliferation of mass communications. What we want to problematize is the assumption that museums and other cultural institutions would fulfill their function better if they received more visitors, and that television and radio are successful because they reach audiences of millions. (We found proof that this assumption is common to both in the fact that museums and the media, and the state and private companies, all evaluate their results by means of a quantification of their clientele and almost never conduct qualitative studies on the way their messages are received and processed.)

I will go even further. Sometimes a complicity can be detected between quantitative evaluations of consumption, the neglect of qualitative—and diverse—needs of different sectors, and a certain authoritarianism. Democratization of culture is thought of as if it were a question of eliminating the distance and difference between artists and the public. Why pursue a connection between artists and receivers? It is the basis of a democratic society to create conditions in which everyone has access to cultural goods, not only materially but in terms of having access to prior resources—education, specialized training in the field—in order to understand the meaning conceived by the writer or painter. But there is an authoritarian component in the desire that the interpretations of the receivers and the meaning proposed by the transmitter completely coincide. Democracy is cultural plurality, an interpretative polysemy. A hermeneutics or a policy that closes the relationship of meaning between artists and public is empirically unattainable and conceptually dogmatic.

It is not a question either of just looking for a cooperative and plural cultural community. Differences based on inequalities are not settled with formal democracy. It is not enough to give equal opportunities to everyone if each sector arrives at consumption, or enters a museum or a bookstore, with disparate cultural capitals and habitus. Although cultural relativism, which admits the legitimacy of differences, is a conquest of modernity, we cannot share the conclusion that some draw from the fact that modernizing democratization must not handle values or hierarchize them.

We can conclude that a democratizing policy is not only one that socializes "legitimate" goods but one that problematizes what must be understood by culture and what are the rights of the heterogeneous. Therefore, what must first be questioned is the value of that one which the hegemonic culture excluded or underestimated in order to constitute itself. It must be asked if the predominant cultures—the Western or the national, the state or the private—are capable only of reproducing themselves or also of creating the conditions whereby marginal, heterodox forms of art and culture are manifested and communicated.

Along these lines, the study of consumption, which we propose as a referent for evaluating cultural policies, cannot stop at knowing the effects of hegemonic actions. It must problematize the principles that organize that hegemony, that consecrate the legitimacy of one type of symbolic goods and one mode of appropriating them. A policy is democratic as much for constructing spaces for collective recognition and development as for raising the reflexive, critical, sensitive conditions whereby what hinders that recognition is pondered. Perhaps the central theme of cultural policies today is how to construct societies with democratic projects shared by everyone without making everyone the same, where disintegration is elevated to diversity and inequalities (between classes, ethnic groups, or other groups) are reduced to differences.

Notes

1. These positions of Paz appear in several of his books. We are following here especially *El ogro filantrópico* and *Los hijos del limo*, chapters 3–6.

2. As far as we know, the first to do so was Blas Matamoro, who compiled a *Diccionario de Jorge Luis Borges*, in which he brings together aphorisms and brief texts culled from the writer's essays, prologues, film reviews, and journalistic interviews. It is from his book that we have taken some quotes.

3. Piglia collects his theses on Borges, presented in courses and lectures, through de Renzi, a character in his novel *Respiración artificial* (162-75), and in interviews published in the volume *Crítica y ficción*. In this book he says that in the novel his interpretations of Borges are "exasperated" in order to produce a "fictional" effect, but he does not contradict them. Perhaps Piglia is, after Borges, best at carrying out the task of fictionalizing personal statements in interviews, and confusing the difference between critical discourse and fiction.

4. Paternosto has collected his illuminating analyses of pre-Columbian art and of its correspondences with the art of our century in his book *Piedra abstracta. La escultura inca: una visión contemporánea.*

5. The research to which I refer is that carried out by E. Cimet, M. Dujovne, N. García Canclini, J. Gullco, C. Mendoza, F. Reyes Palma, and G. Soltero: *El público como propuesta. Cuatro estudios sociológicos en museos de arte.* I had the opportunity to elaborate some of the problems that I will discuss at the end of this chapter with the other members of the team, to which I must add the names of Eulalia Nieto, who collaborated in one period of the work, and Juan Luis Sariego, who intervened in designing the survey and processing the data. To the extent that I now make a new reading of those materials, with problems that were only partly present when the investigation took place, it is obvious that the other participants are not responsible for the conclusions suggested here.

4 | The Future of the Past

Facing the Historical Patrimony: Fundamentalists and Modernizers

The modern world is not made only by those who have modernizing projects. When scientists, technologists, and entrepreneurs search for clients they also have to take into account what resists modernity. Not only in the interest of expanding the market, but also in order to legitimize their hegemony, the modernizers need to persuade their addressees that—at the same time that they are renewing society—they are prolonging shared traditions. Given that they claim to include all sectors of society, modern projects appropriate historical goods and popular traditions.

The need traditionalists and renovators have to support each other leads to frequent alliances of cultural groups and religious fundamentalists with economic groups and technocratic modernizers. To the extent their positions are, on certain points, objectively contradictory, these alliances often break down or give rise to explosive tensions. To understand the ambivalent development of modernity, it is necessary to analyze the sociocultural structure of those contradictions.

Nevertheless, in the studies and debates about Latin American modernity the question of the social uses of the patrimony continues to be absent. It would appear that the historical patrimony were the exclusive domain of restorers, archaeologists, and museologists: specialists in the past. In this chapter I will inquire into how historical meaning intervenes in the constitution of agents that are central to the constitution of modern identities (such as schools and museums), and what is the role of rites and commemorations in the renewal of political hegemony. It is necessary to analyze the functions of the historical patrimony in order to explain why fundamentalisms—that is, the dogmatic idealization of those referents that appear foreign to modernity—have been reactivated in the past few years.

Precisely because the cultural patrimony is presented as being alien to debates about modernity, it constitutes the least suspicious resource for guaranteeing social complicity. That group of goods and traditional practices that identify us as a nation or as a people is valued as a gift, something we receive from the past that has such symbolic prestige that there is no room for discussing it. The only operations that are possible—to preserve it, restore it, disseminate it—are the most secret basis of the social simulation that keeps us together as a group. In the presence of the magnificence of a Maya or Inca pyramid, of colonial palaces, indigenous ceramics from three centuries ago, or the work of an internationally recognized national painter, it occurs to almost no one to think about the social contradictions that they express. The perennial character of these goods makes us imagine that their value is beyond question and turns them into a source of collective consensus, beyond the divisions among classes, ethnic groups, and other groups that fracture society and differentiate ways of appropriating that patrimony.

For that very reason, it is in the patrimony that the ideology of the oligarchic sectors—that is, substantialist traditionalism—survives best today. It was these groups—hegemonic in Latin America from the time of national independence to the 1930s, "natural" owners of the land and the labor power of the other classes—that set the high value on certain cultural goods: the historical centers of the great cities, classical music, humanistic knowledge. They also incorporated some popular goods under the name of "folklore," a label that indicated its differences with respect to art as much as the subtlety of the cultured gaze, which was capable of recognizing the value of the generically human even in the objects of the "others."

The confrontation between this ideology and modern development— since the industrialization and massification of European societies in the eighteenth and nineteenth centuries—reactively generated a metaphysical, ahistorical view of the "national being," whose superior manifestations, deriving from a mythical origin, supposedly exist today only in the objects that recall it. The conservation of those archaic goods would have little to do with their current utility. To preserve a historic site, or certain furniture and customs, is a task with no other end than that of guarding aesthetic and symbolic models. Their unaltered conservation would attest to the fact that the essence of that glorious past survives the processes of change.

The contemporary interest of the traditional patrimony would reside in "spiritual" benefits that are difficult to ponder, but upon whose permanence would depend the present well-being of the people. Faced with the "catastrophes" of modernization, of new technologies, and of anonymous cities, the countryside and its traditions will represent the last hope for "redemption." The Argentine folklorist Félix Coluccio was asked at the end of 1987: what are the provinces to you? He replied:

> They are the soul of the country. When I think of a possible salvation, I see that it could only come from there. The permanence of cultural values, the respect for tradition and, above all, the fact that communities do something transcendent in respecting their identity are most secure in the interior of the country. (Ulanovsky, 18)

The Staging of Power

To understand the essential relations of modernity with the past requires an examination of the operations of cultural ritualization. In order for traditions today to serve to legitimize those who constructed or appropriated them, they must be staged. The patrimony exists as a political force insofar as it is dramatized—in commemorations, monuments, and museums. In our America, where it is only within the last few years—and not in all countries—that the majority of the population has become literate, it is not surprising that culture has been predominantly visual. To be cultured, then, is to grasp a body of knowledge—largely iconographic—about one's own history, and also to participate in the stagings in which hegemonic groups have society present itself with a scene of its origin. In contrast to the usual analyses of ideology, which explain the organization of social meaning through the production and circulation of ideas, I will limit myself principally to the visual and dramatic construction of meaning.

The dramatization of daily life and of power began to be studied by symbolic interactionists and structuralists only a few years ago, but it had been recognized prior to that by writers and philosophers who saw in it a key ingredient in the constitution of the bourgeoisie, of the culture of the town, of the city. Antecedents to the conception of life as theater can be found in Plato's *Laws* or in Petronius's *Satyricon*, but what is interesting here is the modern meaning of dramatization that some people make not before divinity but before other people, in the way Diderot, Rousseau, and Balzac began to observe it: social performance as staging, simulacrum, mirror of mirrors, without an original model. In the midst of secularization, which brought social norms down from heaven to earth, and from the realm of sacred rites to that of daily debate, it would seem that the cultural patrimony is the site most resistant to this process.

The dramatization of the patrimony is the effort to simulate that there is an origin, a founding substance, in relation with which we should act today. This is the basis of authoritarian cultural policies. The world is a stage, but what must be performed is already prescribed. The practices and objects of value are found cataloged in a fixed repertory. To be cultured implies knowing that repertory of symbolic goods and intervening correctly in the rituals that reproduce it. For that reason the notions of collection and ritual are key to deconstructing the links between culture and power.

The "philosophical" foundation of traditionalism is summarized in the certainty that there is an ontological correspondence between reality and representation, between society and the collections of symbols that represent it. What is defined as patrimony and identity claims to be the faithful reflection of the national essence. Hence its principal dramatic performance is the mass commemoration: civic and religious celebrations, patriotic anniversaries, and, in dictatorial societies, especially restorations. The historical patrimony that is celebrated consists of founding events, the heroes who played the main roles in them, and the fetishized objects that evoke them. The legitimate rites are those that stage the desire for repetition and perpetuation of order.

Authoritarian politics is monotonous theater. The relations between the government and the people consist of staging what is supposed to be the definitive patrimony of the nation. Historic sites and squares, palaces and churches, serve as the stage for representing the national destiny, traced from the beginning of time. Politicians and priests are the vicarious actors in this drama.

Bertolt Brecht, who applied his professional knowledge to uncover the way nonprofessional actors utilize theatrical techniques, observed how Hitler constructed his roles in diverse situations: the music lover, the unknown soldier in the Second World War, the happy and generous comrade of the people, the troubled friend of the family. Hitler did everything with great emphasis, especially when he represented heroic personalities; he extended his leg and completely supported the sole of his foot in order to achieve his majestic gait. But it was not enough that the protagonist learn diction and spectacular movements—as Hitler did by taking classes from the actor Basil in Munich and as more recent politicians have in Hollywood. Today we know that all politics is made in part with theatrical resources: the inaugurations for which it is not known if there will be a budget to carry them off, public recognition of rights that will be denied in private.

Brecht said it more eloquently than I can:

> The messages of the men of state, it was written half a century ago, are not impulsive and spontaneous outbursts. They are elaborated and reelaborated from many points of view and they set a date for their presentation.

Even so, it is rumored among the public—"because the people are transformed into the public"—that no one suspects what the statesman is going to say. When the moment arrives, however, he does not speak like someone extraordinary but like a man of the street. He wants those who hear him to identify with him. And so

> he begins a personal duel with other individuals, with foreign ministers or with politicians. He launches furious imprecations in the style of Homeric heroes, broadcasts his indignation, and gives the impression that he is making a great effort not to lunge at the throat of his adversary: he challenges him, calling him by name, makes fun of him. (163)

The contention and the suspense—what is not named—are as important as what is said. The dramatic sense of the commemoration is accentuated by silences, while the ritual staging is offered so that all can share in a knowledge that is a set of implied understandings. It is true nonetheless that such a situation can have a positive value. Every group that wants to differentiate itself and affirm its identity makes tacit or hermetic use of identification codes that are fundamental to internal cohesion and to protect itself from strangers. In conservative regimes, whose cultural policy tends to be reduced to administration of the preexisting patrimony and to reiteration of established interpretations, ceremonies are events that ultimately only celebrate redundancy. They seek the maximum identification of the public-people with the accumulated cultural capital, with its distribution and its effective use. There is nothing better than old buildings and their style, the history of school practice, and conventional images for representing it. For patrimonial conservatism, the ultimate purpose of culture is to be converted into nature. To be natural like a gift.

The school is a key stage for the theatricalization of the patrimony. Through systematic courses, it transmits knowledge about the goods that constitute the natural and historic common estate. In teaching geography, it says what the territory of the nation is and where it ends; in the study of history, events are related through which those boundaries succeeded in being fixed in struggle against external and internal adversaries. Few have formulated this with the clarity of Domingo F. Sarmiento, founder of the lay school system in Argentina ("father of the classroom," says the hymn the students sing) and one of the organizers of modern society in that country. His motto "civilization or barbarism" differentiates the indigenous-mestizo—uncultured—pole of society from the progressive and educated development (defined by the Creole groups) that made possible the nation's existence. The liberal education he founded, which had the merit of being liberated from religious tutelage, nevertheless separates a legitimate patrimony—sacred from a certain point of view—in which the "better" inhabitants of the country could recognize themselves, and excludes the original inhabitants of the territory. With that founding cut, the school program separates the historic deeds that were establishing the correct ways of occupying the national space: "The passage from the uncultured and rude nomad to the working settler, from the vagabond to the farmer" (Batallán and Díaz).

These meanings are not "inculcated" only through the conceptual contents of educational instruction. They are the motive for celebrations, festivals, expositions, and visits to mythic places, an entire system of rituals in which the "naturalness" of the demarcation establishing the original and "legitimate" patrimony is periodically ordered, remembered, and secured. Batallán and Díaz demonstrate that everyday ritual, school discipline, and its peculiar language collaborate in this task: when the prevailing order is transgressed, teachers are accustomed to saying that in school "you don't have to behave like savages"; when it is time to move from the playground to the classroom, they announce that "the time of the Indians is over."

At this point we can clarify that we are not denying here the need for commemorative ceremonies of founding events, which are indispensable for giving density and historical roots to the contemporary experience of any group. Nor do we pretend to ignore the value of school rituals, recognized by ethnographic studies as valuable for forming bonds between teachers and students, shaping consensus about developing activities, and implementing the learning required by "mechanizations." But, as such studies show, excessive ritualization—with just one paradigm, used dogmatically—conditions its practitioners to behave in a uniform way in identical contexts, and renders them incapable of acting when the questions are different and the elements involved are articulated in a different way (Rockwell, 21–22; see also Safa).

In social processes, relations that are highly ritualized with a unique and exclusive historical patrimony—national or regional—create difficulties in performance in changing situations, in autonomous learning processes, and in the production of innovations. In other words, substantialist traditionalism disables people from living in the contemporary world, which is characterized—as we will have occasion to analyze later on—by its heterogeneity, mobility, and deterritorialization.

Nevertheless, traditionalism often appears as a resource for enduring the contradictions of contemporary life. In this epoch in which we doubt the benefits of modernity, temptations mount for a return to some past that we imagine to be more tolerable. In the face of impotence in confronting social disorders, economic impoverishment, and technological challenges, in the face of the difficulty in understanding them, the evocation of distant times reinstates in contemporary life archaisms that modernity had displaced. Commemoration becomes a compensatory practice: if we cannot compete with advanced technologies, let us celebrate our handicrafts and old techniques; if modern ideological paradigms seem useless for accounting for the present and no new ones arise, let us reconsecrate the religious dogmas or the esoteric cults that provided the foundation for life before modernity.

The exhumation of the premodern is not limited to individual flights. The latest Latin American dictatorships accompanied the restoration of social order with an intensification of the celebration of the events and symbols they represent: the commemoration of the "legitimate" past—which corresponds to the "national essence," to morals, to religion, and to the family—becomes the preponderant cultural activity. To participate in social life is to comply with a system of ritualized practices that leave out "the foreign," whatever challenges the consecrated order or promotes skepticism. In order that coups d'état become unnecessary in the future, Argentine military officials recommended a return to the era of the original grandeur of the Nation, which was interrupted at the end of the nineteenth century by the "combination of scientific rationalism, the machine age, romanticism, and democracy."[1] It is obvious that to return so far into the past the present must be emptied of many cultural products, as was seen during the last dictatorship in Argentina when books, exhibitions of paintings, movies and television programs, foreign music, and even folk songs and irreverent tangos were banned.

Even after Argentina regained democracy, fundamentalist movements continue to assail modernity, political and sexual liberalism, and artistic and scientific experimentation. They attack the staging of *Galileo Galilei* and other works by Brecht, along with those of Dario Fo that satirize religious fanaticism. The church threatened with excommunication deputies who—in 1986!—discussed the legalization of divorce, pluralism in public education, and cultural creation.

In Mexico, groups of Catholic fanatics invaded art museums in January 1988 to prevent the exhibition of paintings of the Virgin of Guadalupe that altered the orthodox image. They demanded expulsion from the country for the director of the Museum of Modern Art and psychiatric imprisonment for the artists who portrayed the Virgin with the face of Marilyn Monroe, and Christ with the face of the actor Pedro Infante and wearing boxing gloves. Public spaces in which any religious ceremony has been prohibited by law since last century were symbolically reconquered by those who imagine they can conjure away the contradictions of the present with celebrations of the Virgin in museums and with the restoration of traditional iconography. They seem not to recognize that canonical images are the product of relatively arbitrary figurative conventions: the faces of many virgins allowed by the church have been modeled on those of lovers of kings, popes, and of the artists themselves; with regard to the Virgin of Guadalupe, the Renaissance morphology of her face, the brown color of her skin that favored her identification with indigenous people, and the many changes she has undergone throughout history—from cinematographic representations to the pop and kitsch images of Chicano art (Conde, 18)—make any pretension of subjecting her rating to a pure model completely ridiculous. Rather, they suggest that the extension of this fervor is based on the fusion of the Hispanic and the Indian, on the diversity of later intercultural contexts in which it was inserted, and on the always hybrid versatility of its reinterpretations.

Traditionalist commemoration often establishes itself on an ignorance of the past. Given that this version of the cultured is sustained by oligarchic groups, it can be supposed that their "ignorance" results from an interest in preserving the privileges they conquered in the idealized period. But how do we explain that this need to deny the complexity of the past, the impurities of *mestizaje*, and the innovations with which culture accompanies social changes receives ardent support from the popular sectors? We will return to this question in the chapter dedicated to the popular. Anticipating our discussion, for now we note that the ultimate purpose of authoritarian celebration seems to go beyond the interests of the hegemonic class that sponsors it. What such diverse groups attempt to do in spiritualizing the production and consumption of culture, in detaching it from the social and the economic, in eliminating all experimentation and reducing the symbolic life of society to the ritualization of a dogmatically affirmed national or cosmic order is, at bottom, to neutralize the instability of the social.

Are National Museums Possible after the Crisis of Nationalism?

If the patrimony is interpreted as a fixed repertory of traditions condensed in objects, then it needs a warehouse stage to contain and protect it and a display-window stage to exhibit it. The museum is the ceremonial headquarters of the patrimony, the place where it is kept and celebrated, where the semiotic regime with which hegemonic groups organized it is reproduced. To enter a museum is not simply to go into a building and look at works; rather, it is a ritualized system of social action.

For a long time museums were seen as gloomy spaces where traditional culture would be preserved, solemn and boring, withdrawn in upon itself. "Museums are the last resort on a rainy Sunday," said Heinrich Böll. Since the 1960s an intense debate over their structure and function, with daring renovations, has changed their meaning. They are no longer only institutions for preserving and exhibiting objects; nor are they deadly refuges of minorities.

The number of visitors to museums in the United States, which reached fifty million in 1962, surpassed the total population of that country in 1980. In France, museums receive more than twenty million people a year, and the Pompidou Center alone surpasses eight million, evidence of the attraction that a new type of institution can arouse: in addition to the Museum of Modern Art, it offers temporary exhibits on science and technology, books, magazines, and records for self-service use—in short, the stimulating atmosphere of a multifaceted cultural center. European statistics indicate that museum attendance is growing, while the number of theater and movie spectators has been decreasing in the last few years (Ministry of Culture of Spain, 43). Museums, as mass communication media, can play a significant role in democratizing culture and in changing the concept of culture.

Other signs of vitality are found in the architectural and curating renovation that has refreshed traditional museums (the Louvre, the Whitney in New York, the National Gallery in Washington) and converted some into outstanding testimonies to aesthetic innovation (the Guggenheim, the Pompidou, the Neue Staatsgalerie in Stuttgart). "They put an end to the pilgrimages on one's knees" to "museums without light, with hidden restrooms, and nonexistent cafeterias," where art was an object of work and not of pleasure, exclaimed Marta Traba on discovering the new museums in the United States. They sometimes replace the public square, she said, because they are meeting places where we can spend the day, eat, and enjoy ourselves (15).

Changes in the conception of the museum—insertion in cultural centers, creation of ecomuseums, community, school, and on-site museums—and various scenic and communicational innovations (new atmospheres, educational services, video introductions) prevent us from continuing to talk about these institutions as simple warehouses of the past. Many museums are again assuming the role given to them since the nineteenth century, when they were opened to the public, complementing the school: to define, classify, and conserve the historical patrimony, to link symbolic expressions capable of unifying a nation's regions and classes, to give order to the continuity between the past and the present, between one's own and the foreign. Today we should recognize that the alliances, whether involuntary or deliberate, of museums with mass media and tourism have been more effective for cultural diffusion than artists' attempts to take art out into the street.

The crisis of the museum is not over. An abundant bibliography continues to question the obstinate anachronism of many of them, and the violence they do to cultural goods by tearing them out of their original context and reordering them according to a spectacular view of life. Debates continue over the changes an institution marked since its origins by the most elitist strategies requires in order to relocate itself in the industrialization and democratization of culture.[2]

It is undeniable, in any case, that many museums in the United States, Europe, and Japan are key instruments today for those countries in the renewal of their domestic and international cultural hegemony, and for reconstructing ritual relations with knowledge and art. This is not the situation in Latin America. Therefore, reflection on the place of museums in patrimonial policy can serve to help us find explanations for our deficient cultural development and our peculiar inscription in Western modernity.

Why are museums so bad in Latin America? Not all are, of course. Some are cited as examples by the specialized bibliography: in Mexico, the National Museum of Anthropology and the National Museum of Cultures; the Gold Museum in Bogotá; the Children's Museum in Caracas; and several other art museums in these and other countries. But against these exceptions are hundreds of museums that appear improvised but that have always been that way, where the precontemporary conception persists of piling up pieces in glass cases that reach to the ceilings of monumental buildings.

In Peru, one of the countries with the greatest archaeological and historical wealth on the continent, a large part of the patrimony has been looted by
nationals and foreigners. Only 25 percent of that country's sixty museums
have acquisition programs, barely four have curators, and six offer daily
guided visits. Only seven museums have insured their collections and one
has humidity control in its storage facilities. The lack of inclination on the
part of governmental organizations to correct this situation—or at least to
become aware of its seriousness—can be measured by the fact that when
Alfonso Castrillón gathered these data in the first survey of Peruvian museums, conducted in 1982, he could not obtain funding for his study and the
National Institute of Culture refused to respond to the survey because it
judged it to be "indiscreet" (Castrillón, 7–9).

The belated actions in favor of the patrimony tend to be the work of
civil society, private corporations, or community groups. In some countries
that were able to build good history and art museums—Brazil, Colombia,
Venezuela—many of them belong to banks, foundations, and nongovern-
mental associations. They are concentrated in the big cities and operate
without any connection among each other or with the educational system,
in part because they depend on private organizations, but also because of
the lack of an organic cultural policy at the national level. They act more as
conservators of a small portion of the patrimony, a resource for tourist promotion and advertising by private corporations, than as molders of a collective visual culture.

It is logical that, among Latin American countries, Mexico, because of the
nationalist orientation of its postrevolutionary policy, should be the one
that has been most concerned with expanding visual culture, preserving its
patrimony, and integrating it into a system of museums and archaeological
and historical centers. In the first half of the twentieth century, the documentation and diffusion of the patrimony was done through temporary and
traveling exhibits, cultural missions, and muralism. There were studies on
traditions and collections of objects were formed, but without the consecrating gesture of long duration that involves the exhibition in museums of
a definitively established national culture. Educational policy took priority
over conservation, mass public awareness over the concentration of goods
in buildings.

Beginning in the 1950s, when the revolution was institutionalized and
modernizing currents were imposed on governmental policy, the patrimony
was arranged in differentiated museums. Industrial and tourist development, and the greater professionalization of artists and social scientists, con-

tributed to separating the historical from the artistic, the traditional from the modern, the cultured from the popular. With the goal of creating spaces appropriate to exhibition and consecration for each sector, a complex network of museums arose that doubles every six years and, together with the schools and the mass media, constitutes the stages for classifying and valorizing cultural goods. Although Mexico has a powerful literature, its cultural profile was not established primarily by writers: from the codices to muralism, from the death's-heads of José Guadalupe Posada to paintings and short stories, from the handicraft markets to the mass audiences of the museums, the conservation and celebration of the patrimony, its knowledge and its use, is basically a visual operation.

The big Mexican museums invalidate several stereotypes with which these institutions tend to be disqualified. They show that the main problem facing the museums today is not their decadence. Many are self-absorbed, and simply agglomerate objects; but there are also notable experiments in architectural, curating, and educational renovation. Another commonplace, which attributes the expansion of the audience to the increase in tourism, is contradicted by the figures. The Mexican museums of anthropology and history alone (not counting art museums) received 6,916,339 visitors in 1988, of whom foreigners made up no more than 20 percent.[3]

1. With the goal of understanding the strategies with which private and state institutions stage the cultural patrimony, we will analyze two cases that are representative of the curating policies displayed in Mexico. We choose them also because they coincide with those tried in other Latin American countries in order to insert the cultured traditional into modernity. The first strategy is the *aestheticist spiritualization* of the patrimony. The second is *historical and anthropological ritualization*. We will analyze both policies with the intention of determining whether their modes of consecrating national culture can be sustained in this epoch of the radical crisis of nationalisms.

The aestheticization of the patrimony is appreciated in exemplary fashion in the Rufino Tamayo Museum of Mexican Pre-Hispanic Art in Oaxaca, created by the painter, with the help of Fernando Gamboa, to exhibit his collection. It follows, in part, the exhibition guidelines of the classic European museums—for example, the British Museum and the Louvre—which still persist in institutions that claim to be advanced, as in the collection of indigenous art at the Menil Museum in Houston. The antique objects are separated from the social relations for which they were produced; criteria of autonomization of sculptures and paintings inaugurated by modern aesthetics are imposed upon cultures that integrated art with religion, politics, and economics; the objects are converted into *works* and their value is reduced to the formal game that they establish through their proximity to others in that neutral space—apparently existing outside of history—that is the museum. Detached from semantic and pragmatic references, these pieces are seen according to the meaning fixed for them by the aesthetic relations that the arbitrary syntax of the exhibit program establishes.

Those who organized the Tamayo Museum think that the artistic value of the objects is the most important justification for their being displayed. They wrote at the entrance that

> if the anonymous authors of the works exhibited here had not been artists, if their hands had not been guided by a creative spirit, these works would be forgotten today; they would have disappeared the moment the end they served disappeared.

They do not deny that the material presented possesses "an immense importance as an archaeological, historical, and cultural document, but, above and beyond everything else, it exists today as an independent artistic value, accessible to any awakened sensitivity." The museum prides itself on being the first in the country

> that exhibits works of the indigenous Mexican past as nothing more than art, as an artistic phenomenon. For this reason, there has been a refusal in this museum to arrange the collections by paying attention to the different cultures. To present them, the criterion of chronological order has been adopted, but without rigidity.

Therefore, there is also a lack of contextual information. On the pretext of exalting the ancient art of Mexico, it is robbed of one of the keys to its value: the everyday or ceremonial function for which the original users made it.

The aestheticist approach to curating does not eliminate the ceremonial nature of the museum. It creates another type of ritual, not the one that gave social meaning to the pieces, but the one of those lay temples founded to celebrate the supremacy of the cultured gaze. The solemnity of the buildings, the complexity of the messages they transmit, and the difficulties in understanding them oblige one to behave in them as someone who docilely represents a dramatic text that prescribes the manner in which the visitors must move about, speak, and above all keep quiet if they want their action to have meaning.

It is undeniable that this type of museum has contributed to bringing people closer to cultures, to making them known among themselves, and to giving us visual proofs of a common universal history. By making it clear that our people and our ancient artists have a creative history, but at the same time are not the only ones who create, we are indebted to them for having shaken the meager certainties of ethnocentrism long before the mass media did. But their use of the aesthetics of the fine arts to bring together in the Louvre, the British Museum, and the Metropolitan Museum in New York Egyptian statues, Persian temples, and African masks, or to bring together in the Tamayo Museum in Oaxaca the products of diverse ethnic groups that predate Mexican national integration, reinforces the bad habits of political and intellectual expansionism. Although they contribute to conceiving a solidary beauty above geographical and cultural differences, they also engender a uniformity that hides the social contradictions present in the birth of those works. The statues are no longer invoked, and in those museums it is impossible to know how and why they used to be invoked. It seems as if the pots had never been used to cook with, nor the masks for dancing. Everything is there to be looked at.

Fascination in the face of beauty annuls astonishment in the face of the different. It asks for contemplation, not the effort that should be made by someone who arrives in a different society and needs to learn its language, its ways of cooking and eating, of working and rejoicing. These museums serve little to relativize their own habits because they are not like the anthropologist who, in going to a different group decenters his or her own universe, but rather like the computer or the video that brings the information to our house and adapts it to known schemas. They deliver to those familiar with the cultured aesthetic a domestic view of universal culture.

2. The National Museum of Anthropology stages the Mexican patrimony in a different way. Without neglecting aesthetic veneration, it resorts to the *monumentalization* and *nationalist ritualization* of culture. Its origin lies in the National Museum, founded in 1825, but its name, location, and functions changed several times. The last stage, which generated its international fame, begins on September 17, 1964, with the inauguration in Chapultepec Forest of a modern building of 45,000 square meters, with twenty-five exhibition rooms, large workshops, laboratories, warehouses, cubicles for researchers, a library of 250,000 volumes, a theater, an auditorium, a restaurant, and a bookstore.

There are a number of national museums in Mexico but none is considered—whether inside or outside the country—as being as representative of Mexicanness as this one. This privilege tends to be attributed to the splendor of the building, the size and diversity of its collection, and to its being the most visited: in 1988 it received 1,379,910 visitors. All these elements are con-

tributing factors, but I think that its success resides above all in the skillful utilization of architectural and curating resources to fuse two readings of the country: that of science and that of political nationalism.

The convergence of these two perspectives is represented in the structure of the museum and in the routes it proposes. The building forms a gigantic rectangle with two lateral wings that close at the far end of the museum, leaving a semiopen patio in the center. If we enter on the right, we begin with the scientific introduction: the first room is dedicated to explaining human evolution, based on the questions of the common spectator. "What the bones tell us" is the title of one of the sections. The pieces are selected for their scientific value, many for their beauty, and also so as to ensure that all continents are equally represented. The room has a final synthesis where it is affirmed that "all peoples resolve the same needs with different resources, and in different ways all cultures are equally valuable."

The following sections describe the history of Mesoamerica from its origins, then each region and each of the main ethnic groups that today constitute Mexico. The initial legitimation of all cultures scientifically establishes the praise of the indigenous people that the museum stages by showing the products of their creativity and the high level of knowledge attained by some groups.

If we enter on the left, the first rooms present us with the extreme zones of the country, the cultures of the north and of the Maya. In this case the route

ends with the scientific discourse, which serves then to totalize and justify the order of the objects and the explanations received. The confusion provoked by the indigenous pieces culminates in the most consistent form of legitimation that modern culture offers: scientific knowledge.

Whichever of the two itineraries is followed, it is clear that the central hall, situated at the rear of the building where the two lateral wings are joined, is the most outstanding. One has to go up a ramp to enter and see the culture of the Mexicas, who inhabited the central region of the country, where Tenochtitlán was built and where the capital is today. Not only for this reason does the museum represent the unification established by political nationalism in contemporary Mexico, but also because it brings together original pieces from all regions of the country in the city that is the seat of power. We know that this was not done without protests, and that there were cases in which local resistance was successful in retaining objects in their native sites.[4] But the bringing together of thousands of testimonies from all over Mexico attests to the triumph of the centralist project, announcing that here the intercultural synthesis is produced.

This concentration of grandiose and diverse objects is the first basis for the monumentalization of the patrimony. It was enough to bring together so many gigantic pieces in a single building: the Sun Stone or Aztec Calendar, the enormous head of the fire serpent, the wall of skulls, large masks and facade lintels, stelas and stones inscribed with bas-reliefs, mural paintings, sculptures, columns, statuary columns, and colossal idols dedicated to birth and death, the wind and the water, tender and mature corn, fertility and war. Not only the size of many pieces generates the monumental effect but also their multicolored heterogeneity and visual exuberance.

The most emphatic monuments are those that refer to the nation's founders. The hall of origins opens with a large mural in which various people arrive in America via the Bering Strait and look out from a mountaintop upon the great expanse of earth and ice populated with many animals whom it is supposed they will hunt with their lances. Shortly afterward, the same effect is produced by the enormous paintings that display Pleistocene fauna.

Another key reference in national history is Teotihuacán. Upon entering this section, large letters above the map of Mexico warn us: PLACE OF GODS. We cross a low room with a large display window replete with pots and miniatures, pass under a minutely decorated lintel that is even lower, and soon opens up an enormous hall eight meters high, where, on the right, a wall of the Temple of Quetzalcóatl erupts, facing reproductions of large paintings from the Palace of the Plumed Snails, and, on the left, the giant sculpture of Chalchiuhtlicue, goddess of water, and farther on, a photo-mural of the image of the Pyramid of the Sun, six by fourteen meters in size.

This example is of interest in observing that monumentalist rhetoric was not constructed only with the gigantic but also through its contrast with the

small, and even through the accumulation of miniatures. The same thing happens in the Mexica room when, behind the large Sun Stone, we find a market with more than three hundred miniature human figures who are selling vegetables, animals, pottery, grains, crates, and baskets, all minuscule,

in some fifty booths. The agglomeration of miniatures in this market and in the display windows that extend fifteen to twenty meters along one wall magnify the individual pieces.

When the discursive strategy enlarges meaning, the bringing together of miniatures can have a monumentalizing effect. It brings us closer to the abstract or invisible entity alluded to and allows us to apprehend it in a single gaze. Lévi-Strauss noted that the paintings of the Sistine Chapel are a reduced model, despite their imposing dimensions, because the theme they illustrate is the end of time (44). Every miniature that is exhibited as a symbol of national identity, or of the cosmic or historic powers that engendered Mexicanness, delivers a blow to an unembraceable totality through the accumulation of observations about the real. An inversion of the process of knowledge is produced in the museum. While in order to know the objects of daily life we tend to analyze each one of its parts, in the face of the symbols that offer the reduced scale and the "concrete" image of the abstract entity, we feel that the totality appears to us. Even when the three hundred miniatures doing business in the Mexica market do not have all the realistic details, what Lévi-Strauss says in a different context can be applied to them: "The intrinsic virtue of the reduced model is that it compensates the renunciation of the perceptible dimensions with the acquisition of intelligible dimensions" (46).

The Museum of Anthropology proposes a monumentalized version of

the patrimony through the exhibition of giant pieces, the mythified evocation of real scenes, and the accumulation of miniatures. The visitor is seduced—but not overwhelmed—by this battery of resources. The monumentalization is not brutally imposed. There are plaques with clear explanations and orientations that contextualize the objects with photos, drawings, maps, and dioramas. On the ground floor of every room there are optional routes, and at the end of some of them there are various exits: leading to the next section, to the patio or the garden, to the rooms on upper floor. On the top floor, wide window lattices allow one to see the patio, only partially covered, which does not close off the space between the buildings: it opens a view to the Chapultepec Forest that surrounds the museum. This sensation of openness and lightness is reinforced because the roof that covers it (which is fifty-four by eighty-two meters) has only one visible support—the large central column—and the visitor is unaware of the system of cables that supports the weight from the central post. The patio is not a closed space; "it is a protected space" (Granillo Vázquez, 32).

The greatest museum's achievement lies in its presenting a traditionalist vision of Mexican culture in a modern architectural package and by using recent curating techniques. Everything is directed toward exalting the archaic patrimony, supposedly pure and autonomous, without imposing that perspective in a dogmatic way. It presents it in an open fashion that allows one to admire the monumental and at the same time to linger in a reflexive relationship, sharing intimate moments, with what is exhibited.

The Museum of Anthropology illustrates well the complex insertion of

the traditional patrimony in modern nations because it is at once an open and a centralized structure. The tension between monumentalism and miniaturization, between the archaic and the recent, gives verisimilitude to the museum as a staged synthesis of Mexican nationality. The museum, which presents itself as national, wants to be the vehicle of totality and seeks to make this claim credible by its gigantic size, its twenty-five rooms, and its five kilometers of corridors. One of the most frequent commentaries that we heard from those leaving after their first visit is that "you can't see everything in just one visit."

The simulated "infinitude" of the museum is a metaphor of the infinitude of the national patrimony, but also of the capacity of the exhibition to include it. The museum resembles a faithful testimony to reality. If the visitor is not able to see everything, nor to stop at all the works, nor to read all the plaques, that is his or her problem. The virtue of the institution is to offer at once the totality of the cultures of Mexico and the impossibility of knowing them, the vastness of the nation and the difficulty for each individual to appropriate it on his or her own.

To achieve this result, the resources of staging and ritualization are decisive. The atmospheres introduce the external world into the museum. In going through the room on the origins of American civilizations, suddenly a pit is opened exposing the remains of the mammoth discovered near Santa Isabel Iztapán in 1954. Not only is the hole with the skeleton reproduced, but

so is the moment of the discovery—the pick and the shovel, the brush and the meterstick, the archaeologist's box of tools, his chair, on which his open notebook and pencil are lying—as if the researcher had just gotten up a moment ago and as if we were present at the discovery. It is as if a Mexico replete with historical treasures disseminated outside had been contained, as if it were erupting, inside the museum. Nevertheless, one turns around and there are display windows with bones neatly arranged—the scene of a group of hunters facing an elephant, spectacular but artificially realized—and, in

addition, dozens of visitors, to bring us back to the fact that we are in a museum. The staging goes together with the distancing. Modern ritual includes the possibility of separating ourselves and looking, as spectators, upon what we are participating in.

These two fluctuations—between monumentalization and miniaturization, between exterior and interior—are complementary. History is linked with the quotidian thanks to the fact that what reality presents as undefined and undefinable is assimilated by the imaginary duplication of the curating, by means of "a contradiction toward the minuscule or an expansion toward the immense." It is not a simple technical resource, as Pietro Bellasi has shown; these stagings of the quotidian that play with "megalization" and "miniaturization"—which are common in the linguistic operations dealing with alterity—are ritual acts of "metabolization of the other" (235-36). The other is made "soluble," digestible, when, in the same act in which its grandeur is acknowledged, it is reduced and becomes intimate.

The Museum of Anthropology in Mexico City makes visible still other key operations in the modern treatment of the patrimony and broadens the repertory by including the popular. More: it says that national culture has its source and its axis in the indigenous. This opening is made, however, by marking the limits of the ethnic, equivalent to those that are practiced in social relations. One procedure consists of separating ancient culture—the pre-Columbian indigenous—from contemporary culture. To accomplish this operation, the museum utilizes the difference between archaeology and ethnography, which is translated architecturally and scenographically in the separation between the ground floor (dedicated to pre-Hispanic material) and the upper floor (where indigenous life is represented). The other operation is to present this high part while eliminating the features of modernity: it describes the Indians without the objects of industrial production and mass consumption that we often see in their communities today. We cannot know, therefore, the hybrid forms that the traditional ethnic assumes in mixing with capitalist socioeconomic and cultural development. The quantity of photos and atmospheres suggests a contact with the contemporary lives of the Indians. But these images—except in the Nahua section—exclude any element capable of making modernity present. Although current information is given out in the guided visits, most of the public is left without knowing anything of what the crisis in agrarian production, in its techniques and social relations, and the new conditions imposed on handicrafts by their insertion in urban markets, or on fiestas and ancient fairs by interacting with tourism, have meant for traditional cultures for decades.

Nor do other ethnic groups appear that have had and have a significant role in the formation of modern Mexico. Spaniards, blacks, Asians, Jews, Germans, and Arabs are never mentioned. The anthropological vision is reduced to the pre-Hispanic and the traditional indigenous.

This outline becomes curious when we note that a central aim of the museum is to exhibit the great ethnic cultures as part of the modern project represented in the building of the nation. The museum has to consent to a few signs of modernity so that its discourse is believable: it speaks of the conquest, and gives the number of inhabitants of some states with the goal of emphasizing the high or low proportion of Indians. But it does not explain what historical processes and what social conflicts devastated their populations and changed their way of life. It prefers to expound a "pure" and unified cultural patrimony under the sign of Mexicanness. We already analyzed what is achieved by simultaneously exalting the singular indigenous cultures of each group in order to subordinate them to the common character of the Indian and the unity of the nation. But does not all museifying involve a process of abstraction? Can national identity be affirmed—within or outside of museums—without reducing ethnic and regional peculiarities to a constructed common denominator? Is there a criterion that makes it possible to differentiate legitimate abstraction from that which is not?

Everything depends on who the subject is that selects the patrimonies of diverse groups, combines them, and constructs the museum. In the national

museums, the repertory is almost always decided by the convergence of state policy and the knowledge of social scientists. Rarely can the producers of the culture that is exhibited intervene in these decisions.

And the public? It is almost always called as a spectator. Both the study of visitors to the Museum of Anthropology conducted in 1952 (Monzón)—when it was in a different building and had a different format—and the one done in 1981 (Kerriou) register the fact that the relation of visitors to the museum is predominantly visual and pays very little attention to conceptualization. The two works talk of the enormous attraction that the material—above all the most spectacular material—provokes in the public. In the more recent investigation, 86 percent characterized this museum as the best in Mexico. Both studies observed a stronger interest in the archaeological pieces than in the ethnographic ones and, according to the latest poll, 96 percent of those interviewed went through the rooms on the ground floor, whereas only 57 percent visited the second floor. Half of those who did not visit the upper part of the museum attributed it to a "lack of time," which reveals an option in the use of time and also confirms how difficult it is to see everything the museum exhibits. Along the same line goes the response of the majority when asked why they are interested in coming back to the museum: "To finish seeing it." The pressure to see everything contributes to skipping over the plaques: 55 percent said they had read only "some" of them.

In short, it is a museum in which scientific guidelines organize the material and give consistent explanations, where the specialization of anthropological sciences is reproduced in an exhibition divided between the archaeological and the ethnographic. But museology subordinates conceptual knowledge to the monumentalization and nationalist ritualization of the patrimony. The state gives foreigners, and especially the nation (the two polls and the statistics on attendance show a high majority of Mexican visitors), the spectacle of its history as the basis of its unity and political consciousness.

The architect Ramírez Vázquez, who directed the construction, relates an anecdote that is like the founding mandate of the museum:

> Torres Bodet [the Secretary of Education] brought me to an interview with Lic. López Mateos and told him: "Mr. President, what directions do you give to the architect on what that museum should achieve?" The response was: "That on leaving the museum, the Mexican feels proud to be Mexican." . . . And when we were leaving, the President said: "Ah, I also want it to be so attractive that people say 'Did you go to the museum yet?' the same way they say 'Did you go to the theater yet?' or 'Did you go the movie theater yet?' " (Granillo Vázquez, 32)

What Purpose Do Rites Serve? Identity and Discrimination

Some Mexican authors, among them Carlos Monsiváis and Roger Bartra, have shown, with respect to other discourses—literature, cinema—that certain representations of the national are understood more as the construction of a spectacle than as a realistic correspondence with social relations. "National myths are not a *reflection* of the conditions in which the masses live," but rather the product of operations of selection and "transposition" of deeds and characteristics chosen according to the projects of political legitimation (Bartra, especially 225-42).

To radicalize this desubstantialization of the concept of national patrimony it is necessary to question that central hypothesis of traditionalism according to which cultural identity is supported in a patrimony constituted through two movements: the occupation of a territory and the formation of collections. To have an *identity* would be above all to have a country, a city, or a neighborhood, an *entity* in which everything shared by those who inhabit that place becomes identical and interchangeable. In those territories identity is staged, celebrated in fiestas, and also dramatized in daily rituals.

Those who do not constantly share in that territory, or inhabit it, or therefore have the same objects and symbols, the same rituals and customs, are the others, the different ones. They have a different stage and a distinct work to represent.

When a territory is occupied, the first act is to appropriate its land, fruit, minerals, and, of course, the bodies of its people, or at least the product of their labor power. Inversely, the first struggle of the natives to recover their identity is to rescue those goods and place them under their sovereignty; this is what happened in the battles for national independence in the nineteenth century and in the later struggles against foreign interventions.

Once the patrimony—or at least a fundamental part of it—is recovered, the relation to the territory returns to being as it was before: a natural relation. Inasmuch as it was born in those lands, in the middle of that landscape, identity is something about which there can be no doubt. But since, at the same time, it holds the memory of what was lost and reconquered, the signs that evoke it are celebrated and guarded. Identity has its sanctuary in monuments and museums; it is everywhere, but it is condensed in collections that bring together the essential.

Monuments present the collection of heroes, scenes, and founding objects. They are placed in a square, a public territory that does not belong to anyone in particular but to "everyone," to a clearly delimited social group: those who inhabit the neighborhood, the city, or the nation. The territory of the square or the museum becomes ceremonial by virtue of containing the symbols of identity, objects and souvenirs of the best heroes and battles, something that no longer exists but is preserved because it alludes to origins and essence. It is there that the model of identity—the *authentic* version—is conserved.

Therefore patrimonial collections are necessary, commemorations renew affective solidarity, monuments and museums are justified as places where the meaning we find in living together is reproduced. It has to be acknowledged that traditionalists have served to preserve the patrimony, to democratize access to and use of cultural goods, in the midst of the indifference of other sectors or the aggression of "modernizers" from both inside and outside the community. But today the ideology in whose name those actions are almost always carried out is unrealistic and inefficient: a humanism that wants, in schools and museums, and in cultural diffusion campaigns, to reconcile the traditions of classes and ethnic groups that are separated from those institutions.

In spite of integrating social sectors more democratically than conservative authoritarianism, the liberal version of traditionalism does not prevent the patrimony from serving as a place of complicity. It disguises the fact that monuments and museums are often testimonies to domination more than to a just and solidary appropriation of territorial space and historical time. The signs and rites that celebrate the patrimony call to mind that phrase of Benjamin's that says that all documents of culture are always in some way documents of barbarism.

Even in cases where the commemorations do not consecrate the appropriation of the goods of other peoples, they hide the heterogeneity and the divisions of the people represented. It is rare that a ritual alludes openly to the conflicts among ethnic groups, classes, and other groups. The history of all societies shows rites to be devices for neutralizing heterogeneity and reproducing order and social differences in an authoritarian manner. The rite is distinguished from other practices in that it is not discussed, it cannot be changed or carried out halfway. It is carried out and then one ratifies his or her belonging to an order, or it is transgressed and one remains excluded, outside of the community and of communion.

The most well known theories about ritual, from Van Gennep to Gluckman, understand it as a way of articulating the sacred and the profane, for which reason they almost always study it in the context of religious life. But what is the sacred to which political and cultural ritual refer? A certain social order that cannot be modified, and therefore is seen as natural and superhuman. The sacred, then, has two components: *it is what overflows human understanding and explanation, and what exceeds the possibility of changing it.* The museums analyzed here ritualize the patrimony by organizing the deeds with reference to a transcendental order. In the Tamayo Museum, the objects of the past are resignified in relation to the idealist aesthetic of the fine arts; in the Museum of Anthropology, the cultural deeds of each ethnic group yield to the national discourse. In both cases, the material exhibited is reordered in terms of an alien conceptual system.

Pierre Bourdieu, one of the few authors to present the investigation of rituals in lay form, asking about their purely social function, observes that the goal of separating those who are rejected is as important as the goal of integrating those who share them. The classic rites—passing from infancy to adulthood, being invited to a political ceremony for the first time, entering a museum or a school and understanding what is being presented there—are, more than rites of initiation, "rites of legitimation" and "of institution" (Bourdieu 1982): they institute a lasting difference between those who are participants and those who remain outside.

One of the distinctive features of traditionalist culture is its "naturalizing" of the barrier between the included and the excluded. It does not know the arbitrary aspects of differentiating this territory from that, of determining that repertory of types of knowledge to teach in school or this collection of goods to exhibit in a museum, and, by means of an indisputable ritualization, it solemnly legitimizes the separation between those who accede and those who do not. Ritual, then, in the symbolic world, sanctions the distinctions established by social inequality. Every act of instituting pretends, through cultural staging, that an arbitrary social organization is that way and cannot be any other way. Every act of institution is "a well-founded delirium," Durkheim said, and "an act of social magic," concludes Bourdieu.

Therefore, this author adds, the watchword that sustains the performative magic of ritual is "convert yourself into what you are." You who have received culture as a gift and carry it with you as something natural, incorporated into your being, act as what you are, an heir. Effortlessly enjoy museums, classical music, the social order. The only thing you cannot do, traditionalism affirms when it is obliged to be authoritarian, is abandon your destiny. The worst adversary is not the one who does not go to museums or understand art but the painter who wants to transgress the inheritance by putting an actress's face on the Virgin, the intellectual who questions whether the heroes celebrated in patriotic festivals really were heroes, the musician specialized in the baroque who mixes it with jazz and rock in his compositions.

Toward a Social Theory of the Patrimony

With what theoretical resources can we rethink the contradictory social uses of the cultural patrimony, dissimulated beneath the idealism that sees it as an expression of the collective creative genius, the humanism that attributes to it the mission of reconciling divisions "on a higher plane," and the rites that protect it in sacred spaces? Evidence that the historical patrimony is a key stage for the production of the value, identity, and distinction of the modern hegemonic sectors suggests recourse to social theories that have addressed these questions in a less complacent way.

If we consider the uses of the patrimony from the perspective of studies on cultural reproduction and social inequality, we find that the goods gathered in history by each society do not *really* belong to everyone, although they *formally* appear to belong to everyone and to be available for everyone's use. Sociological and anthropological investigations into the ways each society's knowledge is transmitted through schools and museums demonstrate that diverse groups appropriate cultural heritage in different and unequal ways. It is not enough that schools and museums are open to all, that they are free and promote their diffusing action among all social layers. As we saw in the study of the public in art museums, as we descend the economic and educational scale the capacity to appropriate the cultural capital transmitted by those institutions diminishes.[5]

This diverse capacity of relating to the patrimony originates, in the first place, in the unequal way in which social groups participate in its formation and maintenance. There is no more obvious evidence than the numerical predominance of old military and religious buildings all over America while popular architecture became extinct or was replaced, in part because of its precariousness and in part because it was not maintained with the same care.

Even in countries where the official discourse adopts the anthropological notion of culture, which confers legitimacy on all forms of organizing and symbolizing social life, a hierarchy of cultural capitals exists: art is worth more than handicrafts, scientific medicine more than popular medicine, and written culture more than culture transmitted orally. In the most democratic countries, or where certain movements managed to include the knowledge and practices of indigenous people and peasants in the definition of national culture, the symbolic capital of the subaltern groups has a place, but one that is subordinate, secondary, or on the margins of the hegemonic institutions and apparatuses. Therefore the reformulation of the patrimony in terms of cultural capital has the advantage of not representing it as a set of stable and neutral goods with values and meanings that are fixed once and for all, but rather as a *social process* that, like the other kind of capital, is accumulated, reconverted, produces yields, and is appropriated in an unequal way by different sectors.[6]

Although the patrimony serves to unify each nation, the inequalities in its formation and appropriation require that it also be studied as a space of material and symbolic struggle between classes, ethnic groups, and other groups. This methodological principle corresponds to the complex character of contemporary societies. In archaic communities, virtually all members shared the same knowledge, held similar beliefs and tastes, and had more or less equal access to the common cultural capital. Nowadays regional and sectoral differences, originating in the heterogeneity of experiences and the technical and social division of labor, are used by the hegemonic classes to obtain a privileged appropriation of the common patrimony. Certain neighborhoods, objects, and types of knowledge are consecrated as superior because they were generated by the dominant groups or because these groups have the information and training necessary for understanding and appreciating them, that is, for better controlling them.

The cultural patrimony functions as a resource for reproducing differences between social groups and the hegemony of those who achieve a preferential access to the production and distribution of goods. In order to configure the cultured form of the traditional, the dominant sectors not only define what goods are superior and deserve to be conserved, but they also have at their disposal the economic and intellectual means and the work and leisure time to imprint greater quality and refinement on those goods. In the popular classes one sometimes finds extraordinary imagination for building their houses out of junk in a marginal neighborhood, using manual abilities acquired in their work, and giving appropriate technical solutions to their lifestyle. But it is difficult for that result to compete with those who possess a historically accumulated knowledge, employ architects and engineers, and count on vast material resources and the possibility of comparing their designs with international advances.

The products generated by the popular classes tend to be more representative of local history and more adequate to the present needs of the group that makes them. In this sense, they constitute their own patrimony. They can also achieve a high aesthetic and creative value, as is proven by the handicrafts, literature, and music of many popular regions. But they have less possibility of carrying out various operations that are indispensable for converting those products into a generalized and widely recognized patrimony: to accumulate them historically (especially when they suffer extreme poverty or repression), to turn them into the basis of an objectivized knowledge (relatively independent of individuals and of simple oral transmission), to expand it by means of institutional education, and to perfect them through investigation and systematic experimentation. It is known that some of these points are carried out by certain groups—for example, the accumulation and historic transmission within the strongest ethnic groups; what I am pointing out is that structural inequality prevents the bringing together of all the requisites that are indispensable for intervening fully in the development of the patrimony in complex societies (on these points, see the texts of Antonio Augusto Arantes and Eunice Ribeiro Durham in Arantes).

In any case, the advantages of the traditional elites in the formation and uses of the patrimony become relative in view of the changes generated by the culture industries. The massive redistribution of traditional symbolic goods by electronic channels of communication generates more fluid interactions between the cultured and the popular, the traditional and the modern. Millions of people who never go to museums, or only distantly find out what they are exhibiting through school, today watch television programs thanks to which those goods come into their homes. It seems unnecessary to go and see them: the pyramids and the historic centers travel all the way to the table where the family eats; they become topics of conversation and mingle with the affairs of the day. Television presents advertising messages in which the prestige of the monuments is used to associate those virtues with a car or a liquor. The video clip repeated daily during the World Cup of soccer in Mexico City in 1986, which dissolved the images of pyramids into other modern ones, and of the pre-Columbian ball game into dances that mimicked present-day soccer, proposed a continuity without conflict between tradition and modernity.

In the midst of the crossings that mix the historical patrimony with the symbolism generated by the new communications technologies, how do we discern what is a society's *own* patrimony, that which a cultural policy should favor? Political discourse still chiefly associates the unity and continuity of the nation with the traditional patrimony, with ancient spaces and goods that would serve to make the population cohesive. It is known from the appearance of radio and cinema that these media play a decisive role in the formation of symbols of collective identification. But the cultural mass market is of little interest to the state and in large measure is left in the hands of private enterprise. Occasional attempts appear on state television stations to promote the traditional and erudite forms of culture, but the new communications technologies are frequently seen as something alien to the cultural area. Rather, they are linked to national security and the political-ideological manipulation of foreign interests, as is revealed by their dependence in many countries on ministries of the interior and not on the educational sector.

A cultural policy that takes into account the legal character of the patrimony and its transformation in contemporary societies could be organized by the difference proposed by Raymond Williams between the archaic, the residual, and the emergent, rather than by the opposition between traditional and modern.

The *archaic* is what belongs to the past and is acknowledged as such by those who today relive it, almost always "in a deliberately specialized way." On the other hand, the *residual* is formed in the past but is still active within cultural processes. The *emergent* designates new meanings and values, new practices and social relations (Williams 1980, 143-46).

The least effective cultural policies are those that cling to the archaic and ignore the emergent, since they are not able to articulate the recovery of historical density with the recent meanings that generate innovative practices in production and consumption.

Perhaps where the crisis in the traditional way of thinking about the patrimony is most acute is in its aesthetic and philosophical valorization. The fundamental criterion is that of authenticity, as proclaimed by the pamphlets that talk about folkloric customs, the tourist guides when they exalt "native" crafts and festivals, and the shop signs that guarantee the sale of "genuine popular art." But the most disturbing thing is that this criterion is employed in the bibliography on patrimony to demarcate the universe of goods and practices that merit being considered by social scientists and cultural policies. It is as if it could not take into account the fact that the current circulation and consumption of symbolic goods brought to an end the conditions of production that in a different time made possible the myth of originality, in both elite and popular art and in the traditional cultural patrimony.

Since Benjamin's famous 1936 text, analysis has been done of how the technical reproducibility of painting, photography, and cinema atrophies "the aura" of artistic works, that "unique phenomenon of a distance" (Benjamin 1969b, 222) that the existence of a unique work has in only one place to which pilgrimages are made in order to contemplate it. When books, journals, and television sets reproduce the paintings of Berni, Szyslo, or Tamayo, the original image is transformed by repetition on a mass scale. The problem of the authenticity and uniqueness of the work changes its meaning. We warn, then, with Benjamin, that "the authentic" is a modern and transitory invention: "At the time the medieval picture of a Madonna could not yet be said to be 'authentic.' It became 'authentic' only during the succeeding centuries and perhaps most strikingly so during the last one" (243). On the other hand, it becomes clear that the current change is not only an effect of new technologies, but also a global historical tendency: the desire of contemporary masses "*to bring* things 'closer' spatially and humanly" (223).

Although it is still different to ask oneself about the original work in archaeology and the visual arts than it is in cinema and video (where the question no longer makes sense), the kernel of the problem is that the insertion of culture in social relations changed. Most spectators are not linked with tradition through a ritual relationship, through devotion to unique works with a fixed meaning, but rather by means of unstable contact with messages that are diffused on multiple stages and propose diverse readings. Many techniques of reproduction and exhibition disguise this historical turn: the museums that solemnify objects that were for daily use, the books that spread the national patrimony by packaging it with pompous rhetoric, thereby neutralizing the attempted rapprochement with the reader. But the multiplication of "noble" images also facilitates the creation of those everyday museums assembled in the room by each person who puts on the wall a poster with a photo of Teotihuacán together with a reproduction of a Toledo, souvenirs from trips, newspaper clippings from last month, a friend's drawing—in short, a patrimony of one's own that gets renewed with the flow of life.

This extreme example is not meant to suggest that museums and historical centers have become insignificant and do not merit being visited, nor that the effort at understanding required by a pre-Hispanic ceremonial center or a painting by Toledo can be reduced to clipping reproductions of them and putting them up in one's room. It is not the same thing, of course, to preserve the memory in individual form or to pose the problem of assuming the collective representation of the past. But the example of the private museum suggests that it is possible to introduce more freedom and creativity into relations with the patrimony.

There was a time when museums produced copies of ancient works in order to put them on display outdoors and in contact with visitors. Later the reproduction of paintings, sculptures, and objects sought to expand them for use in education and in the tourist market. In many cases the new pieces, created by archaeologists or restoration technicians, achieved such faithfulness that it became almost impossible to tell them apart from the originals—not to mention cases in which recent technologies improve our relation to the works: an Andean song or a Beethoven symphony recorded fifty years ago sounds better "cleaned up" by a sound technician and reproduced on a compact disc.

The difference between the original and the copy is basic in the scientific and artistic investigation of culture. It is also important to distinguish between them in the diffusion of the patrimony. There is no reason to confuse the recognition of the value of certain goods with the conservative utilization that certain political tendencies make of them. Objects and practices exist that merit being specially valorized because they represent discoveries in knowledge, formal and perceptible achievements, or founding events in the history of a people. But there is no reason for this recognition to lead to constituting "the authentic" in the nucleus of an obsolescent conception of society, and to claim that museums, like temples or national parks of the spirit, are custodians of "true culture," a refuge against the adulteration that would overwhelm us in mass society. The maniacal opposition that the conservatives establish between a sacred past in which the gods inspired the artists and the peoples, and a profane present that renders that heritage banal, has at least two difficulties:

a) It idealizes some moment from the past and proposes it as a sociocultural paradigm of the present, decides that all the attributed testimonies are authentic and therefore preserve an irreplaceable aesthetic, religious, or magical power. The refutations of the authenticity suffered by so many "historic" fetishes oblige one to be less ingenuous.

b) It forgets that all culture is the result of a selection and a combination—constantly renewed—of its sources. In other words, it is a product of a staging in which what is going to be represented is chosen and adapted in accordance with what the audience can listen to, see, and understand. Cultural representations, from popular accounts to museums, never present *the facts*, neither everyday nor transcendental; they are always re-presentations, theater, simulacrum. Only blind faith fetishizes objects and images by believing that truth is deposited in them.

This is known in modernity, but it occurs much earlier. Umberto Eco puts it well when he says that the reconstruction of a Roman villa in the J. Paul Getty Museum in California is not very different from the act of a Roman patrician in having reproductions made of large sculptures from the time of Pericles; he too was "an avid nouveau riche who, after having collaborated in bringing Greece into crisis, assured its cultural survival in the form of copies" (Eco 1986, 54).

A testimony or an object can be more realistic, and therefore significant, for those who relate to it by asking themselves about its current meaning. That meaning can circulate and be captured through a careful reproduction, with explanations that locate the piece in its sociocultural setting, with an approach to curating that is more interested in reconstructing its meaning than in promoting it as spectacle or fetish. Inversely, an original object may hide the meaning it had (it may be original but have lost its relation to its origin) because it is decontextualized, its link to the dance or food in which it was used is cut, and an autonomy is attributed to it that did not exist for its first owners.

Does this mean that the distinction between an original stela and a copy, between a painting by Diego Rivera and an imitation, has become a matter of indifference? Not at all. As misleading as the position that absolutizes an illusory purity is that of those who—resigned to or seduced by commercialization and falsifications—make postmodern relativization into a historical cynicism and propose to adhere happily to the abolition of meaning.

In order to work out the historical and cultural meaning of a society it is important to establish, if possible, the original meaning that cultural goods had and to differentiate the originals from the imitations. It also seems elementary that when pieces are deliberately constructed as replicas, or there is uncertainty about their origin or period, that information should be indicated on the plaque, although museums often hide this for fear of losing the visitor's interest. This is a stupid assumption: sharing with the public the difficulties archaeology or history have in discovering a still uncertain meaning can be a legitimate technique for arousing curiosity and attracting interest in knowledge.

In summation, cultural and research policy with respect to the patrimony has no reason to reduce its task to one of rescuing the "authentic" objects of a society. It seems that we should be more interested in the processes than the objects, and not for their capacity to remain "pure" and equal to themselves, but rather for their sociocultural representativeness. In this perspective, the research, restoration, and diffusion of the patrimony would not have as their central end the pursuit of authenticity or the reestablishment of it but the reconstruction of *historical verisimilitude* and the provision of shared bases for a reelaboration in accord with the needs of the present. In almost all the literature on patrimony it is still necessary to effect that operation of rupture with the naive realism that epistemology long ago carried out. Just as scientific knowledge cannot reflect life, neither can restoration, curating, nor more contextualized and didactic diffusion succeed in abolishing the distance between reality and representation. Every scientific or pedagogical operation on the patrimony is a metalanguage: it does not make things talk but rather talks of and about them. The museum and any patrimonial policy treat objects, buildings, and customs in such a way that, rather than exhibit them, they make intelligible the relations between them and propose hypotheses about what they mean for those of us who see and evoke them today.

A patrimony that is reformulated by taking into account its social uses—not with a defensive attitude, of simple rescue, but with a more complex vision of how society appropriates its history—can involve diverse sectors. There is no reason to reduce it to a problem for specialists in the past. It interests functionaries and professionals concerned with constructing the present, indigenous people, peasants, migrants, and all sectors whose identity tends to be upset by the modern uses of culture. To the extent that the study and promotion of the patrimony assume the conflicts that accompany them, they can contribute to supporting the nation, no longer as something abstract but as what unites and makes cohesive—in a solidary historical project—the social groups concerned about the way in which they inhabit their space.

Would it not be possible to leave behind the stagnation that exists in Latin American political theory with regard to the nation, and the skepticism produced by economic and social processes in which the national seems to dissolve, if we were to advance in this type of analysis about its symbolic configuration? The discussion wavers, however, between *dogmatic fundamentalisms* and *abstract liberalisms*. The fundamentalists cling to the New Spain tradition, the synthesis of Catholicism and hierarchical social order, and so they always sabotaged the development of modernity. Incapable of understanding everything modern that has become installed since the nineteenth century at the core of Latin American development, they can only operate when the contradictions of underdeveloped modernization cause the social pacts that support it to explode. They lack new proposals since they cannot explain why the elective forms of liberal sociability and the capitalist rules of the market are failing in the peripheral countries. They can only offer a mystical adherence to a set of obsolescent religious and patriotic goods without any productive relation to contemporary conflicts. Their limited persuasion is noted in the scant recruitment of believers, their low verisimilitude in the need to ally themselves with military power or the most authoritarian sectors of the right. Their biggest risk: to forget everything traditions owe to modernity.

For its part, the failure of the liberal concept of the nation is not the result of a rejection of modernity but of an abstract promotion of it. In Sarmiento's social and academic project, and in its equivalents in other countries, the traditions that are representative of the original inhabitants are rejected in order to invent a different history in the name of positive knowledge. The Mexican project, as it is enunciated by the Museum of Anthropology, takes charge of ethnic heritage but subordinates its diversity to the modernizing unification expressed simultaneously by scientific knowledge and political nationalism.

There can be no future for our past while we waver between the reactive fundamentalisms against the modernity achieved, and the abstract modernisms that resist problematizing our "deficient" capacity to be modern. To leave behind this "western," this maniacal pendulum, it is not enough to be interested in how traditions are reproduced and transformed. The postmodern contribution is useful for escaping from the impasse insofar as it reveals the constructed and staged character of all tradition, including that of modernity: it refutes the originary quality of traditions and the originality of innovations. At the same time, it offers the opportunity to rethink the modern as a project that is relative, doubtable, not antagonistic to traditions nor destined to overcome them by some unverifiable evolutionary law. It serves, in short, to make us simultaneously take charge of the impure itinerary of traditions and of the disjointed, heterodox achievement of our modernity.

Notes

1. The formulation appears in a speech by the Secretary of Culture, Raúl Casa, but it was quite common in the official discourse of that time. See Andrés Avellaneda's study and documentary compilation.

2. To name just a few titles: those of Hudson, León, Binni and Pinna, Poulot. And of course the collection of the journal *Museum*, published by UNESCO. The best anthology in Spanish can be found in Schmilchuk.

3. Information provided by the Instituto Nacional de Antropología e Historia.

4. A famous example, the dispute between the federal government and the government of Oaxaca over the treasure of Tomb 7 from Monte Albán, is presented in all its political and cultural complexity in the account Daniel Rubín de la Borbolla gave in an interview with Ulises Ladislao (14-15).

5. We are enunciating a general principle, established by investigating the social laws of cultural diffusion; see especially the works of Bourdieu and Passeron and of Bourdieu and Darbel. I do not affirm a mechanical determination of the economic or educational level over the capacity of each subject to appropriate the patrimony, but rather what polls and statistics reveal about the unequal way in which the institutions that transmit the patrimony permit its appropriation, as a result of how they are organized and of their articulation with other social inequalities.

6. I adopt here the concept of cultural capital utilized by Bourdieu to analyze cultural and educational processes, although this author does not employ it in relation to the patrimony. Here I indicate its richness for dynamizing the notion of patrimony and situating it in social reproduction. A more systematic use should—as with any importation of concepts from one field to another—state the epistemological conditions and limits of its metaphoric use in an area for which it was not developed. Cf. Bourdieu 1979, especially chapters 2 and 4, and 1980a, chapters 3, 6, and 7.

5 | The Staging of the Popular

In this history the popular is the excluded: those who have no patrimony or who do not succeed in being acknowledged and conserved; artisans who do not become artists, who do not become individuals or participate in the market for "legitimate" symbolic goods; spectators of the mass media who remain outside the universities and museums, "incapable" of reading and looking at high culture because they do not know the history of knowledge and styles.

Artisans and spectators—are these the only roles assigned to popular groups in the theater of modernity? The popular tends to be associated with the premodern and the subsidiary. In production, it maintains relatively suitable forms for the survival of preindustrial enclaves (artisanal workshops) and local forms of recreation (regional forms of music, neighborhood forms of entertainment). In consumption, the popular sectors are always at the end of the process, as addressees, spectators obligated to reproduce the cycle of capital and the ideology of the dominators.

The constitutive processes of modernity are thought of as chains of oppositions juxtaposed in a Manichaean fashion:

145

The bibliography on culture tends to assume that there is an intrinsic interest on the part of the hegemonic sectors to promote modernity and a fatal destiny on the part of the popular sectors that keeps them rooted in traditions. From this opposition, modernizers draw the moral that their interest in the advances and promises of history justifies their hegemonic position: meanwhile, the backwardness of the popular classes condemns them to subalternity. If popular culture modernizes, as indeed happens, this is a confirmation for the hegemonic groups that there is no way out of its traditionalism; for the defenders of popular causes it is further evidence of the way in which domination prevents them from being themselves.

The preceding chapter documented the fact that traditionalism is today a trend in many hegemonic social layers and can be combined with the modern, almost without conflict, when the exaltation of traditions is limited to culture, whereas modernization specializes in the social and the economic. It must now be asked in what sense and to what ends the popular sectors adhere to modernity, search for it, and mix it with their traditions. A first analysis will consist in seeing how the oppositions modern/traditional and cultured/popular are restructured in changes occurring in handicrafts and fiestas. Next I will stop to analyze some manifestations of urban popular culture where the search for the modern appears as part of the productive movement of the popular sphere. Finally, we will have to examine how, together with the traditional, other features that had been fatally identified with the popular are being transformed: their local character, their association with the national and the subaltern.

To refute the classic oppositions from which popular cultures are defined, it is not enough to pay attention to their current situation. It is necessary to deconstruct the scientific and political operations that staged the popular. Three currents play roles in this theatricalization: folklore, the culture industry and political populism. In the three cases we will see the popular as something constructed rather than as preexistent. The pitfall that often impedes our apprehending the popular and problematizing it consists in presenting it as an a priori proof for ethical and political reasons: who is going to dispute a people's way of being, or doubt its existence?

Nevertheless, the late appearance of studies and policies referring to popular cultures shows that they became visible only a few decades ago. The *constructed* character of the popular is even clearer upon reviewing the conceptual strategies with which it was formed and their relations with the various stages in the establishment of hegemony. In Latin America, the popular is not the same if it is staged by folklorists and anthropologists for museums (beginning in the twenties and thirties), by communications specialists for the mass media (since the fifties), and by political sociologists for the state or for opposition parties and movements (since the seventies).

In part, the current theoretical crisis in research on the popular derives from the indiscriminate attribution of this notion to social subjects formed in different processes. The artificial separation among disciplines that set up disconnected paradigms collaborates in this juxtaposition of discourses that allude to diverse realities. Are the ways in which anthropology, sociology, and communications studies treat the popular incompatible or complementary? The attempts of the last few years to develop unifying views will also have to be discussed; we choose the two most commonly used approaches, that is, the theory of reproduction and the neo-Gramscian conception of hegemony. But through this itinerary we should be concerned above all with the schism that conditions interdisciplinary divisions and opposes tradition to modernity.

Folklore: A Melancholic Invention of Traditions

Elaborating a scientific discourse on the popular is a recent problem in modern thinking. Except for pioneering works like those of Bakhtin and Ernesto de Martino, knowledge dedicated in a specific way to popular cultures, locating them in a complex and consistent theory of the social and using rigorous technical procedures, is a novelty of the last three decades.

Some will accuse this affirmation of being unjust because they will remember the long list of studies on popular customs and folklore that have been carried out since the nineteenth century. We acknowledge these works for having made visible the question of the popular and for having established uses of this notion that are still common today. But their gnosiological tactics were not guided by a precise delimitation of the object of study, nor by specialized methods, but rather by ideological and political interests.

The people begin to exist as a referent in the modern debate at the end of the eighteenth and the beginning of the nineteenth centuries, with the formation in Europe of national states that tried to embrace all levels of the population. However, the Enlightenment believes that this people, to whom recourse was necessary in order to legitimize a secular and democratic government, is also the bearer of that which reason wants to abolish: superstition, ignorance, and turbulence. Therefore, a complex device was developed, in Martín Barbero's words, one "of abstract inclusion and concrete exclusion" (1987a, 15-16). The people are of interest as legitimators of bourgeois hegemony, but bothersome as the locus of the uncultured because of everything they lack.

The Romantics are aware of this contradiction. Preoccupied with welding together the split between the political and the quotidian, between culture and life, various writers are busy getting to know "popular customs" and promoting folkloric studies. Renato Ortiz has synthesized their innovative contribution in three points: against Enlightenment, which saw cultural processes as intellectual activities, restricted to the elites, the Romantics exalted feelings and popular ways of expressing them; in opposition to the cosmopolitanism of classic literature, they were dedicated to particular situations and emphasized the differences and value of the local; in the face of the contempt of classical thought for "the irrational," they reclaimed that which surprises and alters social harmony, passions that transgress the order of "decent men," the exotic habits of other peoples and also of peasants themselves (Ortiz 1985).

The restlessness of writers and philosophers—the Grimm brothers, Herder—to know popular cultures empirically was formalized when the first Folklore Society was founded in 1878. In France and Italy, that name later comes to refer to the discipline that specializes in subaltern knowledge and expressions. In the face of the requirements of positivism that guided the new folklorists, the works of the Romantic writers remained as lyrical uses of popular traditions to promote their artistic interests. Now knowledge of the popular wants to be situated within the "scientific spirit" that drives modern knowledge. To achieve this, in addition to distancing themselves from the amateur "connoisseurs," they need to critique popular knowledge. The intention also existed among the positivists to unite the scientific project with a social redemption enterprise. According to Rafaelle Corso, folkloric work is "a movement of elite men who, through persistent propaganda, strive to awaken the people and enlighten them in their ignorance." Knowledge of the popular world is no longer required only to form modern integrated nations but also to free the oppressed and to resolve the struggle between classes.

Along with positivism and sociopolitical messianism, the other feature of the folkloric task is the apprehension of the popular as tradition—that is, the popular as praised residue: deposit of peasant creativity, of the supposed transparency of face-to-face communication, of the profundity that would be lost by the "external" changes of modernity. The precursors of folklore saw with nostalgia that the role of oral transmission was diminishing in the face of the reading of daily newspapers and books; beliefs constructed by ancient communities in search of symbolic pacts with nature were lost when technology taught them how to dominate those forces. Even in many positivists there remains a Romantic restlessness that leads to defining the popular as traditional. It acquires the taciturn beauty of that which is becoming extinguished and that we can reinvent, outside present-day conflicts, by following our desires for what we should have been. Antiquarians had struggled against what was being lost by collecting objects; folklorists created museums of popular traditions.

A key notion for explaining the methodological tactics of the folklorists and their theoretical failure is that of *survival*. The perception of popular objects and customs as remains of an extinguished social structure is the logical justification of their decontextualized analysis. If the mode of production and the social relations that gave rise to those "survivals" disappeared, why worry about finding their socioeconomic meaning? Only researchers affiliated with idealist historicism are interested in understanding traditions in a wider framework, but they reduce them to testimonies of a memory that they presuppose to be useful for strengthening historical continuity and contemporary identity.[1]

In the end the Romantics become accomplices to the enlightened. In deciding that the specific character of popular culture resides in its faithfulness to the rural past, they are blinded to the changes that were refining it in industrial and urban societies. In assigning to it an imagined autonomy, they suppress the possibility of explaining the popular by the interactions it has with the new hegemonic culture. The people are "rescued" but not known.

I remember the European trajectory of classic folkloric studies because the motivations of their interest in the popular, its uses and its contradictions, are being repeated in Latin America. In countries as different as Argentina, Brazil, Peru, and Mexico, folkloric texts since the end of the nineteenth century have produced a vast body of empirical knowledge about ethnic groups and their cultural expressions: religiosity, rituals, medicine, fiestas, and handicrafts. In many works a profound interpenetration with the Indian and mestizo world can be seen, an effort to give it a place within national culture. But their theoretical and epistemological difficulties, which seriously limit the value of their reports, persist in current folkloric studies. Even in the countries that are the most up-to-date in the analysis of popular culture—such as the four named—this current controls most of the specialized institutions and bibliographic production.

A first obstacle to folkloric knowledge proceeds from the delineation of the object of study. The *folk* is seen, in a way similar to Europe, as a property of isolated and self-sufficient indigenous or peasant groups whose simple techniques and little social differentiation preserve them from modern threats. Cultural goods—objects, legends, musical forms—are of greater interest than the actors who generate and consume them. This fascination with the products—the neglect of the social processes and agents that engender them, and of the uses that modify them—leads to the objects being valued more for their repetition than for their change.

In the second place, many folkloric studies in Latin America were born through the same impulses that gave rise to them in Europe: on the one hand, the need to root the formation of new nations in the identity of their past; on the other hand, the Romantic inclination to rescue popular sentiments in the face of the Enlightenment and liberal cosmopolitanism. Thus conditioned by political nationalism and Romantic humanism, it is not easy for studies on the popular to produce a scientific body of knowledge.

The association of folklorists and anthropologists with nationalist movements converted scholars of popular cultures into recognized intellectuals during the first half of the century, as can be appreciated, for example, in the official functions entrusted to Peruvian and Mexican indigenists. Since the 1940s and 1950s, with the advance of modernizing trends in cultural politics and social research, the fondness for traditional cultures becomes a resource of those who need to relocate their intervention in the academic field. Renato Ortiz finds that the development of Brazilian folkloric studies owes much to objectives with as little scientific basis as those that fixed the terrain of nationality in a fusion of black, white, and Indian; gave intellectuals working in popular culture a symbolic resource through which to raise their consciousness and express the peripheral situation of their country; and made it possible for those intellectuals to affirm themselves professionally in relation to a modern system of cultural production from which they feel excluded (in Brazil the study of folklore is done mainly outside of universities, in traditional centers like the Geographic Historical Institutes, which have an anachronistic view of culture and ignore modern techniques of intellectual work). Ortiz adds that the study of folklore is also associated with advances in regional consciousness, which is opposed to the centralization of the state:

> At the moment when a local elite loses power, a flourishing of studies of popular culture is produced; an author like Gilberto Freyre could perhaps be taken as a paradigmatic representative of the elite that endeavors to reequilibrate its symbolic capital through a regional ideology. (1985, 53)

In Mexico a large body of anthropological and folkloric studies was condi-tioned by the postrevolutionary objective of constructing a unified nation beyond the economic, linguistic, and political divisions that were fracturing the country. The influence of the Finnish school on folklorists—under the slogan "Leave theory behind; what is important is to collect"—promoted a flat empiricism in the cataloging of materials, the analytical treatment of in-formation, and a poor contextual interpretation of the facts, even among the most conscientious authors. Therefore, most of the books on traditional handicrafts, fiestas, poetry, and music enumerate and exalt popular products without locating them in the logic present in social relations. This is even more visible in the museums of folklore or popular art. They exhibit vessels and textiles while stripping them of any reference to the daily practices for which they were made. Those that include the social context are the excep-tions, such as the National Museum of Cultures in Mexico City, created in 1982. Most limit themselves to listing and classifying those pieces that repre-sent traditions and stand out for their resistance or indifference to change.

Despite the abundance of descriptions, folklorists give few explanations about the popular. Their perceptive gaze at what for a long time escaped macrohistory and other scientific discourse, and their sensitivity to the pe-ripheral, must be acknowledged. But they almost never say why it is impor-tant or what social processes give traditions a current function. They do not succeed in reformulating their object of study in accord with the develop-ment of societies where cultural facts rarely have the features that define and valorize folklore. They are neither produced manually or artisanally, nor are they strictly traditional (transmitted from one generation to another), nor do they circulate in oral form from person to person, nor are they anony-mous, nor are they learned and transmitted outside of educational and mass communications institutions or programs. Undoubtedly, the folkloric ap-proximation remains useful for knowing facts that in contemporary soci-eties retain some of these features. It has little to say as soon as we want to in-clude the industrial conditions in which culture is now produced.

The main thing missing in works on folklore is that they do not ask about what happens to popular cultures when society becomes mass-based. Folk-lore, which arose in Europe and America as a reaction against aristocratic blindness toward the popular and as a response to the first industrialization of culture, is almost always a melancholic attempt at subtracting the popular from the massive reorganization of society, fixing it in artisanal forms of production and communication, and guarding it as an imaginary reserve of nationalist political discourses.

...ave a global synthesis of the ideology of work, the strate-
...cultural policy with which the folkloric current succeeded
...pular, not only in many countries but in international orga-
...as to read the Charter of American Folklore, drawn up by a
...group of specialists and approved by the Organization of
Am... ...tes (OAS) in 1970. How does it characterize the future of folklore in the race of the advance of what it identifies as its two biggest adversaries—the mass media and "modern progress"? We can summarize its basic
affirmations in this way:

- Folklore is constituted by a series of traditional goods and cultural
  forms, mainly of an oral and local character, that are always unalterable.
  Changes are attributed to external agents, for which reason it is recommended to train functionaries and specialists so that they "do not adul-
  terate folklore" and "know which are the traditions that there is no reason to change."
- Folklore, understood in this way, constitutes the essence of the identity
  and the cultural patrimony of each country.
- Progress and modern communications media, in accelerating the "final
  process of the disappearance of folklore," destroy the patrimony and
  make it "lose its identity" for American peoples.

From this curious exaltation of local culture on the part of an international organization, the charter traces some policy guidelines for the "conservation," "rescue," and study of traditions. Its proposals concentrate on
museums and schools, festivals and contests, legislation and protection. The
brief treatment of the mass media is limited to suggesting "use them well,"
disqualifying what they broadcast as being "a false folklore."[2]

Prosperous Popular Cultures

The persistence of these notions in cultural policies, curating or tourist
strategies, and even in research centers is incompatible with the current development of the symbolic market and the social sciences. The reformulation of the popular-traditional that is occurring in the self-criticism of some
folklorists and in new research by anthropologists and communications
specialists allows us to understand the place of folklore in modernity in a
different way. It is possible to construct a new perspective for analyzing the
popular-traditional by taking into account its interactions with elite culture

and the culture industries. I will begin to systematize it in the form of six refutations of the classic view of the folklorists.

a) Modern development does not suppress traditional popular cultures. In the two decades that have passed since the issuing of the charter, the supposed process of folklore's extinction did not become more marked, despite advances in mass communications and other technologies that either did not exist in 1970 or were not used then in the culture industry: video, cassettes, cable television, satellite transmission—in short, the series of technological and cultural transformations that result from the combining of microelectronics and telecommunication.

Not only did this modernizing expansion not succeed in erasing folklore, but many studies reveal that in the last few decades traditional cultures *have developed by being transformed.* This growth is the result of at least four types of causes: *(a)* the impossibility of incorporating the entire population into urban industrial production; *(b)* the need of the market to include traditional symbolic structures and goods in the mass circuits of communication in order to reach even the popular layers least integrated into modernity; *(c)* the interest of political systems in taking folklore into account with the goal of strengthening their hegemony and legitimacy; *(d)* continuity in the cultural production of the popular sectors.

Studies on handicrafts show a growth in the number of artisans, the volume of production, and its quantitative weight: a report by Sistema Económico Latinoamericano (SELA) calculates that the artisans of the fourteen Latin American countries analyzed represent 6 percent of the general population and 18 percent of the economically active population (cited in Lauer 1984, 39).[3] One of the main explanations for this increase, given by Andean as well as Mesoamerican authors, is that the deficiencies of agrarian exploitation and the relative impoverishment of products from the countryside drive many communities to search for an increase in their incomes through the sale of handicrafts. Although it is true that in some regions the incorporation of peasant labor power into other branches of production reduced artisanal production, there exist, inversely, communities that had never made handicrafts or only made them for their own consumption, and in the last few decades they were drawn into that work in order to ease the crisis. Unemployment is another reason why artisanal work is increasing, both in the countryside and in the cities, bringing into this type of production young people from socioeconomic sectors that never before were employed in this field. In Peru, the largest concentration of artisans is not in areas of low economic development but in the city of Lima: 29 percent

(Lauer 1982). Mexico shares its accelerated industrial reconversion with an intense support of artisanal production—the greatest volume on the continent and with a high number of producers: 6 million. It is not possible to understand why the number of handicrafts continues to increase, nor why the state keeps adding organizations to promote a type of work that, while employing 28 percent of the economically active population, barely represents 0.1 percent of the gross national product and 2 to 3 percent of the country's exports, if we see it as an atavistic survival of traditions confronted by modernity.

The incorporation of folkloric goods into commercial circuits, which tends to be analyzed as if their only effects were to homogenize designs and eliminate local brands, demonstrates that the expansion of the market needs to concern itself also with the sectors that resist uniform consumption or encounter difficulties in participating in it. With this goal, production is diversified and traditional designs, handicrafts, and folkloric music are utilized that continue to attract indigenous people, peasants, the masses of migrants, and new groups, as well as intellectuals, students, and artists. Through the varied motivations of each sector—to affirm their identity, stress a national-popular political definition or the distinction of a cultivated taste with traditional roots—this broadening of the market contributes to an extension of folklore.[4] As debatable as certain commercial uses of folkloric goods may seem, it is undeniable that much of the growth and diffusion of traditional cultures is due to the promotion of the record industry, dance festivals, fairs that include handicrafts and, of course, their popularization by the mass media. Radio and television amplified local forms of music on a national and international scale, as has happened with the Peruvian criollo waltz and the *chicha*, the *chamamé* and the quartets in Argentina, the music of the Northeast and gaucho songs in Brazil, and the *corridos* of the Mexican Revolution, which are included in the repertory of those who promote New Song in the electronic media.

In the third place, if many branches of folklore are growing it is because in the last few decades Latin American states have increased their support to its production (credits to artisans, scholarships and subsidies, contests, etc.), conservation, trade, and diffusion (museums, books, sales tours, and halls for popular events). The state has various objectives: to create jobs that reduce unemployment and the exodus from the countryside to the cities, to promote the export of traditional goods, to attract tourism, to take advantage of the historical and popular prestige of folklore to cement hegemony and national unity in the form of a patrimony that seems to transcend the divisions among classes and ethnic groups.

But all these uses of traditional culture would be impossible without one basic fact: the continuity in the production of popular artisans, musicians, dancers, and poets interested in maintaining and renewing their heritage. The preservation of these forms of life, organization, and thought can be explained by cultural reasons but also, as we said, by the economic interests of the producers, who are trying to survive or increase their income.

We are not overlooking the contradictory character that market stimuli and governmental bodies have on folklore. The studies we cite talk of frequent conflicts between the interests of the producers or users of popular goods and the merchants, promoters, mass media, and states. But what can no longer be said is that the tendency of modernization is simply to promote the disappearance of traditional cultures. The problem, then, cannot be reduced to one of conserving and rescuing supposedly unchanged traditions. It is a question of asking ourselves how they are being transformed and how they interact with the forces of modernity.

b) Peasant and traditional cultures no longer represent the major part of popular culture. In the last few decades, Latin American cities came to contain between 60 and 70 percent of their country's inhabitants. Even in rural areas, folklore today does not have the closed and stable character of an archaic universe, since it is developed in the variable relations that traditions weave with urban life, migrations, tourism, secularization, and the symbolic options offered both by the electronic media and by new religious movements or by the reformulation of old ones. Even recent migrants, who maintain forms of sociability and celebrations of peasant origin, acquire the character of "urbanoid groups," as the Brazilian ethnomusicologist José Jorge de Carvalho puts it. Hence current folklorists feel the need to be concerned at once with local and regional production and with salsa, African rhythms, indigenous and Creole melodies that dialogue with jazz, rock, and other genres of Anglo-Saxon origin. Traditions are reinstalled even beyond the cities: in an interurban and international system of cultural circulation. Although there was always a current of traditional forms that united the Ibero-American world, Carvalho adds, now

> there exists a flood of hybrid forms that also unite us, it being possible to identify relationships between new Brazilian popular rhythms and new expressions from Bolivia, Peru, Venezuela, the Caribbean, Mexico, and so on. It is not possible to understand tradition without understanding innovation. (8-10)

c) The popular is not concentrated in objects. The current study of culture by anthropology and sociology situates popular products in their economic conditions of production and consumption. Folklorists influenced by semiotics identify the *folk* in behaviors and communicational processes. In none of these cases is it accepted that the popular is congealed in patrimonies of stable goods. Not even traditional culture is seen as an "authoritative norm or static and immutable force," writes Martha Blache, "but as a wealth that is utilized today but is based on previous experiences of the way a group has of responding to and linking itself with its social environment." Rather than a collection of objects or objectivized customs, tradition is thought of as "a mechanism of selection, and even of invention, projected toward the past in order to legitimize the present" (27).

The interactionist and ethnomethodological influence also contributes to conceiving of the formation and the changes of social signification as a product of interactions and rituals. From its perspective, popular art is not a collection of objects, nor the subaltern ideology a system of ideas, nor customs fixed repertories of practices: all are dynamic dramatizations of collective experience. If rituals are the domain in which each society manifests what it wants to situate as perennial or eternal, as Roberto da Matta explains (24), then even the most durable aspects of popular life manifest themselves better than in the inert objects in the ceremonies that bring them to life. (Although da Matta does not establish an exclusive relation between ritual and the past, he emphasizes that even what is tradition in society is better revealed in interactions than in motionless goods.)

d) The popular is not a monopoly of the popular sectors. In conceiving of the *folk* as social practices and communicational processes more than as packages of objects, the fatalist, naturalizing link is broken that associated certain cultural products with fixed groups. Folklorists pay attention to the fact that in modern societies the same person may participate in diverse folkloric groups, and is capable of being synchronically and diachronically integrated into various systems of symbolic practices: rural and urban, neighborhood and factory, microsocial and mass media-based. There is no folklore belonging only to the oppressed classes; nor are the only possible types of interfolkloric relations those of domination, submission, or rebellion. In the last instance, we are coming to no longer consider

> groups as organizations that are stable in their composition and in their permanence, endowed with common characteristics. There is no set of individuals that is folkloric in itself; there are, however, situations that are more or less favorable for a person to participate in folkloric behavior. (Blache, 29)

The evolution of traditional fiestas and of the production and sale of handicrafts reveals that these are no longer exclusive tasks of ethnic groups, nor of broader peasant sectors, nor even of the agrarian oligarchy; ministries of culture and commerce, private foundations, beverage companies, and radio and television stations also intervene in organizing them (cf., e.g., Stromberg; Good Eshelman; Lauer 1982). Folk or traditional cultural facts are today the multidetermined product of actors that are popular and hegemonic, peasant and urban, local, national, and transnational.

By extension, it is possible to think that the popular is constituted in hybrid and complex processes, using as signs of identification elements originating from diverse classes and nations. At the same time, we may become more perceptive in the face of the ingredients of so-called popular cultures that are a reproduction of the hegemonic, or that become self-destructive for the popular sectors, or contrary to their interests: corruption and resigned or ambivalent attitudes in relation to hegemonic groups.

e) The popular is not lived by popular subjects as a melancholic complacency with traditions. Many subaltern *ritual* practices that are apparently devoted to *reproducing* the traditional order humorously transgress it. Perhaps an anthology of the scattered documentation on ritual humor in Latin America would make it clear that people resort to laughter in order to have a less oppressive relation with their past. We propose the hypothesis that the attitude is most antisolemn when it is a matter of crossed traditions in conflict. In the carnivals of various countries, dances by indigenous and mestizo people parody the Spanish conquistadores, making grotesque use of their costumes and the warlike paraphernalia they brought along for the conquest. In the Brazilian carnival there is a reversal of the traditional orders of a society where the intersection of blacks and whites, and old ethnic groups and modern groups, seeks resolution in severe hierarchies: night is used as if it were day, men dress up as women, and the ignorant, the blacks, and the workers appear to be "showing the pleasure of living the latest fashions in song, dance, and the samba" (da Matta, 99).

It is unnecessary to optimize these transgressions to the point of believing that, by vindicating people's own histories, they undo the fundamental tradition of domination. Da Matta himself recognizes that in carnival there is a play between the reaffirmation of hegemonic traditions and the parody that subverts them, since the explosion of the illicit is limited to a short, defined period after which reentry into the established social organization takes place. The rupture of the fiesta does not eliminate hierarchies and inequalities, but its irreverence opens a freer, less fatalistic relation to inherited conventions.

In Mexico too, in the Highlands of Chiapas, carnival is a moment of symbolic and humorous working out of superimposed conflicts. Blacks caricature ladinos, some Indians caricature other Indians, and ethnic tensions are staged, ironically recalling the Caste War of 1867–70. Parody is used in Zinacantán, Chamula, and Chenalhó, as in other areas, to disparage those who are different (other Indians, ladinos, whites) and to disapprove of deviations in conduct within the group itself, that is, as an ethnocentric self-affirmation (Bricker). But the interpretation is also possible that this is done to reduce the oppressive character of centuries-old forms of domination.

Because intercultural conflicts have been similar in other areas of Mesoamerica, it is not strange that similar parodying tactics are found in many communities. Nevertheless, the exegesis of these fiestas tends to emphasize only what in ritual humor serves to make fun of the authorities and caricature foreigners. Some authors, such as Bricker, in observing the frequent relation of ritual humor to deviant behaviors, suggest another function: social control. Ridiculing someone who wears ladino clothing or a corrupt functionary would, for indigenous communities, serve to anticipate the sanctions that would be suffered by those who diverge from traditional behaviors or attack the group itself. But no one, this author notes, proves that there is a causal link between ceremonial caricature and a reinforcement of rules. It cannot be affirmed that in societies that make fun of certain types of conduct these types of conduct occur less frequently, nor that the fear of being ridiculed rather than some other fear—supernatural or legal—is the motivation for avoiding them.

To our way of seeing things, this generalized concern with normality goes together with the symbolic elaboration of change and of the relations between tradition and modernity. This is the interpretation suggested to us by fieldwork done in the Purépecha region of Michoacán. I will dwell on one example among the many that manifest this function of humor in fiestas and handicrafts: the devils of Ocumicho.

I again turn my attention to the devils of Ocumicho, a subject I analyzed eight years ago (1989a, chapter 6), taking into account the fact that since then they have become one of the most successful ceramic products in all of Mexico, and that several additional works were published in the 1980s. Today the devils are a tradition as useful to the inhabitants of Ocumicho in identifying themselves in relation to others as are their language and their ancient ceremonies, even though they were born only thirty years ago. Why did they begin to make them? They give an economic explanation and relate two myths.

In the 1960s, the rains diminished and some nearby *ejido* peasants appropriated some of their most fertile lands. Thus they had to expand pottery production—produced until then by a few families for the daily needs of the community—with the aim of selling it and obtaining income to compensate for what had been lost in the countryside. To this explanation they add two myths. One says that the devil—an important figure in the pre-Cortés beliefs of the region as well as during the colonial period—

> passed through Ocumicho and was bothering everyone. He got into the trees and killed them. He entered into dogs and they would do nothing but shake and yelp. Then he followed people, who would get sick and go crazy. It occurred to someone that he had to be given places where he could live without bothering anyone. That's why we made clay devils, so that he could have a place to be.

The other account refers to Marcelino, an orphan child and homosexual initiated into ceramics by his grandmother, who began to make "beautiful figures" thirty years ago; first he made angels and then he dedicated himself to devils following an encounter with the devil in a ravine. Seeing how quickly his sales grew, and that he was invited to handicraft fairs in Mexico City and New York, his neighbors learned and perfected the technique and continued to vary the images, even after Marcelino's death, which happened when he was still young.

Both accounts are told with multiple variants, as happens when different members of a community contribute to giving diverse emphases to the story and updating it. In this way they renew the value of foundational myths for an unstable activity that within a few years brought prosperity to a few families and afforded many others a better survival. Now the devils circulate throughout the entire country and abroad. Their images—which mix serpents, trees, and Purépecha houses with elements of modern life and with biblical and erotic scenes—won a place in urban shops through the attractiveness of this ambivalence. The devils are seen both in sacred scenes—in Nativity scenes and in the Last Supper, replacing the apostles—and in the reproduction of the most everyday scenes of Ocumicho: selling food, a birth, conversation in the door of a house. They pilot airplanes or helicopters, talk on the telephone, work as ambulant salespeople in the cities, fight with the police, and make love with mermaids or with a Purépecha woman mounted on an animal with seven heads. It is an art that speaks of their own life and their migrations (devils up on the roofs of buses going to the United States).

Carmela Martínez, after *Liberty Leading the People*, July 28, 1830, by Eugène Delacroix.

It makes fun of Catholic rites (which are practiced syncretically) and seduces by the freedom with which it re-creates the comings and goings between the traditional and the modern. It is an art that represents but that is made for others (no residents use devils in decorating their houses); it refers to others as adversaries whom the devils laugh at. The least mimetic images

Antonia Martínez, after the anonymous acid engraving, *Bombardment of All the Thrones of Europe and the Fall of All the Tyrants, for the Happiness of the Universe.*

of their traditions represent what the inheritors of those traditions experience when some member of each family travels to the United States for temporary work. Or their experiences when the National Handicrafts Fund and the National Indigenist Institute teach them how to organize in cooperatives ("solidarity groups"), manage credit, and change the themes and the varnish of the pieces, using synthetic paints but with a treatment that simulates antiquity when the work is finished.

In a very few years, the people of Ocumicho succeeded in developing a sophisticated technique, a set of images that were constantly being renewed, and even a mythic support that relates changes to a distant history. For their part, official institutions contribute to staging this art through extensive distribution, invitations to display it at international fairs, contests, and awards that legitimize this mode of producing and innovating.

Is it the opening—whether critical or mocking—toward modernity, and

Guadalupe Álvarez, after Berthaud's engraving, *The Storming of the Bastille.*

not the simple self-affirmation, that better roots the people in traditions? In part, it seems so. But there is something more. It is revealed in a comparative study of Ocumicho and another nearby community that is also a successful producer of ceramics: Patamban (Gouy-Gilbert). The artisans of the latter, who produce earthenware for daily use, having generated their own market based on the quality of their work and in independent marketing actions, consider official institutions as a type of intermediary between them and others. Gouy-Gilbert finds a correspondence between this greater commercial autonomy and the lesser concern with securing a political power of their own or their traditional religious system. On the other hand, as with Ocumicho, access to the market occurs almost exclusively through governmental institutions, and the precariousness of their commercial links and their dependency on outside economic agents make them more sensitive to the reaffirmation of the *signs* of identity (language, dress, system of religious duties) and to the defense of a communally controlled civil power.

Along this line, we can read the humorous meaning of the devils as symbolic resource for elaborating the abrupt transitions between one's own and

Virginia Pascual, after the anonymous engraving, *Caricature against Marie Antoinette.*

the foreign, between the reproduction of the known and the incorporation of new elements into a reformulated perception of oneself:

> The mobilization of all the cultural resources within an ethnic minority (activation of the relations of kinship, of the duty system, of the fiestas, etc.) may correspond as much to an ultimate form of resistance—a kind of congealing of the ethnic cultural patrimony—as to a resource that permits the community to find ways of adapting. (Gouy-Gilbert, 57)

Carmela Martínez, after the anonymous engraving, *The Executioner Guillotines Himself.*

In 1989 we proposed to ten potters of Ocumicho that they make figures using the theme of the French Revolution. Mercedes Iturbe, director of the Cultural Center of Mexico in Paris, brought them images with revolutionary scenes and related the history of the Revolution to them. Like so many painters and filmmakers who constructed from their own imagination the iconography that shows how to *see* that founding event of modernity, the

Anonymous *amate*, produced in Maxela.

Amate of Roberto Mauricio, from San Agustín Oapan, Guerrero.

Sale of *amates* in Cuernavaca.

Negotiating with a retailer.

Purépecha artisans gave their version of the storming of the Bastille, of Marie Antoinette, and of the guillotine.

Fernando del Paso wrote in the exposition catalog that "no people or nation of the world has a monopoly on barbarism and cruelty." The indigenous artisans who produced these works did not know much about the French Revolution but they have a memory of the horrors carried out by the Spanish conquistadores—who were alarmed by the sacrifices taking place in these lands—in order to impose modernity. The long relation of these potters to devils and serpents in their works undoubtedly facilitated their portraying what could have been contradictory and grotesque in the revolution that sought liberty and brotherhood. The presence of the infernal, says del Paso, distances these pieces from naive risk: despite the rustic appearance of their figures, the Purépechas show that they know that "the cruelty of man against man and ingenuousness are not compatible" (61-62).

f) The pure preservation of traditions is not always the best popular resource for reproducing itself and reelaborating its situation. "Be authentic and you'll earn more" is the slogan of many promoters, handicrafts merchants, and cultural functionaries. The studies that some undisciplined folklorists and anthropologists have finally ended up doing on impure handicrafts demonstrate that sometimes the opposite happens.

In an analogous way to the potters of Ocumicho, *amate* painters are making us rethink the apocalyptic alarms about "the inevitable extinction" of handicrafts and the nexus between the cultured and the popular. Thirty years ago, when several Guerrero communities began to produce and sell paintings made on *amate* paper, in part influenced by artists, some folklorists predicted the decline of their ethnic traditions. Catherine Good Eshelman began a study on these crafts in 1977, starting from the then predominant theory about the place of peasant production in Mexican capitalist formation: handicrafts would be a specific form of participation in this unequal system, one more way to extract surplus and weaken ethnic organization. After living for several years in the producing communities and following the cycle of their adaptations, she had to admit that the growing commercial interaction with the national society and market not only allowed them to improve economically, but they were also strengthening their internal relations. Their indigenous origin was not "a folkloric detail" that gave an exotic attraction to their products, nor was it an obstacle to incorporating themselves into the capitalist economy; rather, it was "the mobilizing and determining force in the process" (18). As the author's historic work demonstrates, those communities spent long periods experimenting with strategies, which were often frustrated, until they arrived at the economic and aesthetic achievements of painting on *amate*. Their origin is multidetermined: they were born in the 1950s, when the Nahuas of Ameyaltepec—potters since before the conquest who sold their masks, flowerpots, and ashtrays in nearby cities—transferred the decorations of their ceramics to *amate* paper. The drawings were ancient but their national and international diffusion began when they were put on *amate*, which—in addition to allowing for more complex compositions—weighs less than clay, is less fragile, and is easier to transport.

The "paintings" are made by men and women, adults and children. They show scenes of their work and their fiestas, valorizing in this way ethnic and familiar traditions that they continue to reproduce in their peasant tasks. The artisans themselves control almost all their trade, allow middlemen less interference than in other artisanal branches of production, and take advantage of their stands and itinerant sales to offer works from other communities (masks, carved rocks, and copies of pre-Hispanic pieces).

According to the poll done by Good Eshelman in Ameyaltepec in 1980-81, 41 percent of families earned more than four minimum-wage salaries, and another 42 percent from two to four minimum-wage salaries. There continue to be middlemen who appropriate part of the profit; those who speculate the most are the ones who pay between ten and twenty dollars for each *amate* and resell them in the United States as "genuine Aztec tribal art" for three hundred or four hundred dollars. There are also companies that use the designs of these communities on tablecloths, postcards, and facial tissue boxes, without paying them anything in return. Despite these forms of exploitation, which are common in other types of handicrafts, their incomes and level of consumption are much higher than those of the average Mexican peasant.[5]

Although these artisans engage in profuse commercial activity, which extends across almost the entire country, they are organized so as not to neglect agriculture, nor ceremonial obligations, nor community services. They invest the profits from their crafts in land, animals, housing, and internal fiestas. Inasmuch as all families are employed in the sale of handicrafts, it is in no one's interest to use their resources and labor power as commodities. In commerce they move individually or by family, but they carry out their sales by using collective networks for sharing information about faraway cities and settling in them by reproducing the material and symbolic conditions of their daily life. Dozens of Nahua artisans arrive at a tourist center, rent part of a cheap hotel and immediately put up ropes to hang clothes instead of keeping them in closets, store water in clay jugs inside the room, erect altars, and prepare food or convince someone in the market to cook it their way.

Through the purchase of materials and the consumption of alien goods, they transfer part of their profit to the national and international market, but the more or less egalitarian control of their sources of subsistence and of the handicraft trade allows them to maintain their ethnic identity. Thanks to their concern for certain traditions (collective control of land and the system of reciprocity), the renewal of their artisanal trade, and the readjustment to a complex interaction with modernity, they have achieved a flourishing independence that they would not have obtained by enclosing themselves in their ancestral relations.

Hegemonic Reconversion and Popular Reconversion

The increase of handicrafts in industrialized countries reveals, as I indicated earlier, that modern economic progress does not imply eliminating the productive forces that do not directly serve their expansion if those forces comprise a numerous sector, and even satisfy sectoral needs or those of a balanced reproduction of the system. Inversely and complementarily, the reproduction of traditions does not demand closing oneself off to modernization. In addition to these Mexican cases, others in Latin America—for example, that of Otavalo in Ecuador (Walter)—show that the heterodox (but self-managed) reelaboration of traditions can be a simultaneous source of economic prosperity and symbolic reaffirmation. Modernization does not demand the abolition of traditions; nor is it the fatal destiny of traditional groups to remain outside of modernity.

It is known that in other areas of Mexico and Latin America indigenous people have not achieved this successful adaptation to capitalist development. Voracious middlemen, archaic and unjust structures of peasant exploitation, antidemocratic or repressive governments, and difficulties of the ethnic groups themselves in relocating in modernity keep them in a state of chronic poverty. If it is calculated how many artisans or ethnic groups have achieved a decent standard of living with their traditions or managed to incorporate themselves into modern development and reduce their asymmetry with the hegemonic groups, the results are deplorable. Even worse: the recent reconversion of Latin American economies aggravates the unequal segmentation in the access to economic goods, middle and higher education, new technologies, and more sophisticated consumption. The question we want to ask is whether the struggles to enter these scenes of modernization are the only ones that are in the interest of popular movements in Latin America.

The accumulation of earlier examples does not refute anything of what is known about the labor exploitation and educational inequality. Nor am I suggesting that things would go better for poor artisans if they were to imitate the potters of Ocumicho and the painters of Ameyaltepec—among other reasons, because the unequal structures that order the relations between peasant and industrial production, between handicrafts and art, make it impossible for the fifteen million artisans on the continent to gain access to the economic and symbolic benefits of the upper and middle classes. But to repeat this would not add another title to the bibliography.

Rather it is a question of ascertaining if, in this framework of injustice, what it means to maintain traditions or participate in modernity has the meaning for the popular sectors that traditionalists and modernizers imagine that it does. In following temporary or permanent migrants to the big cities, in hearing them talk about the habits of other nations, about the opportunities and disadvantages of urban life or of the new technologies, and how they skillfully insert themselves into modern commercial rules, what Good Eshelman affirms about the Nahuas that produce and sell *amates* becomes applicable to many of them:

> They are very mundane and sophisticated . . . , they use the life of their community and their customs as a norm for processing information and understanding others. . . . Their commercial success is due precisely to this mental attitude, which is so open and flexible that it allows them to move around in a complicated, varied world in which they have very diverse experiences and economic relations. (52-53)

This fluid relationship of some traditional groups to modernity is also observed in political and social struggles. In view of the invasion of industries and dams, or against the arrival of transnational systems of communication in their daily life, indigenous people and peasants have had to inform themselves about the most advanced scientific and technological discoveries in order to develop their own positions. The Brazilian Indians who are standing up to the destruction of the Amazon forest, and the Tarascans of Santa Fe de la Laguna in Mexico who, at the beginning of the eighties, succeeded in blocking the installation of a nuclear power plant on their communal lands, show how traditions of production and interaction with nature can be affirmed in relation to the challenges of this end of the century. The Organization for the Defense of the Natural Resources and Social Development of the

Juárez Mountain Range, in which Zapotecs and Chinantecs united to protect their forests against the paper industries, does not limit itself to the simple preservation of their resources: it has given form to an education based on their communal forms of work and on a complex ecological vision of the development of the region and of Mexico, supported by their beliefs in nature but shaped in step with those who build roads thinking only of their profits, "not in order to communicate to the communities" (Martínez Luna).

At the same time as the official reconversion, the reconversion with which the popular classes adapt their traditional knowledge and habits is produced. In order to understand the links that are woven between both, it is necessary to include in the analyses of the popular condition—dedicated to the oppositions between isolated subalterns and dominating cosmopolitans—these unconventional forms of integrating themselves into modernity that are heard in communities like Ocumicho, Ameyaltepec, and so many others. The artisans exchange information about buyers in Mexico City and the United States, taxi and hotel rates in Acapulco, how to use telephones for long-distance communication, from whom traveler's checks can be accepted, where the best place is to buy the electronic equipment that they will bring home.

The hard conditions of survival reduce this adaptation, in most cases, to a commercial and pragmatic apprenticeship. But frequently, especially in the new generations, the cultural crossings that we are describing include a radical restructuring of the links between the traditional and the modern, the popular and the cultured, the local and the foreign. It is enough to pay attention to the growing place that images from contemporary art and the mass media have in artisanal designs.

Let me say that when I began to study these changes, my immediate reaction was to lament the subordination of the producers to the tastes of urban consumers and tourists. Then eight years ago I went into a shop in Teotitlán del Valle—a Oaxacan town dedicated to weaving—where a fifty-year-old man was watching television with his father while exchanging phrases in Zapotec. When I asked him about the tapestries with images by Picasso, Klee, and Miró that he had on display, he told me they started to make them in 1968, when some tourists visited who worked in the Museum of Modern Art in New York and proposed that they renovate their designs. He showed me an album of photos and newspaper clippings in English that analyzed the exhibitions this artisan had done in California. In a half hour I saw him move with ease from Zapotec to Spanish and to English, from art to crafts, from his ethnic group to the information and entertainment of mass culture, passing through the art criticism of a metropolis. I understood that my worries about the loss of their traditions was not shared by this man who moved without too many conflicts between three cultural systems.[6]

Art versus Crafts

Why do so few artisans come to be recognized as artists? The oppositions between the cultured and the popular and between the modern and the traditional are condensed in the distinction established by modern aesthetics between art and crafts. In conceiving of art as a disinterested symbolic movement, a set of "spiritual" goods in which form predominates over function and the beautiful over the useful, crafts appear as the other, the kingdom of objects that could never be detached from their practical meaning. Social art historians, who revealed the dependencies of high art with respect to social context, almost never question the division between the cultured and the popular, which in part is superimposed upon the schism between the rural and the urban and between the traditional and the modern. Art corresponds to the interests and tastes of the bourgeoisie and cultivated sectors of the petite bourgeoisie; it is developed in cities, speaks of them, and when it represents landscapes from the countryside it does so with an urban perspective. (Raymond Williams said it well: "Land that is worked is almost never a landscape; the very idea of landscape presupposes the existence of a separated observer" [31].) Crafts, on the other hand, are seen as products of Indians and peasants in accord with their rusticity, the myths that inhabit their decoration, and the popular sectors that traditionally make and use them.

Is it not astonishing to read that in the colloquium on the dichtomy between high art and popular art one of the quickest historians of the West, Marta Traba, said that popular artists remain reduced to "the practical-picturesque" and are incapable of "thinking of a meaning different from that transmitted and used habitually by the community, whereas the 'high' artist is a solitary one whose primary happiness is to satisfy himself or herself thanks to his or her own creation" (68-71)? It is not possible to talk like this when an art historian knows that for more than half a century the constructivists, the Bauhaus movement, and theatrical and visual arts groups have been demonstrating that creativity can also spring from collective messages.

The other common argument that opposes Art to popular art says that producers of the former are singular and solitary whereas popular artists are collective and anonymous. In that same colloquium in Zacatecas we read that Art produces "unique works" that are unrepeatable, whereas crafts are made in series, in the same way that popular music repeats identical structures in its songs, as if they lacked "a project" and were limited "to *wearing out a prototype* to the point of fatigue, without ever getting to present it as a worldview, and, as a result, to defend it aesthetically through all its variables" (ibid., 70). We already referred to the ways and reasons why popular devils vary as much as or more than those of modern art (not to mention those of earlier art, which was obliged by the church to reproduce theologically approved models). We saw that artisans play with the iconic matrices of their community as part of aesthetic projects and creative interrelations with urban audiences. The myths that sustain the most traditional works and modern innovations indicate to what extent popular artists go beyond prototypes, put forward worldviews, and are capable of defending them aesthetically and culturally.

In another time, the Teotitlán del Valle weaver would have been an exception; persons like him were artisans who out of a peculiar creative necessity produced their works by distancing themselves from their own group, without gaining access to the world of high art either. They painted or engraved with high aesthetic value despite being ignorant of the history of the discipline, the conventions adopted in the international market, and the technical language for explaining them. Their personal style coincided at times with the goals of contemporary art, and that made them attractive in museums and galleries.

Today the intense and persistent relations between the communities of artisans and national and international culture make it "normal" for their members to be linked with modern visual culture, even though those who obtain fluent connections are still the minority. I remember the conversation I had with a producer of devils in his house in Ocumicho. We were talking about how the images occurred to him and I suggested that he explain how the devil was conceived among the Purépecha. He told me the myth that I recounted earlier, but he said that that was not all. I asked if they took scenes from their dreams; he downplayed the question and began to take out an illustrated Bible, religious and art books (one on Dalí), and weekly newspapers and magazines in Spanish and English that were rich in graphic material. He did not know the history of art but had a lot of information about contemporary visual culture, which he organized less systematically but controlled with an associative freedom similar to that of any artist.

In the chapter in which we described the transformations of the high arts in the second half of the twentieth century, we concluded that art can no longer be presented as useless or gratuitous. It is produced within a field crisscrossed by networks of dependencies that link it with the market, the culture industry, and with those "primitive" and popular referents that are also the nourishing source of the artisanal. If perhaps art never succeeded in being fully Kantian—finality without end, stage of gratuitousness—now its parallelism with crafts or popular art obliges us to rethink its equivalent processes in contemporary societies, its disconnections and its crossings.

There is no shortage of authors who attack this division. But they have almost always been folklorists and anthropologists concerned with vindicating the artistic value of indigenous cultural production, art historians willing to acknowledge that things of value also exist outside of museum collections. That phase already produced aesthetic and institutional results. It was demonstrated that in popular ceramics, textiles, and altarpieces one can find as much formal creativity, generation of original meanings, and occasional autonomy with respect to practical functions as in high art. This recognition has given certain popular artisans and artists entrée into museums and galleries. But the difficulties in redefining what is specific to art and to crafts, and in interpreting the links between each one and the other, are not arranged with goodwill openings onto what the neighbor is thinking. The way out of the deadlock in which this question is caught is a new type of research that reconceptualizes the global changes in the symbolic market by taking into account not only the intrinsic development of the popular and the cultured, but also its crossings and convergences. With the artistic and the artisanal being included in mass processes of message circulation, their sources of appropriation of images and forms and their channels of distribution and audiences tend to coincide.

Knowledge of culture and of the popular would be advanced more if the sanitary preoccupation with distinguishing the pure and the uncontaminated in art and crafts were abandoned and if we were to study them starting from the uncertainties that provoke their crossings. Just as the analysis of the high arts requires us to free ourselves from the presumption of absolute autonomy from the field and the objects, the examination of popular cultures demands that we rid ourselves of the assumption that its proper space is self-sufficient indigenous communities isolated from the modern agents that today constitute them as much as their traditions: the culture industries, tourism, economic and political relations with the national and transnational market of symbolic goods.

There are indigenous groups in which aesthetic acts are still given form with considerable independence starting from exclusive traditions, and in which rituals and daily practices of pre-Columbian and colonial origin are reproduced. A risk of the sociology of culture that specializes in modern and urban development—as does almost all sociology—and enunciates general affirmations about Latin America based on censuses, statistics, and polls is to forget this diversity and the perseverance of the archaic.

But the opposite risk—a frequent one among folklorists and anthropologists—is to isolate themselves in those minority groups as if the vast majority of the indigenous people of the continent had not for decades been living processes of migration, *mestizaje*, urbanization, and diverse interactions with the modern world. In this way the examination of the crossings between artisans and art leads into a profound debate over the oppositions between tradition and modernity, and therefore between the two disciplines that today, through their separation, stage that divorce: sociology and anthropology.

Before getting into that polemic, I want to say that another reason for being interested in the art/craft opposition as a sociocultural process—and not only as an aesthetic question—is the need to encompass a more extensive universe than that of singular products consecrated as (cultured or popular) art. In the same way that many works with pretensions of being Art agree on repeating aesthetic models from earlier centuries—and thus in settings with low legitimacy: art gardens, supermarkets, neighborhood cultural centers—most artisanal production has no aesthetic aspirations. In the Latin American countries that are richest in handicrafts—Peru, Ecuador, Guatemala, Mexico—most artisans produce in order to survive; they are not looking for ways to renew the forms or the meaning of their work. What we call art is not only that which culminates in great works, but rather a space where society carries out its visual production. It is in this broad sense that artistic work, its circulation, and its consumption shape an appropriate place for understanding the classifications with which the social is organized.

Anthropology versus Sociology

The differences, and the reciprocal ignorance, between these two disciplines derive from their opposed ways of exploring the traditional and the modern. Anthropology was dedicated chiefly to studying indigenous and peasant communities; its theory and method were formed in relation to rituals and myths, customs and kinship in traditional societies. Meanwhile, sociology was developed most of the time through a knowledge of macrosocial problems and processes of modernization.

They have also been opposed in the valorization of what remains and what changes. Today we cannot easily generalize, but for decades anthropologists, along with folklorists, have been experts of the archaic and the local, of premodern forms of sociality and the rescue of survivals. It is not fair to homogenize sociology either, but we know that its origin as a scientific discipline was associated with industrialization, and many still continue to view traditional organization of social and political relations—for example, *compadrazgo* and kinship relationships—as simple "obstacles to development."

In order to justify their studies' preference for the indigenous and peasant world, anthropologists remind us that thirty million Indians continue to exist in Latin America, with separate territories, their own languages (whose speakers are increasing in some regions), histories that predate the conquest, and work and consumption habits that distinguish them from the rest of the population. Their resistance to oppression and deculturation for five centuries continues to be expressed in autonomous social and political organizations: it cannot be thought that this is "a residual phenomenon, an inexplicable anachronism, not even a feature of folkloric color without major importance" (Bonfil 1981, 27). It must be recognized, affirmed, that "ethnic groups are 'potential nations': units capable of being the social field of concrete history" (ibid., 30-31).

This delimiting of the universe of study leads us to concentrate ethnographic description on the traditional features of small communities and to overestimate their internal logic. In focusing so closely on what distinguishes one group from others or resists Western penetration, the growing processes of interaction with the national society and even with the transnational economic and symbolic market are neglected. Or they are reduced to a sterile "contact between cultures." Hence the fact that anthropology has developed few useful concepts for interpreting how indigenous groups reproduce capitalist development internally or construct mixed formations with it. Conflicts, which are rarely admitted, are seen as if they were only produced between two homogeneous blocks: "colonial" society and the ethnic group. In the study of an ethnic group only those egalitarian or reciprocal social relations are examined that permit it to be considered a "community," without internal inequalities, compactly confronting the "invading" power.

Some authors who attempt to take into account modernizing changes acknowledge—in addition to external domination—the appropriation of their elements by the dominant culture, but they only consider those that the group accepts as being in "its own interests" or those to which a meaning of "resistance" can be given. That is why there are so few analyses of the processes in which an ethnic group—or most of the group—admits the remodeling that the dominators do with its culture: it voluntarily subordinates itself to Western forms of production, health-care systems, or religious movements (from Catholicism to Pentecostalism), and incorporates as its own project the modernizing changes and political integration into the national society. Even less common are investigations that examine the procedures whereby the traditional cultures of indigenous people and peasants converge syncretically with diverse modalities of urban and mass culture, establishing hybrid forms of existence of "the popular."

The difficulties increase when the classic style of anthropological ethnography is applied to the popular cultures of the city. How do you study the millions of indigenous people and peasants who migrate to the capitals, the workers subordinated to the industrial organization of work and consumption? It is impossible to respond if marginal sectors are chosen, if small units of analysis are outlined—a neighborhood, an ethnic group, a cultural minority—if only intensive observation techniques and in-depth interviews are used, and if they are examined as closed systems. These works tend to give original and rich information about microsocial questions. But their strategies of knowledge themselves inhibit the construction of an urban anthropology, or a comprehensive view of the meaning of life in the city, on the order of the Chicago School. We can apply what Eunice Durham says of Brazil to almost all anthropology done in Latin America: it has practiced less

an anthropology of the city than an anthropology in the city. . . . It is a question of investigations that operate with themes, concepts, and methods of anthropology but that are turned to the study of populations that live in cities. The city is, therefore, the place of investigation more than its object. (Durham 1986a, 19)[7]

It seems that we anthropologists have more difficulties in entering into modernity than do the social groups we study.

Another characteristic of these works is that they say very little about modern forms of hegemony. As Guillermo Bonfil notes in a text on research in Mexico,

the majority of anthropological studies on popular culture depart from the assumption, whether implicit or explicit, that their object of study is a different culture; and this even when the research refers to nonindigenous peasant communities or urban sectors. (Bonfil Batalla 1988)

The ethnographic tradition, which is distinguished by the hypothesis that "popular cultures are cultures in themselves, they are different cultures" (ibid.) resists thinking about them as subcultures or parts of a system of domination. Even for this author, who includes domination in his analysis and acknowledges unequal distribution of the global patrimony of society among the causes that originate popular cultures, the specific character of anthropological work consists in studying the differences.

Two arguments support this option. One takes up the connection of anthropology to history, which permits "the long duration" and "the diachronic dimension" to be included among the social processes. Since the beginning of colonization, one resource for dominating aboriginal groups was to maintain their difference; although the structure of subordination may have changed, the need remains—for the dominators and the popular classes, for different reasons—for the culture of these to be different. The second argument arises from observing the popular cultures of today. In mestizo peasant communities, including those where the language changed and traditional dress was abandoned, there subsist features of "material culture, productive activities, consumption guidelines, familiar and communal organization, medical and culinary practices, and a large part of the symbolic universe"; de-Indianization provokes in those groups "the rupture of the original ethnic identity" but they continue to have an awareness of being different and consider themselves to be depositories "of a cultural patrimony created throughout history by that same society" (ibid.). In cities, where the rupture is even more radical, many migrants of indigenous or peasant origin

> maintain links with their communities and renew them periodically; they are organized here in order to maintain life as it is there, as far as circumstances permit them to: they occupy small urban spaces that are becoming populated with people from there; they are organized and support each other according to their community and region of origin; they celebrate their fiestas and speak their own language among themselves. (Ibid.)

The concentration of many anthropologists on traditional cultures is related to their critical view of the effects of modernization. They question the value for the whole of society, and especially for popular layers, of a modern development that—in addition to ruining traditional forms of life—engenders mass migrations, uprooting, unemployment, and excessive urban growth. They are energetically opposed to all evolutionism that regards the ethnic and the peasant as backwardness in order to replace it with an urban and industrial growth defined a priori as progress. Hence, in the reactivation of indigenous and peasant traditions, in their knowledge and techniques, in their way of interacting with nature and resolving social problems in a communitarian way, they search for a style of development that is less degraded and dependent (cf. Warman; Bonfil Batalla 1990).

In the last two decades, the sociology of culture and political sociology have forged an opposing model, which sees popular cultures from the point of view of modernization. They begin from the relative success achieved by the projects of national integration, which eliminated, reduced, or subordinated the indigenous groups. One evidence of this is linguistic uniformity. Another is modern education, which includes generalized literacy in the two main languages—Spanish and Portuguese—and also a type of knowledge that enables the members of each society to participate in the labor market and capitalist consumption, as well as in national political systems. A third is a way of organizing familial and labor relations based on modern liberal principles.

It is known that this historical tendency was reinforced in the dualistic sociological theories that saw industrialization as the dynamic factor in Latin American development and attributed to this discipline the mission of struggling against traditional, agrarian, or "feudal" residues. Precisely because popular "backwardness" was criticized and because in that era sociology concentrated on the debate over socioeconomic models, very few investigations were interested in knowing about subaltern cultures. It was in recent years, when all the programs of modernization and social change went into crisis (developmentalisms, populisms, Marxisms) that Latin American sociologists began to study culture, especially popular culture, as one of the elements of articulation between hegemony and consensus.

The works that stood out in the sociology of culture in the eighties were guided by the theory of reproduction and those in political sociology were based on the Gramscian conception of hegemony. There was often a confluence of purpose in explaining how hegemonic classes founded their position on the continuity of a modern cultural capital that guarantees reproduction of the social structure, and on the unequal appropriation of that capital as a mechanism for reproducing those differences. But despite the greater attention given to the empirical knowledge of popular cultures, they often saw their daily life from the perspective of these macrotheories and gathered only what fit into them. This perspective has the merit of questioning the idealizations generated by the excessive autonomization of subaltern cultures, fulfilled by those who see them as manifestations of the creative capacity of the communities or as the autonomous accumulation of traditions that predate industrialization. In situating popular actions in the aggregate of the social formation, the reproductivists understand subaltern culture as the product of the unequal distribution of economic and cultural goods. The Gramscians, who are less fatalistic, relativize this dependency because they grant the popular classes a certain initiative and power of resistance, but always within the contradictory interaction with hegemonic groups.

Along this line, it has been maintained that there is no popular culture in Latin America with the components that Gramsci attributes to the concept of culture: *(a)* a conception of the world; *(b)* specialized producers; *(c)* preeminent social bearers; *(d)* the capacity to integrate into a social whole and bring it "to think coherently and in a unitary way"; *(e)* make possible the struggle for hegemony; *(f)* manifest itself through a material and institutional organization.[8] What is usually called "popular culture" in these multiethnic countries would be closer to the concept of folklore in the Gramscian vocabulary. The problem is that those universes of ancient practices and symbols are perishing and being weakened by the advance of modernity. In the midst of migrations from the countryside to the city that uproot producers and users of folklore, against the action of schools and the culture industry, the traditional set of symbols can only offer "scattered, fragmented states of consciousness in which heterogeneous elements and diverse cultural strata taken from very different universes coexist" (Brunner 1988, 151-85). Folklore maintains a certain cohesion and resistance in indigenous communities, or rural areas, and in "urban spaces of extreme marginality," but even there the demand for formal education is growing. Traditional culture is exposed to a growing interaction with industrially and mass-produced information, communication, and forms of entertainment:

> The populations or favelas of our big cities have been filled with transistor radios; in rural areas the installation of television relay towers increases; rock is the universal language at young people's parties that cuts across diverse social groups. (Ibid., 172)

A way of understanding the conflict between these two paradigms would be to suppose that the bifurcation between anthropology and sociology corresponds to the existence of two separate modalities of cultural development. If on one side traditional forms of production and communication persist, and on the other urban and mass circuits, it seems logical that there are different disciplines for studying each one. Are the positions in favor of the constant resistance of the popular cultures and regionally inexorable modernization not true—the first in the Andean and Mesoamerican regions and the second in the southern cone and the big cities? The question seems to resolve itself provided that one of the research tendencies does not become generalized, or claim that only one cultural policy exists. Although this precision has a certain relevance, it leaves unresolved the basic problems of a comprehensive analysis of the relations between tradition, modernity, and postmodernity.

Another way of addressing the question is to start with the analogy that appears in dealing with the crisis of the popular and that of elite culture. We also concluded in the chapters on art that there is not only one form of modernity but rather several unequal and sometimes contradictory ones. Both the transformations of popular cultures and those of high art coincide in demonstrating the heterogeneous implementation of the modernizing project in our continent, the diverse articulation of the liberal rationalist model with ancient aboriginal traditions, with Catholic colonial hispanism, and with each country's own sociocultural developments. Nevertheless, in exploring the features of this heterogeneity the division between disciplines again arises. Whereas anthropologists prefer to understand it in terms of difference, diversity, and cultural pluralism, sociologists reject the perception of heterogeneity as the "mere superimposition of cultures" and speak of a "segmented and differential participation in an international market of messages that 'penetrates' the local structure of culture everywhere and in unexpected ways" (Brunner 1988, 215-18).

It is fitting to add for the moment that both tactics for approaching the problem have demonstrated their fruitfulness. The anthropological training for unmasking what may be ethnocentric in the generalization of a modernity born in the metropolises is indispensable, as is, on the other hand, that of recognizing the local forms of symbolizing conflicts and of using cultural alliances to construct social pacts and mobilize each nation in a project of its own. At the same time, the sociological view serves to avoid the illusory isolation of local identities and informal loyalties, to include in the analysis the reorganization of the culture of each group by the movements that subordinate it to the transnational market or at least require it to interact with it.

Notes

1. Nicole Belmont (259-68) makes a critique of the notion of survival along this line.

2. The OAS convened a meeting on traditional popular culture with the goal of bringing the Charter of American Folklore up-to-date. This took place in Caracas July 20-24, 1987, under the auspices of the Center for Traditional and Popular Cultures of Venezuela and the Inter-American Center of Ethnomusicology and Folklore. Some of the arguments that follow I put forth

on that occasion; my specific critique of the charter was published later that year ("Las artes populares en la época de la industria cultural," 3-8).

3. SELA's estimate does not include countries that do not belong to this system, but the only country absent from it that does have significant artisanal production is Brazil.

4. Since the beginning of the 1980s, authors from various countries have been interested in the revitalization that commercialization and consumption of nontraditional sectors have made possible for folklore (e.g., Ribeiro et al., Becerril Straffton).

5. At the time that the poll mentioned earlier was conducted, at the beginning of the eighties, thirty-five of every one hundred Mexican homes had incomes below the monthly minimum wage, that is, a little less than one hundred dollars (Aguilar Camín 1988, 214).

6. For an analysis of artisanal modernization in Teotitlán del Valle, see Cohen and Schneider.

7. Another study by the same author (1986b) shows what the change of direction we suggest here can mean for research.

8. This is the way in which it is formulated by Brunner ("Notas sobre cultura popular, industria cultural y modernidad," in *Un espejo trizado,* 151-85).

6 | The Popular and Popularity: From Political to Theatrical Representation

While the staging of local cultures by the folklorists was convincing, it was thought that the mass communications media were the great threat to popular traditions. In reality, the process of homogenization of the indigenous cultures of America began long before radio and television: in the ethnocidal operations of the conquest and colonization, in the violent Christianization of groups with diverse religions, during the formation of national states, in monolingual schooling, and in colonial or modern organization of urban space.

One cannot even attribute the origin of the massification of popular cultures to the electronic media. This error was proposed by early studies on communication, according to which *mass culture* would replace the traditional cultured and popular. "The mass" was conceived of as a field definable within the social structure, with an intrinsic logic like that of literature and art until the middle of the twentieth century: a subculture determined by the position of its agents and the range of its audiences.

Impressed by the sudden growth in readers of newspapers and magazines and of radio and television audiences, communications specialists believed that the symbolic changes were a set of effects resulting from the greater quantitative impact of the messages. Today the electronic media are relocated in a more general trend of modern societies. Industrialization and urbanization, generalized education, and union and political organizations have been reordering social life according to mass laws since the nineteenth century, before the appearance of the press, radio, and television.

The notion of mass culture arose when societies were already massified. In Latin America the transformations promoted by modern communications media are interwoven with the integration of nations. Monsiváis states that on the radio and in film Mexicans learned to recognize themselves as a totality beyond ethnic and regional divisions: ways of speaking and dressing, tastes and codes of behavior that previously were distant and disconnected are now joined in the language with which the media represent the masses that are invading the cities and give them a synthesis of national identity (Monsiváis 1984). Martín Barbero says that the national projects were consolidated thanks to the encounter of the states with the masses that communications technologies have promoted. If making a country is not only to succeed in having what is produced in one region reach another part, if it requires a unified political and cultural project, a symbolic consumption that favors the advance of the market, then the integration proposed by the media does not casually converge with nationalist populisms. For each country to cease being "a country of countries," it was decisive that radio take up, in a solidary way, the oral cultures of diverse regions and reclaim the proliferating "vulgarities" in urban centers. Like film, and as in part television later did, they translated "the idea of the nation into sentiment and the commonplace" (Martín Barbero 1987b).

In the third stage—after the first sociopolitical massification, and the second one driven by the alliance of media and populism—mass communications appeared as agents of developmentalist innovation. While production was being industrialized and the goods of modern consumption—autos, electrical appliances—multiplied, television advertised them and updated the information and the tastes of consumers. Artists then convert the new objects and machines into icons and aspire to be promoted and interviewed by the media. Popular art, which had won diffusion and social legitimacy thanks to radio and film, is reelaborated in view of the audiences that now learn about folklore through television programs.

In the midst of these changes in function the names vacillate: mass culture, culture for the masses, culture industry? A history of so-called mass culture could be made just out of a record of abandoned notions. It would be an impressive account because it covers a period of no more than thirty or forty years.

In the middle of the century there was talk of *mass culture*, although it was soon noticed that the new media, such as radio and television, were not the property of the masses. It seemed more exact to call it *culture for the masses,* but that designation lasted only as long as it could sustain the one-directional view of communication that believed in the absolute manipulation of the media and assumed that its messages were destined for the masses as submissive receivers. The notion of *culture industry*—useful to the Frankfurt School in producing studies as renovating as they were apocalyptic—continues to be useful when we want to refer to the fact that more and more cultural goods are not generated artisanally or individually but rather through technical procedures, machines, and labor relations equivalent to those that engender other industrial products; nevertheless, this focus tends to say little about *what* is produced and *what* happens to the receivers. This notion also does not, strictly speaking, include the electronic and telematic processes in which cultural production involves informational and decisional processes that go beyond the simple industrial manufacture of symbolic goods.

In short, we are not going to summarize hastily a history that is still open and uncertain. We only observe that in this movement we confront at once the difficulty of incorporating into cultural studies:

- new industrial, electronic, and informational *processes of production* that reorder what we used to call cultured and popular;
- other *formats* that at times appear as a new type of goods (from photography and comics to television and video);
- massive and transnational *processes of circulation* that do not correspond only to innovations in technology and format but are applicable to any symbolic good, whether traditional or modern;
- new types of *reception* and *appropriation,* whose variety goes from the individual concentration that obliges one to spend many hours in front of the television or the computer screen, to the horizontal uses of video by alternative education groups to strengthen communication and critical integration.

It is impossible to synthesize such varied formats and processes under only one name. Some terms, such as those of mass culture or culture for the masses, can be used with the caveat that they designate only one aspect and not the most recent; the notions of culture industry, electronic culture, or tele-information are pertinent for naming technical or particular aspects. But the most difficult task is still to explain the global cultural processes that are occurring through the combination of these innovations. New symbolic frameworks are evolving in which neither the media nor mass culture operate in isolation, nor can their efficacy be evaluated by the number of receivers, but rather as parts of a recomposition of social meaning that transcends previous modes of classification.

Communications: The Construction of the Spectator

What is left in this process of what was called popular? On the one hand, electronic communications media show significant continuity with traditional popular cultures insofar as both are imaginary stagings of the social. There is no reality that folklore represents authentically, insofar as the media deforms it. The romantic idealization of fairy tales resembles too much that of soap operas, and the fascination with horror stories is not far from that presented by police stories (and it is known that the newspapers and television programs of this genre are the most popular). The narrative structures of melodrama, black humor, the construction of heroes and antiheroes, the events that do not copy but on the contrary transgress the "natural order" of things are so many other coincidences that make so-called mass culture the great competitor of folklore.

The media puts itself "in charge of adventure, serial fiction, mystery, fiestas, humor, a whole zone that is looked down upon by high culture" (Ford 1988, 36-38), and incorporates the hegemonic culture with an efficacy that folklore has never achieved. Radio in all Latin American countries—and film in some—stages the language and myths of the people that the dominant painting, narrative, and music almost never collected. But at the same time it induces another articulation of the popular with the traditional, with the modern, with history, and with politics.

What is the people for the manager of a television station or a market researcher? Audience numbers, the average number of records a singer sells per month, statistics that can be shown to advertisers. For the media, the popular is not the result of traditions, nor of collective "personality," nor is it defined by its manual, artisanal, oral—in a word, premodern—character. Communications specialists see contemporary popular culture as constituted starting with the electronic media—not as the result of local differences, but rather of the diffusing and integrating action of the culture industry.

The notion of the popular constructed by the media, and in large part accepted by studies in this field, follows the logic of the market. "Popular" is what sells massively, what the multitudes like. As a matter of fact, what matters to the market and the media is not the popular but popularity. The media is not concerned with maintaining the popular as culture or tradition; the culture industry is more interested in constructing and renewing the *simultaneous* contact between broadcasters and receivers than it is in the formation of historical memory. It is also disturbed by the word "people," which evokes images of violence and insurrections. The displacement of the noun *people* by the adjective *popular*, and even more by the abstract noun *popularity*, is a neutralizing operation useful for controlling the "political susceptibility" of the people (Bollème). While the people may be the place of tumult and danger, popularity—adhesion to an order, consensus on a system of values—is measured and regulated by opinion polls.

The political demonstration spectacularizes the presence of the people in a way that lacks predictability: who knows how the invasion of a crowd in the streets will end? In contrast, the popularity of singers or actors within closed spaces—a stadium or a television channel—with a programmed beginning and end, at precise times, is a controlled spectacle: even more so if that mass acclaim is diluted in the ordered transmission of domestic television sets. What is theatrical in the big shows is based as much on the syntactical and visual structure and the grandiloquence of the spectacle as on the ratings and the magnitude of the popularity; but it is a question of an almost secret spectacularization, which is finally submerged in the intimate discipline of domestic life. The people seem to be a subject that is presented; popularity is the extreme form of re-presentation, the most abstract, one that reduces it to a number and to statistical comparisons.

For the market and for the media the popular does not matter as tradition that lasts. On the contrary, a law of constant obsolescence accustomed us to the fact that the popular, precisely because it is the place of success, is also the place of the ephemeral and of oblivion. If what is sold this year continued to be valuable next year, new records and jeans would cease to be purchased. The mass popular is that which does not remain and is not accumulated as experience nor enriched with what is acquired.

The communicational definition of popular also abandons the ontological character assigned to it by folklore. The popular does not consist of what the people are or have, but what becomes accessible, what they like, and what merits their frequent adhesion or use—with which a distortion is produced that is symmetrically opposed to that produced by folklore: the popular is given to the people from outside. This heteronomous way of defining subaltern culture is generated, in part, by the omnipresence attributed to the media. We still have not left behind the glare that provoked communications specialists to see the rapidity with which television multiplied its audience in the stage of the primitive accumulation of audiences. It is curious that this belief in the unlimited capacity of the media to establish scripts of social behavior continues to impregnate critical texts of those who work for a democratic organization of culture and blame the media for succeeding by itself to distract the masses from their reality. Much of the bibliography reduces the problematic of mass communications to the maneuvers whereby a transnational system imposes tastes and opinions on the subaltern classes.

Since the 1970s, this conceptualization of the popular as a subordinate, passive, and reflected entity has been questioned theoretically and empirically. It does not hold up in the face of post-Foucauldian conceptions of power, which cease to see it as concentrated in blocks of institutional structures, imposed vertically, and think of it as a disseminated social relation. Power is not contained in an institution, nor in the state, nor in the communications media. Nor is it a certain potency with which some are gifted: "it is the name that one attributes to a complex strategical situation in a particular society" (Foucault 1980, 93). Therefore the so-called popular sectors coparticipate in those relations of force that are set up simultaneously in production and consumption, in families and individuals, in the factory and the union, in partisan groups and base organizations, and in the mass media and the structures of reception that receive and give new meaning to its messages.

Let us think of a popular fiesta such as the ceremony of the dead or Carnival in various Latin American countries. They were born as community celebrations but one year tourists began to arrive, then press photographers, radio, television, and more tourists. The local organizers put up stands for selling beverages, handicrafts that they always produced, souvenirs that they invent to take advantage of the visit by so many people. In addition, they charge the media for permitting it to photograph and film. Where does the power reside: in the mass media, the fiesta organizers, the vendors of beverages, handicrafts, or souvenirs, or the tourists and media spectators who, if they were to lose interest, would erode the entire process? Of course, the relations tend not to be egalitarian but it is clear that the power and construction of the event are a consequence of a complex and decentered fabric of reformulated traditions and modern interchanges, of multiple actors acting in combination.

For decades—though only now are we realizing it—the links between the media and popular culture have formed part of broader structures of social interaction. To understand them requires moving "from the media to the mediations," argues Martín Barbero in analyzing the influence of radio, between the 1930s and 1940s, for its capacity to unite with the interpellations that since populism have converted "the masses into people and the people into Nation"; the same occurs if the efficacy of film in relation to the process of urbanization is studied, since movies helped migrants learn how to live and express themselves in the city and bring their morality and their myths up-to-date. Radio "nationalized the language"; television unifies the intonations, gives repertories of images in which the national becomes in tune with the international (Martín Barbero 1987a, Part 3).[1]

It will be seen better in the following chapter why communications technologies and the industrial reorganization of culture do not replace traditions, nor homogeneously massify them, but rather change the conditions for obtaining and renewing knowledge and sensitivity. They propose a different type of link between culture and territory, between the local and the international, different codes of identification of experiences, of deciphering their meanings, and ways of sharing them. They reorder the relations of dramatization and credibility with the real. All this is connected, as we know, to the remodeling of culture in terms of commercial investment, although the symbolic changes cited cannot be explained only by the weight that the economic acquires.

At this moment it is interesting to emphasize that, knowing that mass communications stage the popular in a different way, we ignore almost everything about how the popular sectors take up this transformation. Because the refutation of the omnipotence of the media has still not brought us to a knowledge of how they are articulated in reception with the other systems—cultured, popular traditional—for organizing meaning.

It is not enough to admit that discourses are received in different ways and that there exists no lineal nor monosemic relation in the circulation of meaning. If the intersection of "mass media" discourse with other social mediators generates a field of effects, and that field is not definable only from production, to know the action of the culture industry requires an exploration of the processes of mediatization, the rules that govern the transformations between a discourse and its effects.[2] But the scarcity of studies on consumption—which are rather quantitative market and opinion surveys—still permits little advancement in the reformulation of the relations between mass communication and popular reception.

It is, nevertheless, a propitious space for interdisciplinary work. It is a question of a *communicational* problem, which demands methodological concepts and instruments more subtle than those usually used in investigations of the public and the market. But the theory and techniques of *anthropological* observation, and the training of this discipline in obtaining direct knowledge in the microinteractions of daily life, can help in knowing how the discourses of the media are inserted in cultural history and in the habits of perception and understanding of the popular sectors.

Populism: The Simulation of the Actor

There has been a proliferation of sociological and political studies on this trend but rarely do they treat a question that is central for populism: its way of using culture to build power. Two central features of its symbolic practice interest us here: its project of modernizing folklore by converting it into a foundation of order and consensus and, at the same time, reversing the trend of making the people into a mere spectator.

In contrast to the folkloric exaltation of traditions in the name of a metaphysical view of the people as originary creative force, populism selects from the archaic cultural capital what can be made compatible with contemporary development. Only fundamentalist groups freeze the popular in the love of the land and the race, in biological and telluric traits, just as it is imagined that they existed in preindustrial stages. Political populisms utilize what survives of that naturalizing ideology by relocating it in current conflicts. In the patrimonial and civic ritualizations described in chapter 4, popular wisdom and creativity are staged as part of the historic reserve of the nation in the face of new challenges. In state populism, the traditional values of the people, assumed and represented by the state or by a charismatic leader, legitimize the order that these administer and give the popular sectors the confidence that they are participating in a system that includes and recognizes them.[3]

This staging of the popular has been a mix of participation and simulacrum. From Vargas and Perón to recent populisms, the effective revalorization of the popular classes, the defense of labor rights, the diffusion of their culture and their art go together with imaginary stagings of their representation.

Populism made new interactions with modernity possible for the popular sectors, both with the state and with other hegemonic actors: that their demands for work, housing, and health be partially heard; that the subaltern groups learn to deal with functionaries, process paperwork, speak on the radio and television, and get themselves acknowledged. These new citizens succeed in being such within the asymmetrical relations of power, in ritualizations that at times substitute for interaction and the material satisfaction of the demands. In this process the convergence of political populism with the culture industry is important. In taking into account the fact that in modern societies the people exist as a mass, as the public of a system of symbolic production that transcended its artisanal phase, the populists try to ensure that the people not remain as the passive receiver of communicational actions. In addition to promoting premodern forms of communication and political alliances—personal and neighborhood relations—their cultural program constructs scenes in which the people appear participating and performing (protest demonstrations, parades, public rites).

Three changes that have occurred in the last few years weaken this type of constitution of the popular. One derives from the transformations generated by the culture industries. Like other goods, those offered by the political field are resignified as they circulate, according to the logic of publicity, on television, radio, and in the press. To participate in an electoral campaign requires an investment of millions of dollars, as well as adapting the image of the candidates to the one recommended by the opinion polls and replacing the political and reflexive content of the messages through operations to redesign the "product." Posters—one of the last genres of political discourse that until recently simulated artisanal and personalized communication— are today designed by advertising agencies and put up on commission: this is perhaps the most striking symptom of how marketing techniques have replaced militancy and direct social participation. As these actions (like cosmetic surgery to improve the candidate's profile, changing glasses and clothing, and what the communications specialists charge for advising him) are broadcast by the media as part of the preelection spectacle, what we will call a "deverisimization" of political demagoguery is produced. This loss of power, of course, is accompanied by a drop in the representativeness and credibility of the parties because of their inefficacy in confronting social and economic crises.

The other change that deteriorates populism is precisely the economic crisis and the neoliberal reorganization of states. How can the championing of popular interests be staged when there is no surplus to distribute? The stagnation and the recession of the eighties, the constant monetary devaluation, and the burden of the foreign debt not only returned income levels to those of the previous decade; in addition to aggravating poverty, unemployment, and the shortage of basic necessities, they also crushed the symbolic game and the political dramatization of hopes.

It would seem necessary to study how the incredibility of the parties, the low participation in them, and the enormous percentage of people who abstain from elections (or remain undecided a week before) are combined with the overactivity of journalistic information. But this is a new type of political journalism that inflates anecdotes, the spectacular—and even the police—dimension of social conflicts, to the detriment of debates and reflection. In almost all Latin American societies the decline in interest in party activism goes hand in hand with a drop in the circulation of political weeklies compared to the sixties. In contrast, there is growth in the number of readers of current events and entertainment magazines, in which social and political information is concentrated in interviews more than in analysis, and in the daily life or tastes of public personalities more than in their opinions on conflicts that affect the ordinary citizen. Thus publications and radio and television programs generate "satisfactory" interpretations for different groups of consumers, pleasant and entertaining commentaries, melodramatic experiences obtained "in place of the facts," without problematizing the social structure in which those facts are inscribed or presenting the possibility of changing it. The political mediation between popular movements and governmental or party apparatuses is replaced by this symbolic mediation of the press and the information programs in the media, which present the material in order to pretend that we are informed. When problems seem unresolvable and those in charge incompetent, we are offered the compensation of information that is so intense, immediate, and frequent that it creates the illusion that we are participating.

It is clear that these changes are related to the displacement of a culture of productivity by a culture of speculation and spectacle. Classical populism based its championing of the popular on the culture of work. Industrial conversion, by means of technological innovations that reduce the number of workers required and disqualify their traditional knowledge, reinforces employer control over the productive process and labor conditions. Likewise it diminishes union power, as well as that of the politicians who negotiated with it when conflicts were defined more by their social aspect than by their technical requirements. What can still be saved from populism is then displaced onto consumption (cheaper goods and services in shops or state transport) or onto symbolic offers: spectacles of collective identification and guarantees of order and stability.

But is the popular nothing more than the effect of certain acts of enunciation and of staging? It is understandable that the staging of the social and the delegation of representativeness are more brutal in sectors that, for having lacked a voice and writing until recently, and for being ignorant of the complexity of new technologies, are constituted by others. But what is there beneath so many ventriloquists and "producers" of the popular (in the cinematographic and theatrical sense as well as in the other)?

The modernity that created these creators of the popular also generated an attempt to flee from that theatrical circle: to go to the people, listen to them, and see how they act. Let us read their texts, let us go to their spontaneous manifestations, let us allow them to speak. From the Romanticism of the nineteenth century to the writers that become journalists, from the governmental or alternative institutions dedicated to documenting oral memory to the novelists with tape recorders and the educators who organize popular periodicals, they have tried to insure that the people are not rep-resented but rather that they are presented to themselves. Life histories, story contests, chronicles and testimonies, and literary workshops with workers and peasants have sought to ensure that popular *speech* finds a place in the *written* world, and that colloquial discourse—of the village or of the neighborhood—enters the "legitimate" field of culture. The three sectors recently analyzed—folkloric, mass media, and populist—sometimes contribute to this process of making the people speak: they collect narratives, include street interviews in radio and television programs, and share the settings of power with the people.

We cannot valorize everyone equally. There are ethnologists and historians who discuss the methodological conditions necessary for the recording and interpretation of life histories or of direct information: the most advanced debate is taking place in North American postmodern anthropology and is dedicated to revealing how the investigator always interferes in the society that he or she studies and tends to hide the fragmented character of all fieldwork experience and how textual strategies of ethnographic description reduce the conflictive polyphony of each culture to the single coherent voice of scientific description.[4]

There are also writers who use literary techniques to document social processes and at the same time to redefine the divisions of the literary field, the relations between reality and fiction, and the problems involved in processing citations and discursive representation.[5] In these cases there are explicit reflections that contribute to redefining the hierarchies of literary and scientific discourses as well as their methods of linking reality and representation.

But the championing of the popular also gave rise to other movements—in the first place, those constructed by the popular classes themselves: from the political parties and unions to a vast ensemble of ethnic, neighborhood, educational, ecological, feminine and feminist, youth, social work, and "alternative" artistic and political groupings. Nevertheless, such a variety of representatives, definitions, and recovery strategies does not help much to determine precisely what we can understand by popular. Even more so when the attribution of the character of the popular is the result of contradictory processes in which fractions of a movement share or dispute the legitimacy of the designation of popular for parties, unions, or states that wish to bear that name.

Rarely is it recorded how much leftist or alternative populism collaborates in producing this uncertainty. I refer to the movements that seem to imitate the linguistic-cultural habits of the subaltern classes and think they can find the "essence" of the popular in their critical conscience and their transforming impulse. This tendency took shape in Brazil and in other Latin American countries beginning in the 1960s. Writers, filmmakers, singers, professionals, and students, gathered in the Brazilian Popular Centers of Culture (CPC), deployed an enormous diffusing task of culture by redefining it as "conscientization." In the book that synthesized the aesthetic-political ideas of the CPC, Ferreira Gullar wrote that "popular culture is, in short, the raising of consciousness of Brazilian reality. . . . It is, first and foremost, revolutionary consciousness" (84).

At the end of the same decade, the Liberation Cinema Group proposed in Argentina—and later extended it to other countries—an "action cinema" that would break the passivity of the spectacle and promote participation. Confronted by commercial film and film by the author, as well as by rightist sectors of Peronism that limited themselves to ritualizing the popular as a mystic and earthly force, the group favored a "militant cinema," a "culture of subversion," and "the struggle for national emancipation" (Solanas and Getino, 29). It opposed to the "cinema of evasion, a cinema that rescues the truth; to a passive cinema, a cinema of aggression; to an institutionalized cinema, a guerrilla cinema" (ibid., 49). In the same way that the CPC did, it inverted the folkloric characterization of the popular: instead of defining it by traditions, it did so by its transforming power; instead of dedicating itself to conserving art, it tried to use art as an instrument of agitation.

Although the defeats of the seventies attenuated this optimism, its conception of culture and the popular persists in communications and alternative artistic, political, and educational work. According to the register of the Institute for Latin America, these groups number more than one thousand on our continent (García Canclini and Roncagliolo).[6] Many of them have to be acknowledged for having produced—in addition to works aimed at educating and mobilizing the popular sectors in defense of their rights—an empirical knowledge of subaltern cultures, in some countries greater than that of academic institutions. But their political and social action tends to be of limited scope, with difficulties in constructing effectively alternative options because they relapse into the errors of folklorism and populism. As with both of these, they select particular or "concrete" empirical objects, absolutize their immediate and apparent characteristics, and—based on those characteristics—inductively infer the social place and historic destiny of the popular classes. They imagine that the multiplication of microgroup actions will someday bring about transformations in society as a whole, without considering that the big components of popular forms of thought and sensibility—the culture industry, the state—are spaces in which popular interests must be made present or must struggle for hegemony. They isolate small groups, confident of reconquering the utopia of transparent and egalitarian relations with the simple artifice of liberating the popular classes from the always external agents (the media, bureaucratized politics) that corrupt them, and then letting the intrinsic goodness of human nature emerge.

With action or participative research methods they claim to obtain the "true" explanation of popular meaning, but the microsocial outline of their analyses of communities or neighborhoods, or of daily practices, disconnected from the network of macrodeterminations that they explain, prevents them from explaining the restructuring of the popular in the era of the culture industry. The staging of these "base," "authentic" sectors, as if they were autonomous and foreign to the macrosocial structures, inhibits any problematizing of the conditions of legitimacy and validity of popular knowledge. For this reason, they do not utilize epistemological resources that would allow them to separate naive certainties from common sense—what the popular actors say that they do. They assume that allowing them to speak is sufficient for a true knowledge about them to emerge. When these works also do not include a critical reflection on the conditioning circumstances of the researcher-participant, they transfer their political utopias to the object of study and perceive in the popular classes only their questioning acts; they interpret mere symbolic difference as opposition.

It is necessary to apply the critique of ethnocentrism both to the investigators and to the popular informants. We social scientists who have interests in reproducing the intellectual field, as well as those who combine study and activism (in other words, who are conditioned at once by the academic and the political worlds), and the popular sectors themselves, are subject to the tendency of every group to generate schemas of perception and understanding capable of justifying our positions in the social system. Knowledge is constructed once there is a break with premises and their conditions of credibility, with the appearance of common sense, whether it be popular, political, or scientific.

Toward Transdisciplinary Research

We have differentiated three uses of the popular. The folklorists almost always talk of *the traditional popular,* the mass media of *popularity,* and politicians of *the people.* At the same time, we identified some social strategies that underlie each conceptual construction. We saw their incompatibilities and their incommensurability, in Kuhn's sense (diverse ways of seeing the world and of practicing knowledge), which places the study of the popular in a preparadigmatic situation.

Does it make sense to include under the name of *the* popular modalities as diverse as those that folklorists, anthropologists, sociologists, and communications specialists study and those that politicians, writers, and base educators talk about? What is the advantage for scientific work in giving the name popular culture to that of the indigenous person and the worker, the peasant and the city dweller, that generated by different labor conditions, neighborhood life, and the communications media?

These questions have received institutional and communicational responses more than scientific solutions. A group of heterogeneous articles is gathered together or a multithematic symposium is organized and they are placed under the title "popular culture." The formula is used to name a museum or a television program when the aim is to diffuse the diverse cultures of a country. Something like this happens when "popular movements" are organized and under that rubric are placed groups whose common situation of subalternity does not allow them to be sufficiently designated by their ethnicity (Indian), their place in the relations of productions (worker), or their geographical environment (peasant or urban). The popular allows all these situations of subordination to be synthetically included and a shared identity to be given to the groups that converge in a solidary project.

In the social sciences too the incorporation of those multiple uses of "popular" has had positive effects. It extended the notion beyond indigenous and traditional groups, giving recognition to other actors and cultural forms that share the condition of subalterns. It freed the popular from the economicist path imposed upon it by those who reduced it to the concept of class: even when the class theory continues to be necessary for characterizing the location of popular groups and their political struggles, the conceptual broadening allows the inclusion of forms of symbolic elaboration and social movements that are not derived from their place in the relations of production. The denomination *popular* has facilitated the studying of subaltern sectors not only as workers and militants but as "invaders" of lands and consumers.

Nevertheless, scientific discourse and political tasks need to establish a better-defined empirical referent and know if the popular is an ideological construction or corresponds to clearly identifiable social subjects or situations. With the goal of refounding the notion of popular, reproduction theory and the Gramscian conception of hegemony were turned to. The studies on social reproduction make it clear that popular cultures are not simple manifestations of the creative need of the peoples, nor the autonomous accumulation of traditions existing prior to industrialization, nor products of the nominating power of parties or political movements. By situating subaltern actions in the social formation as a whole, reproduction theory transcends the recollection of customs and discovers the complementary meaning of practices developed in distinct spheres. The same society that generates inequality in the factory reproduces it in school, urban life, mass communication, and general access to culture. As the same class receives subordinated places in all those spaces, popular culture may be understood as a consequence of the unequal appropriation of economic and symbolic goods by the subaltern sectors.

The objection to the theory is that, in fixing popular classes in the place assigned to them by social reproduction, all initiative is reserved for the dominant groups. They are the ones that determine the meaning of development, each sector's possibilities of access, the cultural practices that unite or separate the parts of a nation. Attempts have been made to use the Gramscian theory of hegemony to correct the omnipotence of reproductivism. Popular cultures are not a passive or mechanical effect of the reproduction controlled by the dominators; they are also constituted by retaking their own traditions and experiences in the conflict with those who exercise hegemony, more than domination—that is, with the class that, although it directs reproduction politically and ideologically, must allow spaces in which subaltern groups develop practices that are independent and not always functional for the system (their own habits of production and consumption, festive expenditures that go against the logic of capitalist accumulation).

Articulating these concepts of reproduction and hegemony is a still-unresolved problem in social theory. Those who, like Bourdieu, investigate from the perspective of the most radical versions of reproduction theory deny the existence of popular culture understood as difference and dissent; for them, culture is capital that belongs to all of society and that everyone interiorizes through the habitus. The unequal appropriation of that capital only produces struggles for distinction between classes. Developed in relation to a highly unified symbolic market—French society—reproductive theory considers popular culture as an echo of the dominant (Bourdieu 1979, chapter 7, and 1983). This reproductivist model has been questioned in France by authors who share reproduction theory (e.g., Grignon and Passeron). In multiethnic, multicultural nations like those of Latin America, we can argue that no such cultural unification exists, nor do dominant classes so effective at eliminating differences or subordinating them entirely. But this criticism does not eliminate the fruitfulness of reproductivist analyses for explaining why the behavior of the popular classes is often not one of resistance or opposition but rather adapts to a system that includes it.

The neo-Gramscians see culture as part of the struggle for hegemony rather than as a space of distinction and political conflict between classes. Therefore, this model is utilized by those who emphasize autonomy and the capacity for initiative and opposition by subaltern sectors. Although the complex Gramscian conception, enriched by recent anthropologists (Cirese, Lombardi, Satriani, Signorelli), avoids the more naive risks of voluntarist and spontaneist tendencies, it has stimulated unilateral and utopian views like those that we already criticized in "alternative" movements. The difficulties become more acute, both in this current and in the reproductivist one, when their models are used as superparadigms and generate popular strategies to which they attempt to subordinate the totality of the facts: all that is not hegemonic is subaltern, or the inverse. The descriptions then omit ambiguous processes of interpenetration and mixing in which the symbolic movements of different classes engender other processes that cannot be ordered under the classifications of hegemonic and subaltern, modern and traditional.

Before analyzing these hybrid cultures in the next chapter—as well as the notion of coherent and compact social totality that the reproduction and hegemony theories presuppose—we will clarify two crossroads in the study of the popular.

1. The oscillation between reproductivists and neo-Gramscians makes manifest the tension between two basic operations of scientific investigation that run through all research on the popular: I am referring to the confrontation between deduction and induction. We call *deductivists* those who define popular cultures from the general to the particular, according to

characteristics that are imposed—by the mode of production, imperialism, the dominant class, the ideological apparatuses, or the culture industry. The deductivists—as still happens in certain communications studies—believe it legitimate to infer what happens in popular reception from the claimed manipulative power of the state or the media. They do not acknowledge autonomy or difference in subaltern cultures, in their way of relating to one another, of communicating, and of resisting. For the deductivists, the only thing we know of the popular classes is what the hegemonic sectors want to do with them.

Inductivism, in contrast, confronts the study of the popular by starting with properties that it supposes to be intrinsic to the subaltern classes, or with a creativity that other sectors have lost, or a power of opposition that is the basis of their resistance. According to this current, we know nothing more of popular cultures than what the popular classes do and say. Its immanentist conception of the popular leads it to analyze it by following only the account of the actors. Given that the interviewee is defined as indigenous, the investigation consists of "rescuing" what he or she does in his or her own terms and "faithfully" duplicating the discourse of the informant; or, if the person is defined as a worker, given that no one knows better what happens than he or she, we have to believe that his or her condition and class consciousness are as he or she presents them. The divergence between what we think and our practices is neglected, as is the one between the self-definition of the popular classes and what we can know about their life by studying the social laws in which they are inserted. They act as if knowing were simply a matter of gathering together facts according to their "spontaneous" appearance instead of conceptually constructing the relations that give them their meaning in the social logic.

The bifurcation between these tendencies is also manifested in the choice of research techniques. The deductivists prefer surveys and statistics, which permit them to establish the big lines of mass behavior. The inductivists privilege ethnography, prolonged observation in the field, and open interviews, because they are interested in recording what is specific about small groups. Grignon and Passeron have observed that the techniques selected are symptomatic of how the relation of popular culture to society is visualized. Those who opt for quantitative procedures tend to neglect the partial autonomy of the popular classes and emphasize their dependence on macrosocial laws. In contrast, those who renounce surveys and macroanalysis tend to disregard the relations of domination and postulate the relativist legitimacy of the practices of each group: "Ethnographism leads to privileging the most traditional, folkloric, closed, and exotic aspects of peasant cultures" (Grignon and Passeron, 38).

This opposition may seem schematic and Manichaean, although it is easy to give examples of pure deductivists and inductivists. Undoubtedly there are anthropologists, sociologists, and communications specialists who speak of complex interactions between the macro- and the microsocial. By dint of working in the field and letting themselves be challenged by the facts, they succeed in breaking with the presuppositions of ethnocentrism and relativism, and also perceive what escapes their conceptual frameworks and their methods. But it is significant that—despite the evident importance of these processes of interaction—we possess so few methodological concepts and resources for working in them.

2. The other opposition that structures this comparative analysis of the studies of the popular, and of the social movements that represent it, is the one separating *traditionalists* and *modernizers*. On the symbolic level, the divergence expresses the different and unequal developments of distinct sectors in Latin American societies. The choice of one or the other posture corresponds in part to the position of the actors in the social structure. Likewise, the bifurcation of intellectuals with regard to this question has to do with the scientific capital accumulated in the study of tradition and modernity and with the interest in preserving—along with the rights of the discipline—the place acquired by its practitioners in the academic field.

If this sociological explanation were sufficient for understanding why conceptual oppositions reproduce interests of groups that are opposed in society and in the cultural field, a rationalist call would be enough: that the two sides become conscious of the fact that their antagonisms arise from interested, and therefore distorted, representations of social processes. It would be a question of working together, seeking objectivity without prejudices, in order to eliminate divided cultural policies and investigations. A flexible interdisciplinary study in which we admit the quota of truth to the other would mend the splits between folklorists and anthropologists located on one side and sociologists and communications specialists dug in on the other side.

Why do these enterprises of political and epistemological goodwill fail? Clues for answering this question can be found in the analyses of cases presented. The conflict between tradition and modernity does not appear as the crushing of the traditionalists by the modernizers, nor as the direct and constant resistance of popular sectors determined to make their traditions useful. The interaction is more sinuous and subtle: popular movements also are interested in modernizing, and the hegemonic sectors in maintaining the traditional—or part of it—as a historical referent and contemporary symbolic resource. Faced with this reciprocal necessity, both are connected by means of a *game of uses* involving the other in both directions. The asymmetry continues to exist but is more entrenched than it appears to be in the simple antagonistic schema between traditionalists and modernizers, subalterns and hegemonics.

Certainly it would be easier to perceive this in the popular sectors with more education and modern qualifications—workers, for example. But studies are still scarce that, in addition to examining the conditions of exploitation in the productive process, devote a detailed ethnographic attention to the everyday spaces of reproduction of the labor force. The few authors who have done so observe that worker resistance and reconversions tend to be produced by an arduous combination of representations formed in work and cultural forms stemming from ethnic roots and political nationalism. Aware of the difficulties of confronting industrial reconversion or obtaining notably better salaries, workers raise compensatory demands in housing, education, and health and seek how to rearticulate solidarity not only in work but also in consumption, not only in defense of what they have but in the requalification necessary in order to live in a different society (Sariego Rodríguez; Nieto; Gilly, especially 85-89 and 116-21).

A more subtle view of these interactions also appears in studies on the links between artisans and official institutions. The dispute over the use of public resources is produced as much by material goods (credits, loans) as by symbolic ones (contests, awards, ritualizations in which social or national unity is staged). The producers look for governmental institutions that can lend them money and help them in the commercialization and protection of their goods. FONART in Mexico, Artesanías in Colombia, FUNARTE in Brazil, and similar organizations in other countries teach them how to manage bank credit, suggest changes in technique and style in their pieces in order to improve their sales, and stage the products by means of catalogs, display windows, audiovisuals, and advertising. Artisans need the institutions in order to reproduce themselves, but the institutions also need the artisans in order to legitimize their existence through the "service" they provide. Gouy-Gilbert observed that the Purépechas of Patamban and Ocumicho negotiate their role as clients and beneficiaries, take advantage of the competition between institutions, and even know what the image bearers are that the state uses so that an idea of tradition subsists in the collective spirit to which it is possible to refer. These references are limited but manifold, because of the variety of the indigenous communities that in this way permanently offer the spectacle of cultural diversity in a universe condemned to a certain monolithism. (58-59)

When the investigation presents the relations between popular and hegemonic sectors only in terms of confrontation, it gives a biased and unrealistic view of the real for the subjects themselves. That is why policies fail that propose changes in this Manichaean perspective, omitting mutual commitments. "We are very useful," an artisan said to me at a contest, "in order for FONART, the Museum of Anthropology, and anthropologists to exist. But our talking to you or going to FONART helps us to realize where we come from." The interactions between hegemonic and subaltern groups are scenes of struggle, but they are also where both dramatize experiences of alterity and recognition. Confrontation is one way of staging inequality (confrontation in order to defend what is one's own) and difference (thinking about oneself through what constitutes a challenge).

Scientific or Theatrical Definition of the Popular?

What is left after this deconstruction of "the popular"? A bothersome conclusion for researchers: the popular, heterogeneous conglomeration of social groups has no univocal meaning as a scientific concept but rather the ambiguous value of a theatrical notion. The popular designates the positions of certain actors, which situate them against the hegemonic group and not always in the form of confrontations.

But can the popular sectors, redefined in this way, come to constitute themselves as historical subjects and be something more than staging effects? It is clear that in indigenous radio stations and local periodicals, in urban popular movements and base communities, and in groupings to defend their interests in production and consumption, the popular sectors speak and act. But it would be deceiving to limit ourselves to hastily connecting these manifestations and declaring them counterhegemonic. It cannot be ignored that even in the most direct and self-managed experiences there is *action* and *acting*, expression of what is one's own and constant reconstitution of what is understood by one's own in relation to the broader laws of social dramaturgy, as well as reproduction of the dominant order. English historians, and some Latin Americans, were the ones who best perceived that the instability of popular conditions and positions does not permit them to be outlined with the neatness of a census description. Subaltern groups "*are* not, in reality, but rather *are being*," asserts Luis Alberto Romero; therefore "they are not a historical subject but an area of society in which subjects are constituted" (1987, 15-16).

It is possible to advance in this process of reconstructing the notion of the popular if we move from an epic staging to a tragicomic one. The most insistent defect in the characterization of "the people" has been to think of the actors grouped under that name as a compact social mass that advances constantly and combatively toward a renewed future. The most complex investigations say instead that the popular is staged not with this epic unidirectionality but rather with the contradictory and ambiguous sense of those who suffer history and at the same time struggle in it, those who—as in all tragicomedy—are continually working out the intermediate steps, the dramatic tricks, the parodic games that permit those who have no possibility for radically changing the course of the work to manage the interstices with a measure of creativity and to their own benefit.

I find a path for this reformulation of the popular by the social sciences in the importance granted by a few authors to melodrama. Why is this theatrical genre one of those preferred by the popular sectors? In the tango and the soap opera, in mass cinema, and in sensual writing, what moves the popular sectors, says Martín Barbero, is the drama of recognition and the struggle to make oneself recognized, the need to resort to multiple forms of primordial sociality (kinship, neighborly solidarity, friendship) in the face of the failure of the official ways of institutionalizing the social, which are incapable of assuming the density of popular cultures (1987a, 243-44).

But how does one carry out scientific work with this scattered notion, this disseminated existence of the popular, apprehended in one place by the folklorists, in another by the sociologists, and beyond that by the communications specialists? It is a question that no guild can respond to alone. If a path exists, we do not believe it is possible to disregard transdisciplinary work. I do not say interdisciplinary because that tends to mean that diverse specialists juxtapose the knowledge obtained by each in a fragmentary and parallel fashion.

The opening of each discipline into the others leads to an uncomfortable insecurity in studies on popular culture. But it can also be thought to bring research to an interesting period, if we concur with what Italo Calvino said of writers: that their task is more attractive and valuable

the more improbable the ideal bookshelf is in which one would like to be placed, with books that are still not accustomed to being placed together with others and whose proximity could produce electrical discharges and short circuits. (208)

Perhaps the most encouraging thing that is happening with the popular is that some folklorists are not concerned only with rescuing it, communications specialists with diffusing it, and politicians with defending it, that each specialist is not writing only for his or her equals, nor in order to judge what the people are, but rather in order to ask ourselves, together with the social movements, how to reconstruct it.

Notes

1. We refer to this excellent conceptual history of the sociocultural functions of the media for an extensive view of the theme.

2. In *La semiosis social* (Part 3), Eliseo Verón offers a consistent theoretical proposal for analyzing the productivity of meaning in complex societies in a nonlinear way.

3. We cite here three references from different countries: Portantiero and Ipola, Vega Centeno, and González Casanova.

4. See, for example, the works of Clifford and Marcus, and of Rosaldo, *Culture and Truth: The Remaking of Social Analysis.*

5. Two different examples from Argentine literature are Ricardo Piglia, in the texts already cited in chapter 3, and Aníbal Ford (*Desde la orilla de la ciencia. Ensayos sobre identidad, cultura y territorio, Ramos generales,* and *Los diferentes ruidos del agua*).

6. In this book, in which some of these alternative experiences are collected and analyzed, we extend our discussion more on their valorization and critique.

7 | Hybrid Cultures, Oblique Powers

The two preceding chapters seem unbalanced. In arguing against the excessive weight of the traditional in the study of popular cultures, most of the pages went toward demonstrating what there is not of the traditional, authentic, and self-generated in the popular groups. I gave little space to urban popular cultures, to the changes unleashed by migration, to the atypical symbolic processes of dissident youths, and to the masses of unemployed and underemployed that make up what are called informal markets.

Now I am going to defend the hypothesis that it makes little sense to study these "slighted" processes under the aspect of popular cultures. It is on those stages that almost all the conventional categories and pairs of oppositions (subaltern/hegemonic, traditional/modern) employed for talking about the popular explode most visibly. Their new modalities of organization of culture and of hybridization of the traditions of classes, ethnic groups, and nations require different conceptual instruments.

How do we analyze the manifestations that do not fit into the cultured or the popular, that spring from their crossings or on their margins? If this part insists on presenting itself as a chapter, with citations and notes, is it not for the author's lack of professional preparation for producing a series of video clips in which a gaucho and a resident of a favela converse about the modernization of traditions with Mexican migrants who enter the United States illegally, or while they visit the Museum of Anthropology, or wait in line at an automatic teller and comment on how the Rio or Veracruz carnivals have changed?

Style concerns me not only as a way of staging the argumentation of this chapter. It has to do with the possibility of investigating materials not encompassed by the programs with which the social sciences classify the real. I wonder if the discontinuous, accelerated, and parodic language of the video clip is fitting for examining hybrid cultures, if its fruitfulness for breaking down habitual orders and letting emerge the ruptures and juxtapositions ought not culminate—in a discourse interested in knowledge—in a different type of organization of data.

With the goal of progressing in the analysis of intercultural hybridization, I will broaden the debate over the ways of naming it and the styles with which it is represented. First I will discuss a notion that appears in the social sciences as a substitute for what can no longer be understood under the signs of cultured or popular: the formula "urban culture" is used in order to attempt to contain the diverse forces of modernity. Next I will be concerned with three key processes for explaining hybridization: the breakup and mixing of the collections that used to organize cultural systems, the deterritorialization of symbolic processes, and the expansion of impure genres. Through these analyses we will seek to determine precisely the articulations between modernity and postmodernity, between culture and power.

From the Public Space to Teleparticipation

Perceiving that the cultural transformations generated by the latest technologies and by changes in symbolic production and circulation were not the exclusive responsibility of the communications media induced a search for more comprehensive notions. As the new processes were associated with urban growth, it was thought that the city could become the unity that would give coherence and analytical consistency to the studies.

Undoubtedly, urban expansion is one of the causes that intensified cultural hybridization. What does it mean for Latin American cultures that countries that had about 10 percent of their population in the cities at the beginning of the century now concentrate 60 to 70 percent in urban agglomerations? We have gone from societies dispersed in thousands of peasant communities with traditional, local, and homogeneous cultures—in some regions, with strong indigenous roots, with little communication with the rest of each nation—to a largely urban scheme with a heterogeneous symbolic offering renewed by a constant interaction of the local with national and transnational networks of communication.

Manuel Castells already observed in his book *La cuestión urbana* that the dizzying development of cities, in making visible under this name multiple dimensions of social change, made it comfortable to attribute to them the responsibility of vaster processes (93). Something similar occurred to what happened with the mass media. The megalopolis was accused of engendering anonymity; it was imagined that neighborhoods produce solidarity, the suburbs crime, and that green spaces relax . . .

Urban ideologies attributed to *one* aspect of the transformation, produced by the intercrossing of many forces of modernity, the "explanation" of all its knots and crises. Since that book by Castells, much evidence has accumulated showing that "urban society" is not sharply opposed to the "rural world" and that the predominance of secondary relations over primary ones and of heterogeneity over homogeneity (or the opposite, according to the school) is not due only to the population concentration in the cities.

The urbanization predominant in contemporary societies is intertwined with serialization and anonymity in production, with restructurings of immaterial communication (from mass media to the telematic) that modify the connections between the private and public. How can we explain the fact that many changes in thinking and taste in urban life coincide with those in the peasantry, if not because the commercial interactions of the latter with the cities and the reception of electronic media in rural houses connects them daily with modern innovations?

Inversely, living in a big city does not imply becoming dissolved in the massive and the anonymous. The violence and public insecurity, the incomprehensibility of the city (who knows all the neighborhoods of a capital city?), lead us to search for selective forms of sociability in domestic intimacy and in trusting encounters. Popular groups seldom leave their spaces, whether peripheral or centrally located; middle- and upper-class sectors increase the bars on their windows and close and privatize the streets of their neighborhoods. For everyone radio and television, and for some the computer connected to basic services, bring them information and entertainment at home.

Living in cities, writes Norbert Lechner in his study on daily life in Santiago, has become "isolating a space of one's own." In contrast to what Habermas observed in early periods of modernity, the public sphere is no longer the place of rational participation from which the social order is determined. It was like that, in part, in Latin America during the second half of the nineteenth century and the first half of the twentieth. It is enough to record the role of the "press, theater, and the patrician salons in conformity with a Creole elite"; first for restricted sectors, then broader ones, liberalism assumed that the public will should be constituted as "the result of the discussion and publicity of individual opinions" (Lechner, Part 2, 73-74).

Studies of the formation of popular neighborhoods in Buenos Aires in the first half of the century recorded that the microsocial structures of urbanism—the club, the café, the neighborhood society, the library, the political committee—organized the identity of the migrants and Creoles by linking immediate life with the global transformations that were being sought by society and the state. Reading and sports, militancy and neighborhood sociability were united in a utopian continuity with national political movements (Gutiérrez and Romero).

This is coming to an end, partly due to changes in the staging of politics; I am referring to the mix of bureaucratization and "mass mediatization." The masses, called upon since the 1960s to express themselves in the streets and to form unions, were being subordinated in many cases to bureaucratic formations. The last decade presents frequent caricatures of that movement: populist leaderships without economic growth and without surplus to distribute, end up overwhelmed by a perverse mixture of reconversion and recession and sign tragic pacts with the speculators of the economy (Alan García in Peru, Carlos Andrés Pérez in Venezuela, Carlos Menem in Argentina). The massive use of the city for political theatricalization is reduced; economic measures and requests for the collaboration of the people are announced on television. Marches and rallies in streets and squares are occasional or have minor effect. In the three countries cited, as in others, public demonstrations generated by the impoverishment of the majority sometimes adopt the form of disarticulated explosions, attacks on shops and supermarkets, on the margin of the organic paths to political representation.

The city's loss of meaning is in direct relation to the difficulties of political parties and unions in calling people to collective tasks that do not produce income or are of doubtful economic gain. The lesser visibility of macrosocial structures, their subordination to nonmaterial and different circuits of communication that mediatize personal and group interactions, is one of the causes for the decline in the credibility of all-encompassing social movements, such as the parties that concentrated the entirety of labor demands and civic representation. The emergence of multiple demands, enlarged in part by the growth of cultural protests and those relating to the quality of life, raises a diversified spectrum of organizations to speak for them: urban, ethnic, youth, feminist, consumer, ecological movements, and so on. Social mobilization, in the same way as the structure of the city, is fragmented in processes that are more and more difficult to totalize.

The efficacy of these movements depends, in turn, on the reorganization of the public space. Their actions have a low impact when they are limited to using traditional forms of communication (oral, of artisanal production, or in written texts that circulate from person to person). Their power grows if they act in mass networks: not only the urban presence of a demonstration of one or two hundred thousand persons, but—even more—their capacity to interfere with the normal functioning of a city and find support, for that very reason, in the electronic information media. Then, sometimes, the sense of the urban is restored and the massive ceases to be a vertical system of diffusion to become a larger expression of local powers, a complementing of the fragments.

At a time when the city or the public sphere is occupied by actors that technically calculate their decisions and technobureaucratically organize the attention to the demands, according to criteria of revenue and efficiency, polemical subjectivity—or simply subjectivity—retreats to the private sphere. The market reorders the public world as a stage for consumption and dramatization of the signs of status. The streets are saturated with cars, people rushing to fulfill work obligations or to a programmed recreation activity, almost always according to its economic yield.

A separate organization of "free time," which turns it into a prolongation of work and money, contributes to this reformulation of the public. From working breakfasts to work, to business lunches, to work, to seeing what is on television at home, and some days to socially productive dinners. The free time of the popular sectors, compelled by underemployment and wage deterioration, is even less free in having to be busy with a second or third job, or in looking for them.

Collective identities find their constitutive stage less and less in the city and in its history, whether distant or recent. Information about unforeseen social vicissitudes is received in the home and commented upon among family or with close friends. Almost all sociability, and reflection about it, is concentrated in intimate exchanges. Since information on price increases, what the governor did, and even the accidents that happened the previous day in our own city reach us through the media, these become the dominant constituents of the "public" meaning of the city, those that simulate integrating a disintegrated imaginary urban sphere.

Although this is the trend, it would be unjust not to point out that sometimes the mass media also contribute to overcoming fragmentation. To the degree they inform us about the common experiences of urban life—social conflicts, pollution, which streets have traffic jams at what hours—they establish networks of communication and make it possible to apprehend the social, collective meaning of what happens in the city. On a broader scale, it may be affirmed that radio and television, in placing in relation to each other diverse historical, ethnic, and regional patrimonies and diffusing them massively, coordinate the multiple temporalities of different spectators.

The investigations of these processes should articulate the integrating and disintegrating effects of television with other processes of unification and atomization generated by the recent changes in urban development and the economic crisis. The groups that get together now and then to analyze collective questions—parents at school, workers at their workplace, neighborhood organizations—tend to act and think as self-referential and often sectored groups because economic pressure forces them down the economic ladder. This has been studied chiefly by sociologists in the southern cone, where military dictatorships suspended political parties, unions, and other mechanisms of grouping, mobilization, and collective cooperation. The repression attempted to reshape the public space by reducing social participation to the insertion of each individual in the benefits of consumption and financial speculation.[1] Up to a point, the media became the great mediators and mediatizers, and therefore substitutes for other collective interactions.

The dictatorships made this transformation more radical. But in the last decade, when other Latin American governments have shared this neoconservative policy, its effects have been generalized. "To appear in public" is today to be seen by many people scattered in front of the family television set or reading the newspaper in their home. Political leaders and intellectuals accentuate their conditions as theatrical actors, their messages are distributed if they are "news," and "public opinion" is something measurable by opinion polls. The citizen becomes a client, a "public consumer."

"Urban culture" is restructured by giving up its leading role in the public space to electronic technologies. Given that almost everything in the city "happens" thanks to the fact that the media say so, and in seeming to occur the way the media want it to, there is an accentuation of social mediatization and of the weight of the stagings, and political actions are constituted as so many images of the political. Thus Eliseo Verón (1985), pushing things to the extreme, asserts that participating today means having relations with an "audiovisual democracy" in which the real is produced by the images created in the media.

I would put it in somewhat different terms. More than an absolute substitution of urban life by the audiovisual media, I perceive a *game of echoes*. The commercial advertising and political slogans that we see on television are those that we reencounter in the streets, and vice versa: the ones are echoed in the others. To this circularity of the communicational and the urban are subordinated the testimonies of history and the public meaning constructed in longtime experiences.

Historical Memory and Urban Conflicts

From mass culture to technoculture, from urban space to teleparticipation. In observing this trend, we run the risk of relapsing into the linear historical perspective and suggesting that communicational technologies *substitute for* the inheritance of the past and public interactions.

It is necessary to reintroduce the question of the modern and postmodern uses of history. I am going to do so with the most challenging and apparently most solemn reference: monuments. What meaning do they conserve or renew in the midst of the transformations of the city and in competition with transitory phenomena like advertising, graffiti, and political demonstrations?

There was a time when monuments, along with schools and museums, were a legitimizing stage of the traditional cultured. Their gigantic size or distinguished placement contributed to exalting them. "Why are there no statues in short sleeves?" the Argentine television program *La noticia rebelde* asked the architect Osvaldo Giesso, director of the Cultural Center of the city of Buenos Aires. To give a long, drawn-out response would require considering the statues together with the rhetoric of textbooks, the ritualism of civic ceremonies, and the other self-consecrating liturgies of power. One would also have to analyze how the monumentalist aesthetic that governs most historic spaces in Latin America was initiated as an expression of authoritarian social systems in the pre-Columbian world. Spanish and Portuguese colonial expansionism was superimposed on them because of the need to compete with the grandiloquence of indigenous architecture by means of neoclassical giganticism and baroque exuberance. Finally, it would be necessary to analyze how the processes of independence and construction of our nations engendered enormous buildings and murals, portraits of heroes, and calendars of historical events, all designed to establish an iconography representative of the size of the utopias.

What do monuments claim to say within contemporary urban symbolism? In revolutionary processes with broad popular participation, public

The evocation of the originary scene of the city is mixed with images of current urban life. The stone monument, barely elevated above the street and constructed with materials and textures similar to those used in the buildings that surround it, seems to indicate a relation of continuity between the pre-Columbian inhabitants and current ones. But at the same time the crossing of the historical iconography with contemporary signaling suggests combinations that can end up being contradictory or parodic: Are the Indians pedestrians? Are their hands pointing to the political propaganda of today?

Against what is Emiliano Zapata battling now, at the entrance to the city of Cuernavaca? Against the advertising of hotels, beverages, and other urban messages? Against the dense traffic of vehicles that suggest the conflicts in which his energetic figure would be located?

The same Zapata, but a different one also, made by the peasants of a town near Cuetzalán, in the state of Puebla. Without a horse and without the monumental rhetoric of battle, simply angry, a head the size of any man's, on a crude pedestal, like the houses nearby.

The Monument to the Miner, in Guanajuato, demonstrates that horizontal identification with the surroundings does not always succeed in fulfilling the intended exalted purpose. The naturalism of the representation and the ground-level placement of the work do not permit the monument, which is confused with its context, to consecrate what it shows. Is it not indispensable that the monument be separated from the real, that it mark the unreality of the image so that its meaning becomes realistic?

The proud severity of the mother with her son, accentuated by the hieratic treatment of the stone, contrasts with the demonstration in favor of abortion, which offers two other variations of the theme: posters with a suffering face, and the smiles and gestural fluidity of the protesters.

The Hemiciclo Juárez, in the Alameda of Mexico City, is the basis for multiple uses, which correspond to the diverse interpretations of the figure of the hero. First, a demonstration of parents protesting for their disappeared children. Later, feminists struggling in favor of abortion choose the father of anticlericalism to support their defense of voluntary maternity. The central banner partially obscures the images put up earlier, and between them all they propose various levels of resignification of the monument.

The enormous head of Juárez designed by Siqueiros and located on the Calzada Zaragoza at the exit of Mexico City toward Puebla, is a monument and a window, a wall that imposes itself upon and frames the current scene. We see it rewritten by supporters of the Solidarity union in Poland—the nineteenth-century Mexican reformer associated with a European social struggle of the twentieth century. The evocation of the leader of the Reform, designed by a postrevolutionary sculptor who mixes in his image the gigantic cutoff head, in the style of the Olmecs, with broken lines, is of futurist inspiration.

rites and monumental constructions express the historic impulse of mass movements. They are part of the struggle for a new visual culture in the midst of the stubborn persistence of signs of the old order, such as occurred with the first postrevolutionary Mexican muralism and with Russian graphic art in the twenties and Cuban graphic art in the sixties. But when the new movement becomes the system, the projects for change follow the route of bureaucratic planning more than that of participative mobilization. When social organization is stabilized, ritualism becomes sclerotic.

To show the type of tensions that are established between historical memory and the visual scheme of modern cities, I will analyze a group of monuments. It is a small selection from the abundant documentation on monuments of Mexico assembled by Paolo Gori and Helen Escobedo.[2] I am going to begin with a group of sculptures that represent the founding of Tenochtitlán and are located a short distance from the Zócalo in Mexico City.

These examples suffice to show the changes the most solid commemorations of patrimony suffer. Monuments often contain several styles and references to diverse historical and artistic periods. Another hybridization is added later in interacting with urban growth, advertising, graffiti, and modern social movements. The iconography of national traditions (Juárez) is used as a resource for struggling against those who, in the name of other traditions (those of Catholicism that condemn abortion), oppose modernity.

These images suggest diverse ways in which traditions and the monuments that consecrate them are reutilized today. Certain heroes of the past survive in the middle of conflicts that unfold in any modern city between systems of political and commercial signs, traffic signals, and social movements.

Modern development attempted to distribute objects and signs in specific places: commodities in current use, in shops; objects of the past, in history museums; those that claim to be valuable for their aesthetic meaning, in art museums. At the same time, the messages emitted by commodities, historical works, and artistic works, and those that indicate how to use them, circulate through schools and the mass media. A rigorous classification of *things* and of the *languages* that speak about them sustains the systematic organization of the social *spaces* in which they should be consumed. This order structures the life of consumers and prescribes behaviors and modes of perceiving that are appropriate for each situation. To be cultured in a modern city consists in knowing how to distinguish between what is purchased for use, what is commemorated, and what is enjoyed symbolically. The social system requires living in a compartmentalized way.

Nevertheless, urban life transgresses this order all the time. In the movement of the city, commercial interests are crossed with historical, aesthetic, and communicational ones. The semantic struggles to neutralize each other, to perturb the message of the others or change its meaning, and to subordinate the rest to its own logic are stagings of the conflicts between social forces: between the market, history, the state, advertising, and the popular struggle for survival.

While historical objects in museums are removed from history and their intrinsic meaning is frozen in an eternity where nothing will ever happen, monuments open to the urban dynamic facilitate the interaction of memory with change and the revitalization of heroes thanks to propaganda or transit: they continue struggling with the social movements that survive them. In Mexico's museums, the heroes of independence are distinguished by their relation to those of the Reform and the revolution; in the street their meaning is renewed in dialoguing with present contradictions. Without display windows or guards to protect them, urban monuments are happily exposed to their being inserted into contemporary life by graffiti or a popular demonstration. Although sculptors resist abandoning the formulas of classical realism in representing the past or making heroes in short sleeves, monuments are kept up-to-date by the "irreverences" of the citizens.

Graffiti, commercial posters, social and political demonstrations, monuments—languages that represent the main forces operating in the city. Monuments are almost always works with which political power consecrates the founding persons and events of the state. Commercial posters seek to synchronize daily life with the interests of economic power. Graffiti (like the posters and political events of the oppositions) express popular criticism of the imposed order. That is why the publicity announcements that hide or contradict the monuments, and the graffiti written over other graffiti, are so significant. At times the proliferation of announcements drowns out historical identity and dissolves memory in the anxious perception of the novelties that are incessantly renewed by advertising. On the other hand, the authors of spontaneous legends are saying that monuments are inadequate for expressing how the city moves. Is not the need to politically reinscribe monuments evidence of the distance between a state and a people, or between history and the present?

Decollecting

This difficulty in including what we earlier totalized under the formula "urban culture," or with the notions of cultured, popular, and massive, presents the problem of whether the organization of culture can be explained by reference to *collections* of symbolic goods. The disarticulation of the urban also puts into doubt the possibility of cultural systems' finding their key in the relations of the population with a certain type of *territory* and history that would, in a peculiar sense, prefigure the behaviors of each group. The next step in this analysis must be to work with the (combined) processes of *decollecting* and *deterritorialization*.

The formation of specialized collections of high art and folklore was a device in modern Europe, and later in Latin America, for ordering symbolic goods in separate groups and hierarchizing them. A certain type of paintings, music, and books belonged to those who were cultured, even though they did not have them in their houses and even though it was through access to museums, concert halls, and libraries. To know their order was already a way of possessing them that distinguished them from those who did not know how to relate to that order.

The history of art and literature was formed on the basis of collections that were housed in museums and libraries when these were buildings for keeping, exhibiting, and consulting collections. Today art museums exhibit Rembrandt and Bacon in one room, popular objects and industrial design in the following ones, and beyond those are happenings, performances, installations, and body art by artists who no longer believe in the works and refuse to produce collectible objects. Public libraries continue to exist in a more traditional mode, but any intellectual or student works much more in his or her private library, where books are mixed with journals, newspaper clippings, fragmentary bits of information that will be moved often from one shelf to another and whose use requires them to be spread out on several tables and on the floor. The situation of the cultural worker today is what Benjamin glimpsed in that pioneering text in which he described the sensations of moving and unpacking his library among the disorder of the boxes, "the floor strewn with scattered papers," the loss of the order that connected those objects with a history of knowledge, making him feel that the mania of collecting "is no longer of our time" (Benjamin 1969a, 59-66).

On the other hand, there was a repertory of folklore, of the objects of peoples or classes that had different customs and therefore other collections. Folklore was born from collecting, as we saw in an earlier chapter. It was formed when collectors and folklorists moved to archaic societies, investigated and preserved the containers used for cooking, the clothing, and the masks used in ritual dancing, and then gathered them together in museums. The containers, masks, and textiles are now found equalized under the name of "handicrafts" in urban markets. If we want to buy the best designs, we no longer go the mountains or the forests where the Indians who produce them live, because the pieces of diverse ethnic groups are mixed together in shops in the cities.

The aggregate of works and messages that used to structure visual culture and provide the grammar of reading the city diminished their efficacy in the urban space as well. There is no homogeneous architectural system and the distinguishing profiles of neighborhoods are being lost. The lack of urban regulation, and the cultural hybridity of buildings and users intermix styles from various eras in a single street. The interaction of the monuments with advertising and political messages situates the organization of memory and visual order in heteroclite networks.

The agony of collections is the clearest symptom of how the classifications that used to distinguish the cultured from the popular, and both from the massive, are disappearing. Cultures no longer are grouped in fixed and stable wholes, and therefore the possibility disappears of being cultured by knowing the repertory of "the great works," or of being popular because one manages the meaning of the objects and messages produced by a more or less closed community (an ethnic group, a neighborhood, a class). Now these collections renew their composition and their hierarchy with the fashions; they are crossed all the time and, to top it all off, each user can make his or her own collection. The technologies of reproduction permit each person to set up a repertory of records and cassettes in his or her home that combine the cultured with the popular, including those who already do this in the structure of their works: Piazzola, who mixes the tango with jazz and classical music, and Caetano Veloso and Chico Buarque, who appropriate at once the experimentation of the concrete poets, Afro-Brazilian traditions, and post-Webernian musical experimentation.

In addition, there is a proliferation of reproduction devices that we cannot define as either cultured or popular. In them collections are lost, and images and contexts—along with the semantic and historical references that used to bind together their meanings—are destructed.

Photocopiers. Books are unbound; anthologies approach authors incapable of being dealt with in symposia; new bindings group together chapters of diverse volumes following the logic not of intellectual production but of their uses: to prepare for an exam, to follow the tastes of a professor, to pursue sinuous itineraries absent in the routine classifications of bookstores and libraries. This fragmentary relation with books leads us to lose the structure in which the chapters are inserted; we descend, Monsiváis once wrote, into the "Xerox grade of reading." It is also true that the freer handling of texts, their reduction to notes, as desacralized as the tape-recorded class— which sometimes never passes to the written page because it is transferred directly to the screen of a computer—induces more fluid links among the texts and among students and knowledge.

Videocassette recorders. One forms his or her personal collection by mixing football games and Fassbinder films, North American series, Brazilian soap operas, and a debate over the foreign debt—what the channels broadcast when we are watching them, when we are working, or when we are sleeping. The recording may be immediate or delayed and with the possibility of erasing, rerecording, and verifying how it turned out. The video recorder resembles television and the library, says Jean Franco: "it permits the juxtaposition of very different topics starting from an arbitrary system and directed to communities that transcend the limits between races, classes, and sexes" (1987, 56). In truth, the video recorder goes farther than the library. It reorders a series of traditional or modern oppositions: between the national and the foreign, leisure and work, news and entertainment, politics and fiction. It also intervenes in sociability by allowing us to not miss a social or family gathering because we are watching a program and by promoting networks for borrowing and exchanging cassettes.

Videos. This is the most intrinsically postmodern genre. Intergenre: it mixes music, image, and text. Transtemporal: it gathers together melodies and images of various epochs and freely cites deeds out of context; it takes up what was done by Magritte and Duchamp, but for mass audiences. Some works take advantage of the versatility of video to create works that are brief but dense and systematic: *Fotoromanza* by Antonioni, *Thriller* by John Landis, *All Night Long* by Bob Rafelson, for example. But in most cases all action is given in fragments; it does not ask us to concentrate or to look for a continuity. There is no history to speak of. Not even art history or the media matter: images are plundered from everywhere and in any order. In a two-minute video, the German singer Falco summarizes the story of *The Black Vampire* by Fritz Lang; Madonna dresses like Marilyn Monroe, copying the choreography of *Gentlemen Prefer Blondes* and the facial expressions of Betty Boop: "Those who remember love the homage and the nostalgia. Those who have no memory of it or who were not born yet also love it as their eyes follow the treat that is being sold to them as something brand-new" (McAllister, 21-23). There is no interest in indicating what is new and what comes from before. To be a good spectator one has to abandon oneself to the rhythm and enjoy the ephemeral sights. Even the videos that present a story downplay or ironize it by means of parodying montages and abrupt accelerations. This training in a fleeting perception of the real has had so much success that it is not limited to discotheques or a few entertainment programs on television; in the United States and Europe there are channels that broadcast them twenty-four hours a day. There are business, political, music, advertising, and educational videos that are replacing the business manual, the pamphlet, the theatrical spectacle, and the more or less reasoned staging of politics in electoral meetings. They are cold, indirect dramatizations that do not require the personal presence of interlocutors. The world is seen as a discontinuous effervescence of images, art as fast food. This ready-to-think culture allows us to de-think historical events without worrying about understanding them. In one of his films Woody Allen made fun of what he had understood by speed-reading *War and Peace*: "It talks about Russia," he concluded. *Le Nouvel Observateur* says seriously that it finds a new way of reinterpreting the student revolts of 1968 using this aesthetic: they were a "revolt clip: hot montage of shock images, rupture of rhythm, cutoff ending" (43).

Video games. These are like the participative version of videos. When they take the place of movies—not only in the public's free time but in the space of the movie theaters that close for lack of viewers—the operation of cultural displacement is clear. From contemporary cinema they take the most violent aspects: war scenes, car and motorcycle races, karate and boxing matches. They familiarize directly with the sensuality and efficacy of technology; they provide a mirror-screen where power itself and the fascination of battling with the big forces of the world are staged by taking advantage of the latest techniques and without the risk of direct confrontations. They dematerialize and disembody danger, giving us only the pleasure of winning out over others, or the possibility, in being defeated, that the only thing lost is coins in a machine.

As studies on the effects of television established long ago, these new technological resources are not neutral, nor are they omnipotent. Their simple formal innovation implies cultural changes, but the final sign depends on the uses different actors assign to them. We cite them here because they crack the orders that used to classify and distinguish cultural traditions; they weaken historical meaning and the macrostructural conceptions to the benefit of intense and sporadic relations with isolated objects, with their signs and images. Some postmodern theorists argue that this predominance of immediate and dehistoricized relations is coherent with the collapse of the great metaphysical narratives.

Actually, there are no reasons to lament the decomposition of rigid collections that, by separating the cultured, the popular, and the massive, promoted inequalities. Nor do we think that there are prospects for restoring the classic order of modernity. We see in the irreverent crossings occasions for relativizing religious, political, national, ethnic, and artistic fundamentalisms that absolutize certain patrimonies and discriminate against the rest. But we wonder if extreme discontinuity as a perceptive habit, the diminution of opportunities for understanding the reelaboration of the subsistent meanings of some traditions and for intervening in their change, do not reinforce the unconsulted power of those who continue to be concerned with understanding and managing the great networks of objects and meanings: the transnationals and the states.

Among the decollecting and dehierarchizing strategies of the cultural technologies must be included the existing asymmetry in production and use between the central and the dependent countries and between consumers of different classes within the same society. The possibilities for taking advantage of technological innovations and adapting them to their own productive and communicational needs are unequal in the central countries—generators of inventions, with high investment in renovating their industries, goods, and services—and in Latin America, where investments are frozen because of the debt and austerity policies, where scientists and technicians work with ridiculous budgets or have to emigrate, and where control of the more modern cultural media is highly concentrated and depends a great deal on outside programming.

Of course it is not a question of returning to the paranoid denunciations and conspiratorial conceptions of history that accused the modernization of quotidian and mass culture of being an instrument of the powerful in order to better exploit. The question is to understand how the dynamic itself of technological development remodels society and coincides with or contradicts social movements. There are different kinds of technologies, each with various possibilities for development and articulation with the others. There are social sectors with diverse cultural capitals and dispositions for appropriating them with different meanings: decollecting and hybridization are not the same for the adolescents from the popular classes who go to public video-game parlors as they are for those from the middle and upper classes who have the games at home. The meanings of the technologies are con-structed according to the ways they are institutionalized and socialized.

The technological remodeling of social practices does not always contra-dict traditional cultures and modern arts. It has extended, for example, the use of patrimonial goods and the field of creativity. Just as video games triv-ialize historical battles and some videos trivialize experimental art trends, computers and other uses of video make it easy to obtain data, visualize graphics and innovate them, simulate the use of pieces and information, and reduce the distance between conception and execution, knowledge and ap-plication, information and decision. This multiple appropriation of cultural patrimonies opens up original possibilities for experimentation and com-munication with democratizing uses, as is appreciated in the use some pop-ular movements make of video.

But new technologies not only promote creativity and innovation; they also reproduce known structures. The three most frequent uses of video—consumption of commercial movies, porno films, and the recording of fam-ily events—repeat audiovisual practices initiated by photography and the Super 8. On the other hand, video art—explored mainly by painters, musi-cians, and poets—reaffirms the difference and the hermetism in a way simi-lar to that of art galleries and movie clubs.

The coexistence of these contradictory uses reveals that the interactions of new technologies with previous culture makes them part of a much big-ger project than the one they unleashed or the one they manage. One of these changes of long standing that technological intervention makes more evident is the reorganization of the links between groups and symbolic sys-tems; the decollections and hybridizations no longer permit a rigid linking of social classes to cultural strata. Although many works remain within the minority or popular circuits for which they were made, the prevailing trend is for all sectors to mix into their tastes objects whose points of origin were previously separated. I do not want to say that this more fluid and complex circulation has evaporated class differences. I am only saying that the reor-ganization of the cultural stagings and the constant crossings of identities require that we ask ourselves in a different way about the orders that sys-tematize the material and symbolic relations among groups.

Deterritorializing

The most radical inquiries into what it means to be entering and leaving modernity are by those who assume the tensions between deterritorialization and reterritorialization. With this I am referring to two processes: the loss of the "natural" relation of culture to geographical and social territories and, at the same time, certain relative, partial territorial relocalizations of old and new symbolic productions.

In order to document this transformation of contemporary cultures I will analyze first the transnationalization of symbolic markets and migrations. Then I propose to explore the aesthetic meaning of this change by following the strategies of some impure arts.

1. There was a method of associating the popular with the national that, as we noted in earlier chapters, nourished the modernization of Latin American cultures. Carried out first in the form of colonial domination, then as industrialization and urbanization under metropolitan models, modernity seemed to be organized in politicoeconomic and cultural antagonisms: colonizers versus colonized, cosmopolitanism versus nationalism. The last pair of opposites was the one handled by dependency theory, according to which everything was explained by the confrontation between imperialism and national popular cultures.

Studies of economic and cultural imperialism served to get to know some devices used by the international centers of scientific, artistic, and communicational production that conditioned, and still condition, our development. But this model is insufficient for understanding current power relations. It does not explain the planetary functioning of an industrial, technological, financial, and cultural system whose headquarters is not in a single nation but in a dense network of economic and ideological structures. Nor does it take into account the need of metropolitan nations to make their borders flexible and integrate their economies and their educational, technological, and cultural systems, as is occurring in Europe and North America.

The persistent inequality between what the dependency theorists called the First and the Third Worlds maintains with relative effect some of their postulates. But although the decisions and benefits of the exchanges may be concentrated in the bourgeoisie of the metropolises, new processes make the asymmetry more complex: the decentralization of corporations, the planetary simultaneity of information, and the adaptation of certain international forms of knowledge and images to the knowledge and habits of each community. The delocalization of symbolic products by electronics and telematics, and the use of satellites and computers in cultural diffusion, also impede our continuing to see the confrontations of peripheral countries as frontal combats with geographically defined nations.

The Manichaeism of those oppositions becomes even less realistic in the eighties and nineties when several dependent countries are registering a notable increase in their cultural exports. In Brazil, the advance of massification and industrialization of culture did not imply—contrary to what tended to be said—a greater dependency on foreign production. Statistics reveal that in the last several years its cinematography and the proportion of national films on the screens grew: from 13.9 percent in 1971 to 35 percent in 1982. Books by Brazilian authors, which accounted for 54 percent of publishing production in 1973, rose to 70 percent in 1981. Also, more national records and cassettes are listened to, while imported music declines. In 1972, 60 percent of television programming was foreign; in 1983, it fell to 30 percent. At the same time that this trend toward nationalization and autonomy is occurring in cultural production, Brazil is becoming a very active agent in the Latin American market of symbolic goods by exporting soap operas. As it also succeeds in broadly penetrating the central countries, it became the seventh world producer of television and advertising, and the sixth in records. Renato Ortiz, from whom I take these data, concludes that they went "from defense of the national popular to exportation of the international popular" (1988, 182-206).

Although this trend does not occur in the same way in all Latin American countries, there are similar aspects in those of more modern cultural development that reestablish the articulations between the national and the foreign. Such changes do not eliminate the question of how distinct classes benefit from and are represented in the culture produced in each country, but the radical alteration of the stagings of production and consumption—as well as the character of the goods that are presented—questions the "natural" association of the popular with the national and the equally a priori opposition with the international.

2. Multidirectional migrations are the other factor that relativizes the binary and polar paradigm in the analysis of intercultural relations. Latin American internationalization is accentuated in the last few decades, when migrations not only include writers, artists, and exiled politicians as happened since last century, but settlers from all social layers. How do we include in the one-directional schema of imperialist domination the new flows of cultural circulation opened up by the transplants of Latin Americans to the United States and Europe, from the least-developed countries to the most prosperous ones of our continent, from poor regions to urban centers? Are there two million South Americans who, according to the most conservative statistics, left Argentina, Chile, Brazil, and Uruguay in the seventies because of ideological persecution and economic suffering? It is not

accidental that the most innovative reflection on deterritorialization is unfolding in the principal area of migrations on the continent—the border between Mexico and the United States.

From both sides of that border, intercultural movements show their painful face: the underemployment and uprooting of peasants and indigenous people who had to leave their lands in order to survive. But a very dynamic cultural production is also growing there. If there are more than 250 Spanish-language radio and television stations in the United States, more than fifteen hundred publications in Spanish, and a high interest in Latin American literature and music, it is not only because there is a market of twenty million "Hispanics," or 8 percent of the U.S. population (38 percent in New Mexico, 25 percent in Texas, and 23 percent in California). It is also due to the fact that so-called Latin culture produces films like *Zoot Suit* and *La Bamba,* the songs of Rubén Blades and Los Lobos, aesthetically and culturally advanced theaters like that of Luis Valdez, and visual artists whose quality and aptitude for making popular culture interact with modern and postmodern symbolism incorporates them into the North American mainstream.[3]

Whoever is familiar with these artistic movements knows that many are rooted in the everyday experiences of the popular sectors. So that no doubts remain about the transclass extent of the phenomenon of deterritorialization, it is useful to refer to the anthropological investigations on migrants. Roger Rouse studied the inhabitants of Aguililla, a rural town in southwestern Michoacán, apparently only accessible by a dirt road. Its two main activities continue to be agriculture and raising livestock for subsistence, but the emigration that began in the forties was such an incentive that almost all families there now have members who live or have lived abroad. The declining local economy is sustained by the flow of dollars sent from California, especially from Redwood City, that nucleus of microelectronics and postindustrial North American culture in Silicon Valley, where the Michoacanos work as laborers and in services. Most stay for brief periods in the United States, and those who remain longer maintain constant relations with their place of origin. There are so many outside of Aguililla, and so frequent are their connections with those who remain there, that one can no longer conceive of the two wholes as separate communities:

> Through the constant migration back and forth and the growing use of telephones, the residents of Aguililla tend to be reproducing their links with people that are two thousand miles away as actively as they maintain their relations with their immediate neighbors. Still more, and more generally, through

the continuous circulation of people, money, commodities, and information, the diverse settlements have intermingled with such force that they are probably better understood as forming only one community dispersed in a variety of places. (Rouse, 1-2)

Two conventional notions of social theory collapse in the face of these "crossed economies, meaning systems that intersect, and fragmented personalities." One of these is that of "community," employed both for isolated peasant populations and for expressing the abstract cohesion of a compact national state, in both cases definable by relation to a specific territory. It was assumed that the links between the members of those communities would be more intense inside than outside of their space, and that the members treat the community as the principal medium to which they adjust their actions. The second image is the one that opposes center and periphery, also an "abstract expression of an idealized imperial system," in which the gradations of power and wealth would be distributed concentrically: most in the center and a progressive decrease as we move toward surrounding zones. The world functions less and less in this way, says Rouse; we need "an alternative cartography of social space" based instead on the notions of "circuit" and "border."

It also should not be assumed, he adds, that this reordering only includes those on the margins. He notes a similar disarticulation in the economy of the United States, previously dominated by autonomous blocks of capital. In the central area of Los Angeles, 75 percent of the buildings now belong to foreign capital; in all urban centers combined, 40 percent of the population consists of ethnic minorities from Asia and Latin America, and "it is calculated that this number will approach 60 percent in the year 2010" (Rouse, 2). There is an "implosion of the third world in the first," according to Renato Rosaldo (n.d., 9); "the notion of an authentic culture as an autonomous internally coherent universe is no longer sustainable" in either of these two worlds, "except perhaps as a 'useful fiction' or a revealing distortion" (Rosaldo 1989, 217).

When, in the last few years of his life, Michel de Certeau taught in San Diego, he used to say that in California the mix of immigrants from Mexico, Colombia, Norway, Russia, Italy, and the eastern United States made him think that "life consists of constantly crossing borders." Roles are taken and changed with the same versatility as cars and houses:

This mobility rests on the postulate that one is not identified either by birth, by family, by professional status, by friendships or love relationships, or by property. It seems as if all identity defined by status and place (of origin, of work, of residence, etc.) were reduced, if not swept away, by the velocity of all move-

ments. It is known that there is no identity document in the United States; it is replaced by the driver's license and the credit card, that is, by the capacity to cross space and by participation in a game of fiduciary contracts between North American citizens. (Certeau, 10-18)[4]

During the two periods during which I studied the intercultural conflicts on the Mexican side of the border, in Tijuana, in 1985 and 1988, several times I thought that this city is, along with New York, one of the biggest laboratories of postmodernity.[5] In 1950 it had no more than sixty thousand inhabitants; today there are more than a million, with migrants from almost all regions of Mexico (mainly Oaxaca, Puebla, Michoacán, and the Federal District) who have settled there over the years. Some go daily into the United States to work; others cross the border during the planting and harvesting seasons. Even those who stay in Tijuana are linked to commercial exchanges

between the two countries, to North American *maquiladoras* located on the Mexican border, or to tourist services for the three or four million people from the United States who arrive in this city every year.

From the beginning of this century until fifteen years ago, Tijuana was known for a casino (abolished during the Cárdenas government), cabarets, dance halls, and liquor stores where North Americans came to elude their country's prohibitions on sex, gambling, and alcohol. The recent installation of factories, modern hotels, cultural centers, and access to wide-ranging international information has made it into a modern, contradictory, cosmopolitan city with a strong definition of itself.

In interviews we did of primary, secondary, and university students, and of artists and cultural promoters from all social layers, there was no theme more central for their self-definition than border life and intercultural contacts. One of our research techniques was to ask them to name the most representative places of life and culture in Tijuana in order to photograph them later; we also took pictures of other scenes that seemed to condense the city's meaning (publicity posters, casual encounters, graffiti) and selected fifty photos to show to fourteen groups from various economic and cultural levels. Two-thirds of the images they judged most representative of the city, and about which they spoke with the greatest emphasis, were those that linked Tijuana with what lies beyond it: Revolution Avenue, its shops and tourist centers, the minaret that bears witness to where the casino was, the parabolic antennas, the legal and illegal passages on the border, the neighborhoods

where those from different parts of the country are concentrated, the tomb of the Unknown Soldier, "lord of the émigrés," to whom they go to ask that he arrange their "papers" or to thank him for their not having been caught by *la migra* (or Immigration).

The multicultural character of the city is expressed in the use of Spanish, English, and also indigenous languages in the neighborhoods and *maquiladoras,* or among those who sell crafts downtown. This pluralism diminishes when we move from private interactions to public languages, that is, those of radio, television, and urban advertising, where English and Spanish predominate and coexist "naturally."

Along with the poster that recommends the disco club and the radio station that plays "rock in your language," another announces a Mexican liqueur in English. Music and alcoholic beverages—two symbols of Tijuana—coexist under this linguistic duality. "The other choice" is explicitly the liqueur, but the contiguity of the messages makes it possible that it also refers to rock in Spanish. The ambivalence of the image, which the inter-viewees considered analogous to life in the city, also allows us to conclude—following the order of reading—that the other choice is English.

The uncertainty generated by the bilingual, bicultural, and binational os-cillations has its equivalence in the relations with its own history. Some of the photos were chosen precisely because they allude to the simulated char-acter of a good portion of Tijuana culture. The Hot Water Tower, burned in

the 1960s with the intention of forgetting the casino it represented, was rebuilt a few years ago and now is exhibited with pride on magazine covers and in advertising; but in pointing out to the interviewees that the current tower is in a different location than the original one, they argue that the change is a way of displacing and relocating the past.

On several corners of Revolution Avenue there are zebras. In reality they are painted burros. They are there so that North American tourists can be photographed with a landscape behind them in which images from various regions of Mexico are crowded together: volcanoes, Aztec figures, cacti, the eagle with the serpent. "Faced with the lack of other types of things, as there are in the south where there are pyramids, there is none of that here . . . as if something had to be invented for the gringos," they said in one of the groups. In another group, they pointed out that "it also refers to the myth that North Americans bring with them, that it has something to do with crossing the border into the past, into the wilderness, into the idea of being able to ride horseback."

One interviewee told us: "The wire that separates Mexico from the United States could be the main monument of culture on the border."

In arriving at the beach "the line" falls and leaves a transit zone, used at times by undocumented migrants. Every Sunday the fragmented families on both sides of the border gather for picnics.

Where the borders move, they can be rigid or fallen; where buildings are

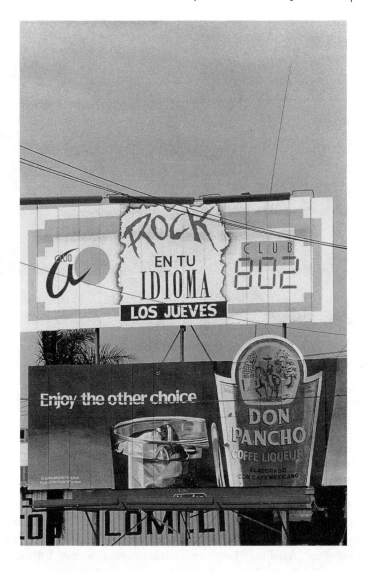

evoked in another place than the one they represent, every day the spectacular invention of the city itself is renewed and expanded. The simulacrum
comes to be a central category of culture. Not only is the "authentic" relativized. The obvious, ostentatious illusion—like the zebras that everyone
knows are fake or the hiding games of illegal migrants that are "tolerated" by
the United States police—becomes a resource for defining identity and communicating with others.

To these hybrid and simulated products, border artists and writers add their own intercultural laboratory. The following is from a radio interview with Guillermo Gómez-Peña, editor of the bilingual journal *La línea quebrada/The broken line,* with offices in Tijuana and San Diego:

> REPORTER: If you love our country so much, as you say you do, why do you live in California?
> GÓMEZ-PEÑA: I am de-Mexicanizing myself in order to Mexicomprehend myself. . . .
> REPORTER: What do you consider yourself, then?
> GÓMEZ-PEÑA: Post-Mexica, pre-Chicano, pan-Latino, land-crossed, Art American . . . it depends on the day of the week or the project in question.

Several Tijuana periodicals are dedicated to reworking the definitions of identity and culture taking the border experience as their starting point. *La línea quebrada,* which is the most radical, says that it expresses a generation that grew up "watching *charro* and science-fiction movies, listening to cumbias and Moody Blues songs, building altars and filming in Super 8, reading *El Corno Emplumado* and *Art Forum.*" Since they live in the interval, "in the crack between the two worlds," and since they are "the ones who didn't go because we didn't fit, the ones who still don't arrive or don't know where to arrive," they decide to assume all possible identities:

> When they ask me my nationality or ethnic identity, I cannot respond with one word, since my "identity" has multiple repertories: I am Mexican but also

Chicano and Latin American. On the border they call me "chilango" or "mex-iquillo"; in the capital "pocho" or "norteño," and in Europe "sudaca." Anglo-Saxons call me "Hispanic" or "Latino," and Germans have more than once confused me with being Turkish or Italian.

With a phrase that would please a migrant as much as a young rocker, Gómez-Peña explains that "our deepest generational feeling is that of the loss that arises from the departure." But there are also things that they have gained: "a view of culture that is more experimental, that is, multifocal and tolerant" (Gómez-Peña, 3-5).[6]

Other artists and writers from Tijuana question the euphemized view of the contradictions and the uprooting they perceive in the *La línea quebrada* group. They reject the celebration of the migrations often caused by poverty in the place from which people migrate, and which is repeated in their new destination. There is no lack of those who, despite not having been born in Tijuana, contest this parodic and detached insolence in the name of their fifteen or twenty years in the city: "people who have arrived recently and want to discover us and tell us who we are."

Both in this polemic and in other manifestations of strong emotions in referring to the photos of Tijuana, we saw a complex movement that we would call *reterritorialization*. The same people who praise the city for being open and cosmopolitan want to fix signs of identification and rituals that differentiate them from those who are just passing through, who are tourists, or . . . anthropologists curious to understand intercultural crossings.

The editors of the other Tijuana journal, *Esquina baja,* devoted a long time to explaining to us why they wanted, in addition to having an organ in which to express themselves,

> to generate an audience of readers, a local journal of quality in all aspects, such as design and presentation . . . in order to counteract a bit that centrist trend that exists in the country, because what there is in the provinces does not succeed in transcending, and is minimized, if it does not first pass through the fine sieve of the Federal District.

We find something similar in the vehemence with which everyone rejected the "missionary" criteria for cultural activities favored by the central government. Against the national programs designed to "affirm Mexican identity" on the northern border, Baja Californians argue that they are as Mexican as the rest, though in a different way. About the "threat of North American cultural penetration" they say that, in spite of the geographic and communicational proximity to the United States, the daily commercial and cultural exchanges make them live inequality intensely and therefore have a less idealized image of those who receive a similar influence in the capital via television messages and imported consumer goods.

Deterritorialization and reterritorialization. In the exchanges of traditional symbols with international communications circuits, culture industries, and migrations, questions about identity and the national, the defense of sovereignty, and the unequal appropriation of knowledge and art do not

disappear. The conflicts are not erased, as neoconservative postmodernism claims. They are placed in a different register, one that is multifocal and more tolerant, and the autonomy of each culture is rethought—sometimes—with smaller fundamentalist risks. Nevertheless, the chauvinist critiques of "those from the center" sometimes engender violent conflicts: acts of aggression against recently arrived migrants and discrimination in school and at work.

The intense crossings and the instability of traditions, bases of the valorizing opening, may also be—in conditions of labor competition—a source of prejudice and confrontation. Therefore, the analysis of the advantages or inconveniences of deterritorialization should not be reduced to the movements of ideas or cultural codes, as is frequently the case in the bibliography on postmodernity. Their meaning is also constructed in connection with social and economic practices, in struggles for local power, and in the competition to benefit from alliances with external powers.

Intersections: From the Modern to the Postmodern

Hybridity has a long trajectory in Latin American cultures. We remember formerly the syncretic forms created by Spanish and Portuguese matrices mixing with indigenous representation. In the projects of independence and national development we saw the struggle to make cultural modernism compatible with economic semimodernization, and both compatible with the persistent traditions.

Decollecting and deterritorialization have antecedents in the utopian reflections and in the practices of artists and intellectuals. Two examples: the aesthetic proclamations of the Brazilian "cannibals" and of the Martín Fierro group in the twenties. The Anthropophagous Manifesto, published in 1928-29, says:

> I am only interested in what is not mine. . . . It was because we never had grammar or collections of old vegetables. And we never knew what was urban, suburban, border, and continental . . . [that] we were never catechized. We live through a sleepwalking right.

The writers of the Martín Fierro group in 1924 affirmed their belief "in the importance of the intellectual contribution of America . . . the independence movement initiated by Rubén Darío." They added that this "does not mean, however, that we will have to renounce, much less pretend to disregard, the fact that every morning we use a Swedish toothpaste, some towels from France, and an English soap."

The constant references to border culture that we found in those interviewed in Tijuana remind us of the descriptions of the port, of the crosses between natives and migrants, "the exacerbation of the heterogeneous," and the "obsessive" cosmopolitanism that Beatriz Sarlo detects in liberal and socialist writers between the twenties and forties in Buenos Aires: Borges the same as González Tuñón, Nicolás Olivari as well as Arlt and Oliverio Girondo. They cultivate "the wisdom of departure, of estrangement, of distance, and of culture shock that can enrich and complicate knowledge about the social margin and the transgressions." Arlt wrote in his *Aguafuertes porteñas*: "Poetic farce, poor charm, the study of Bach or of Beethoven together with a tango of Filiberto or of Mattos Rodríguez." That "culture of mixing" makes "Creole formation" coexist with "an extraordinary process of importation of symbolic goods, discourses, and practices" (Sarlo 1988b, 160, 167, 28).

It is known how many works of Latin American art and literature, valued as paradigmatic interpretations of our identity, were produced outside of the continent, or at least outside of their authors' countries of birth—from Sarmiento, Alfonso Reyes, and Oswald de Andrade to Cortázar, Botero, and Glauber Rocha. The place from which several thousand Latin American artists write, paint, or compose music is no longer the city in which they spent their infancy, nor the one they have lived in for several years, but rather a hybrid place in which the places really lived are crossed. Onetti calls it Santa María; García Márquez, Macondo; Soriano, Colonia Vela. But in truth, although those towns resemble other traditional ones of Uruguay, Colombia, and Argentina, they are redesigned by cognitive and aesthetic patterns acquirable in Madrid, Mexico, or Paris.

It is hardly a process of transnationalization of high art. Almost the same thing happens with the music of Roberto Carlos, so similar to that of José José, and both so similar to that of any singer of filled stadiums or on a Sunday television program in any country on the continent. There are those who believe they can explain this air of family by the power the culture industry exercises over the creators created by it. But something equivalent, though more complex, happens with the more experimental singer-songwriters of urban music. Although the personal profiles of Caetano Veloso, Raymundo Fagner, Mercedes Sosa, Fito Páez, Eugenia León, or Los Lobos are more differentiated than those of Roberto Carlos and José José, each of them opens his or her national repertory to the others, some even to the point of making records or performing together.

In what, then, lies the novelty of postmodern decollection, deterritorialization, and hybridity? In that artistic practices now lack consistent paradigms. Modern artists and writers innovated and altered the models or replaced them with others, but they always had *referents of legitimacy*. The transgressions of modern painters have been made by talking about the art of others. One line of thinking was that painting was in the metropolises: therefore the images of Jacobo Borges, José Gamarra, and Gironella remake, with irony or irreverence, those that from Velázquez to Rousseau had been conceived of as legitimate in European visuality. Other currents opened the cultured gaze to popular images, convinced that Latin American art would be justified by collecting the iconography of the oppressed: Viteri fills his works with rag dolls; Berni braids wires with egg cartons, bottle caps and automobile scrap metal, wigs, and curtain fragments in order to parodically talk about modernity and the *Mundo ofrecido a Juanito Laguna*. Art of European references or art of popular references: always art that is mestizo, impure, that exists by dint of being placed at the crossing of paths that have been composing us and breaking us down. But they thought there were paths and paradigms of modernity so respectable that they were worth discussing.

Postmodern visuality, in contrast, is the staging of a double loss: of the script and of the author. The disappearance of the script means that the great narratives no longer exist that used to order and hierarchize the periods of the patrimony and the flora of cultured and popular works in which societies and classes recognized each other and consecrated their virtues. That is why in recent painting a single work can be at once hyperrealist, Impressionist, and pop, or an altar or a mask can combine traditional icons with what we see on television. Postmodernism is not a style but the tumultuous copresence of all styles, the place where the chapters in the history of art and folklore are crossed with each other and with the new cultural technologies.

The other modern attempt at refounding history was the subjectivity of the author. Today we think that the narcissistic exaltation of the painter or the filmmaker who want to make of their gesturing the founding act of the world is the pseudo-lay parody of God. We do not believe the artist who wants to build with illustrious grammar and is prepared to legislate the new syntax. With the help of art historians, he or she tried to convince us that the pink period follows the blue and that there would be a progression from Impressionism to futurism to Cubism to surrealism. In Latin America, we assumed that the postwar vanguards were the overcoming of socialist realism, of the Mexican muralist school, and the varied tellurisms of other countries; later it seemed to us that the experimental vanguards were replaced by the heroic, committed visuality of the sixties and seventies.

The frenetic vertigo of vanguard aesthetics and the market's game of substitutions, in which everything is interchangeable, removed verisimilitude from the founding pretensions of gesturing. Modern art, which could no longer be a literal representation of an undone worldly order, also cannot be what Baudrillard maintains in one of his first texts: "literality of the gestural of creation" (stains, drips), constant repetition of the beginning, like Rauschenberg, abandoned to the obsession of reinitiating the same canvas many times, feature by feature (102-11). It also is not a metaphor of the political gesturing that dreamed of total and immediate changes. The artistic market and the reorganization of urban visuality generated by the culture industry and the fatigue of political voluntarism are combined to make unrealistic any attempt at making of high art or folklore the proclamation of the inaugural power of the artist or of prominent social actors.

Art and handicrafts markets, while they maintain differences, coincide in a certain treatment of works. Both the artist who, in hanging his or her works, proposes an order of reading and the artisan who arranges his or her pieces following a mythical framework discover that the market disperses and resemanticizes their works upon selling them in different countries and to heterogeneous consumers. The artist is sometimes left with the copies or the slides, and someday a museum may bring those works together, according to the revalorization that they experienced, in a show where a new order will erase the painter's "original" statement. The artisan is left with the possibility of repeating similar pieces, or going to see them—put in a series whose order and discourse are not his or her own—in the popular art museum or in books for tourists.

Something equivalent happens in the political market. Ideological goods that are exchanged, and the positions from which they are appropriated and defended, increasingly resemble each other in all countries. The old nationalist, or at least national, profiles of the political forces have been becoming diluted in alignments generated by common challenges (foreign debt, recession, industrial reconversion) and by the "exits" proposed by the big international currents: neoconservatism, social democracy, social communism.

Without script or author, postmodern visual and political cultures are testimonies to the discontinuity of the world and its subjects, and the co-presence—melancholic or parodic, depending on the spirit—of variations that the market favors for renewing sales and that the political trends test . . . for what?

There is not only one response. Baudrillard said that

> in a technical civilization of operatory abstraction, where neither machines nor domestic objects require much more than a controlling gesture (that gestural abstraction signifying a whole mode of relations and behavior), modern art in all its forms has for its primary function the salvation of the gestural moment, the intervention of the integral subject. It is the part of us, crushed by the technical habitus that art conjures up in the pure gestural complex of the act of painting and its apparent liberty. (108)

I meet many Latin American artists critical of modernity who, for aesthetic, sociocultural, or political motives, refuse this mannerism of the unending inauguration. Although they do not now link their work to the struggle for an impracticable new total order, they want to rethink fragments of the patrimony of their group in their works. I think of Toledo reworking the Mazatecan erotic bestiary, with a style that joins his indigenous knowledge and his participation in contemporary art. Earlier I cited Paternosto and Puente, who reorganize their austere geometrism in order to experiment with pre-Columbian designs and other images that are neither repetitive nor folklorizing; or painters devoted to exploring the exasperated polychrome of our cultures—such as Antonio Henrique Amaral, Jacobo Borges, Luis Felipe Noé, and Nicolás Amoroso—who are concerned with reconstructing the relations among colors, subjective time, and historical memory.

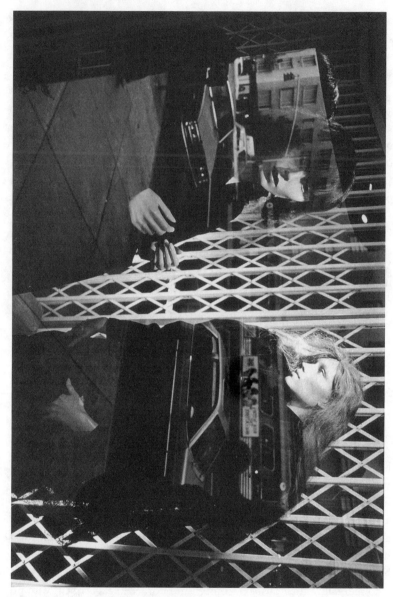

For many artists, recognizing cultural hybridization, and working experimentally with it, serve to deconstruct the perceptions of the social and the language that represent it.

Two mannequins that could be women that could be mannequins. In their fake bodies, they reflect the street, cars, and a bus with an advertisement with four women models. Maybe a man is looking at them and another is about to enter the scene. Who is inside and who is outside the grating?

We see the world through duplications and appearances. It is not strange that this photo, taken by Paolo Gasparini in New York in 1981, is titled *Behind*.

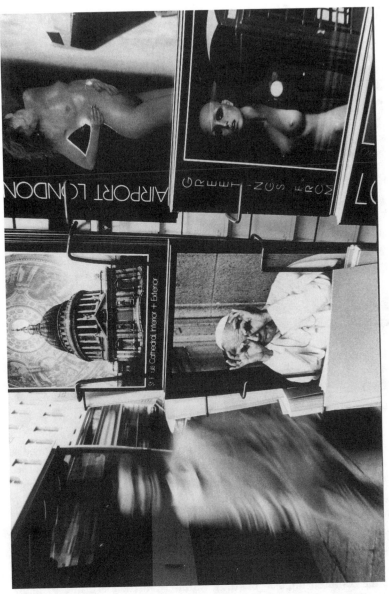

The gaze (London, 1982). The images that are clearly visible are the photographs of the women, the cathedral, and the pope. The "real" image, of the man walking by on the street, is mobile and uncertain. The pope, who seems to be watching from his inert photo, is watched by us, who are watched over by him while we observe the nudes. Who is more real, who controls, in a society where ecclesiastical iconography coexists so fluidly with the erotic? Photos that comment on other photos, display windows that multiply the fiction: these are resources for "becoming conscious" of the fact that we live in a world of metalanguages and oblique powers.

León Ferrari, *Ascension.*

All of them oppose the more extended social function of the mass media, which would, according to Lyotard, strengthen a certain recognizable order of the world, revitalize realism, and "preserve the consciousnesses of doubt." They concur with the theorist of postmodernism in thinking that the task of art consists, in the midst of those easy certainties, in questioning the conditions in which we construct the real.

I do not see in these painters, sculptors, and graphic artists the theological will to invent or impose a meaning on the world. But there is also not the confused nihilism of Andy Warhol, Rauschenberg, and so many practitioners of "bad painting" and the transvanguard. Their critique of artistic genius, and in some cases of elitist subjectivism, does not prevent them from warning that there are arising other forms of subjectivity in charge of new (or not so new) social actors, who are no longer exclusively white, Western, and male. Stripped of any totalizing or messianic illusion, these artists maintain a tense, interrogative relationship with societies, or fragments of them, where they think they see living sociocultural movements and practicable utopias.

I know how narrow the use of these words is among the precipices left behind by the collapse of so many traditions and modernities. But certain works of artists and popular producers allow us to think that the theme of utopias and historical projects is not closed. Some of us understand that the collapse of the totalizing accounts does not eliminate the critical search for meaning—or better yet, for meanings—in the articulation of traditions and modernity. On the condition of recognizing the instability of the social and semantic plurality, perhaps it is possible to continue asking ourselves how to construct meanings of high and popular art in their inevitable mixtures and their interaction with mass symbols.

Impure Genres: Graffiti and Comics

We spoke of artists and writers who open the territory of painting or the text so that their language migrates and is crossed with others. But there are constitutionally hybrid genres—for example, graffiti and comic strips. They are practices that from birth ignored the concept of patrimonial collection. Places of intersection between the visual and the literary, the cultured and the popular, they bring the artisanal nearer to industrial production and mass circulation.

1. Graffiti is for the *cholos* of the border, the youth gangs of Mexico City, and for equivalent groups in Buenos Aires or Caracas—a territorial writing of the city designed to assert presence in, and even possession of, a neighborhood. The battles for control of space are established through their own marks and modifications of the graffiti of other groups. Their sexual, political, or aesthetic references are ways of enunciating modes of life and thought for a group that does not have access to commercial, political, or mass-media circuits to express itself, but that affirms its style through graffiti. Its manual, spontaneous design is structurally opposed to "well"-painted or printed political or advertising legends and challenges those institutionalized languages when it alters them. Graffiti affirms territory but destructures the collections of material and symbolic goods.

The relation of property to territories is relativized in recent practices that seem to express the disarticulation of cities and political culture. Armando Silva describes three principal stages in the evolution of graffiti, which are associated with three cities (1987, 22-24). That of May '68 in Paris (also in

León Ferrari, *The Sermon on the Mount of Doré, 1865,* + *Ku Klux Klan Cross* (p. 94 of *Biblia*).

Berlin, Rome, Mexico City, and Berkeley) was made with antiauthoritarian, utopian slogans and macropolitical ends. New York graffiti, written in marginalized neighborhoods and in the subway, expressed ghetto references with micropolitical purposes; at times incomprehensible for those who did not control that hermetic code, it was the one that most typically wanted to delimit spaces in a disintegrating city and to recover territories.

In Latin America both modalities existed, but in the last few years, as a simultaneous manifestation of urban disorder, loss of credibility in political institutions, and utopian disenchantment, a mocking and cynical graffiti has developed. Silva gives Colombian examples. When the pope's visit in 1986 overwhelmed the streets of Bogotá with processions and propaganda, the walls responded: "Jesus Christ is coming soon. Let's go," "God doesn't do his job. Not even on Sundays."[7] Criticism of the government adopts the open insult, poetic irony—"I cede a cloud in the presidential sector"—or desperation: "Don't believe anyone. Go for a walk."

Some artists see in the intercultural and intertemporal fusions of postmodernism only the opportunity for getting rid of the solemn accounts of modernity. León Ferrari exacerbates the disintegration of religious and political collections in his collages in order to affirm the liberating impulses of modern thought. His montages of sacred icons with Nazi and warlike images, of the threatening angels of Rafael and Dürer with erotic scenes, seek to renew critical irony on history.

The rereading of religious iconography leads Ferrari to find in fundamentalist Christianity bases for the institutionalized terror of modern dictatorships. It is no accident that the god who separates those who fear him from the others, and sends the latter to that type of "concentration camp" that is hell, serves as a justification for totalitarian political doctrines. That hell exalted by Giotto and Michelangelo, in works admired as supreme examples of sensitivity and progress, is associated by Ferrari with torture and the Ku Klux Klan.

In the crisis of hyperinflation and ungovernability of the Argentine economy of 1989 we find a multiplication of legends. While the languages of political parties became unrealistic (36 percent of voters remained undecided a week before the presidential elections), the walls were filled with indignation and skepticism: "Put your representative to work: don't reelect him"; "The country is not for sale; it's already sold," "Yankees go home, and take us with you." As tends to occur with graffiti, they promote anonymous dialogues: "Argentina will soon be paradise: we're all going to walk around naked." Someone responds: "Will there be apples?" Romantic and political idealizations diffused by the mass media are taken up sarcastically: "Silvio Rodríguez was the only one who had a unicorn . . . and the dummy goes and loses it."

Graffiti is a syncretic and transcultural medium. Some graffiti fuse word and image with a discontinuous style: the crowding together of diverse authors' signs on a single wall is like an artisanal version of the fragmented and incongruent rhythm of the video. In others, the strategies of popular language and of university students are changed around, observes Armando Silva. There is also a "synthesis of urban topography" in a lot of recent graffiti that eliminates the border between what was written in bathrooms or on walls (1988, 192). It is a marginal, deinstitutionalized, and ephemeral way of assuming the new relations between the private and public, between daily and political life.

2. Comic strips have become so much a central component of contemporary culture, with such an extensive bibliography, that it would be trivial to insist on what we all know of their novel alliance, since the end of the nineteenth century, between iconic culture and literary culture. They take from art and journalism, are the most read literature, and are the branch of the publishing industry that generates the highest profits. In Mexico, for example, seventy million issues are published every month and their revenues are greater than those of books and magazines combined.

We might remember that comic strips, in generating new narrative orders and techniques by means of an original combination of time and images in a story of discontinuous frames, contributed to demonstrating the visual potential of writing and drama that can be condensed in static images. It has already been analyzed how the fascination with its hybridized techniques led Burroughs, Cortázar, and other cultured writers to use their discoveries. Studies have also been done of the correspondence between the comics' synthesis of various genres, their "heteroclite language," and the attraction they arouse in audiences from various classes and in all family members (Gubern 213ff.).

I am interested in exploring here an author of comic strips who incorporates into his work on gender several of the concerns that run through this book. I am referring to Fontanarrosa. One of his main characters, *Boogie, the Greasy,* comes out of a reworking of the literary and cinematographic thriller, the adventure novel, and the political discourse of the U. S. political right. The other, *Toilet Pereyra,* takes up the folkloric language of gauchoesque songs and legends, and of radio theater and television programs about "the national identity." When it appeared in 1972, it parodied the exuberant kitsch of the folkloric thematic in the media of that era.[8] How does he do it? On the one hand, by exaggerating the linguistic turns and visual stereotypes of "the gaucho"; on the other, by making more evident the fact that this earthly exaltation was excessive when it appeared together with the diffusion of the modern culture of the elites and mass culture by the same electronic media that were promoting folklore. In Fontanarrosa's comics, Toilet is found with, among others, Borges, Zorro, Antonio das Mortes, E.T., Superman, Don Quixote, and Darwin. He cuts across the arts, genres, and epochs.

It has been pointed out that the assiduous use of literary sources makes an

intertextual space of these stories: "Toilet Pereyra is a gauchc
not of the pampa but of gauchoesque literature" (Campra, 40)
that he comes out of the cross between literature and the me
episode of the first book of stories is significant: Toilet finds hin
uation similar to that of Martín Fierro in encountering a group of soldiers,
from which he is saved by an equivalent of Cruz, who invites him to flee with
him "to the Indian camp." Toilet rejects the offer, arguing: "It seems like I already read this somewhere else and I want to be original." The author's
comic strip introduces the preoccupation of art with innovation in mass
culture and, at the same time, Toilet's reply suggests that history has changed
and it is not possible to repeat Martín Fierro.

In moving from humor magazines to being published weekly or biweekly
in the best-selling daily newspaper in Argentina, *Clarín*, this comic strip's
references to contemporary events increase: "I am not obliged to make
something of the present, but I cannot tell anachronistic stories in a newspaper either." Although Fontanarrosa says that for reasons of narrative efficacy he conserves a "certain gauchoesque atmosphere"—"there never appears a late-model car"—the comic strip transcends all folklorism. It works
on "the complicities of the people" and therefore—in contrast to Boogie,
which is published in various countries—attempts at publishing Toilet outside of Argentina did not succeed. But this complicity implies that the author accepts that, for the people, traditions form part of modern processes.
In this sense, I would say that Toilet is, over the course of its seventeen years
of publication and of the thirteen volumes its issues make up, an attempt—
with the ironic sobriety that corresponds to humor—to redefine the opposition between unitarian and federalists.

For a century, Argentines have been discussing whether cultural policy
should opt for the civilization of the metropolises, rejecting the barbarism
of the indigenous, or for an energetic recovery of the national-popular. As
we approach the twenty-first century, when cultural industries like the
comic strip and soap operas cause us to inhabit an international space, faced
with the question of whether we prefer Sarmiento or Rosas, we would do
better to get closer to Toilet Pereyra.

There is a story in which Fontanarrosa thematizes the uncertain situation of territorial borders. The story begins with an opposition between
Toilet and another character whom we will call Pursued. Toilet is sitting
drinking maté; to his situation of rest and serenity are opposed the running
and desperation of the man who is fleeing. There is also an opposition of

the tragic ("Police from fifteen countries are chasing after me!") and the gaucho's humorous reply ("Why so successful?").

In the second scene the humor arises when Pursued clarifies that they are looking for him for having done something that we might call metasmuggling. He does not smuggle across borders but rather smuggles borders themselves: "Landmarks, barriers, stone markers, barbed wire, dotted lines." Toilet represents the person in gaucho mythology who does not recognize borders, the inhabitant of "the immensity of the pampa"; Pursued is the one who transgresses borders to the point of distributing new ones and selling them with defects. Before, he was a common smuggler—he dealt in hides; now he deals with borders: from illegal practice in trade to illegal action in politics.

Halfway through the story, the deceitful mechanisms used by the market to expand, independent of "natural" necessities, are caricatured. To bring wraps of toad skin to Paraguay, to a tropical area, and argue that there is no skin colder than that of the toad is a justification similar to those invented by advertising in its persuasive tactics. The commercial dissemination of products also appears to be mocking the limits between what territories and climates establish as reasonable.

Then the pursuit interrupts the dialogue. But it is no longer the police but Interpol, the international defenders of order. In the face of the transgression of speculative trade, Toilet declares himself a defender of an ethic based

PURSUED: Hide me, sharecropper! Police from fifteen countries are chasing after me!
TOILET: Son of a gun! Why so successful?

PURSUED: I'm a smuggler in borders.
TOILET: And what do you smuggle?
PURSUED: Didn't I just tell you? Borders: landmarks, barriers, stone markers, barbed wire, dotted lines.

on the preservation of nature: "As an ecologist, I don't protect anyone who has skinned God's little animals."

Finally, Toilet joins in solidarity with Pursued and tells him to pretend that he is part of a procession that is passing by. Toilet's dog, Mendieta, discovers that it is not a procession but a demonstration. And in the last frame Toilet gives a new surprise: it is a demonstration, but of police on strike for a raise. There is thus a chain of disguises: Pursued becomes a marcher in a procession that is a demonstration, that it is a demonstration of strikers, but one by the people who usually repress them.

Mendieta provides the moral of the story: "One never knows what one is going to be caught up in tomorrow." The same conclusion, in its ambiguity, contains uncertainty. It can be understood as meaning that we do not know where we are going to be situated tomorrow, or that we do not know where one is going to be, on which side of which border, tomorrow.

Humor is constructed and renewed in this series of displacements. In all of Fontanarrosa's comic strips the hilarity is born of the fact that borders are mobile, and that the characters and themes get confused. In this the indetermination of limits, besides being a humorous technique, is converted into a significant nucleus. The humorist—a professional of resignification, a specialist in slippages in meaning—indicates here that the uncertainty or unforeseen continuity between territories is not an invention

PURSUED: But I sold a defective border and the Chaco-Paraguay War was started.
PURSUED: Before, I smuggled hides: capybara, otter, *astracán* [unborn lamb].
TOILET: Look, I know animals but I've never run across an *astracán*.
PURSUED: The hide of the *astracán* is a kind of intestines you can see.

TOILET: I even saw a polar bear one day. It's so soft the skin of that animal!
PURSUED: You touched it? That animal is fearsome.
TOILET: This one wasn't fearsome. It was plush.
PURSUED: I also brought wraps of hides to Paraguay.
TOILET: To Paraguay? With that heat?

PURSUED: Toad skin. There's no hide colder than that. Cool and light.
PURSUED: Oh, my God! There comes Interpol! Hide me!
TOILET: As an ecologist, I don't protect anyone who has skinned God's little animals, innocent little creatures, good souls of the Lord!

TOILET: Look! There goes a procession! Mix in with the people, and I won't say anything!
PURSUED: Thanks!
TOILET: And he got into the crowd just like that, the bandit.
MENDIETA: But . . . it's not a procession. It's a demonstration.

TOILET: They're policemen on strike, demanding a raise.
MENDIETA: That's the way it is, Don Toilet. One never knows what one is going to be caught up in tomorrow.

of comic-strip authors; they do nothing more than expose a society in which borders can be anywhere. If the comic strip mixes earlier artistic genres, if it succeeds in having characters who are representative of the most stable part of the world—folklore—interact with figures from literature and the mass media, and if it introduces them into diverse epochs, it is doing nothing more than to reproduce the real; better put, it is doing nothing other than to reproduce the staging of advertising that convinces us to buy what we do not need, of the "manifestations" of religion, and of the "processions" of politics.

Oblique Powers

This crossing of some postmodern transformations of the symbolic market and of everyday culture contributes to understanding the failure of certain ways of doing politics that are based on two principles of modernity: the autonomy of symbolic processes and the democratic renewal of the cultured and the popular. Likewise, it can help us explain the generalized success of neoconservative politics and the lack of socializing or more democratic alternatives adapted to the level of technological development and the complexity of the social crisis. In addition to the economic advantages of the neoconservative groups, their action is facilitated by their having better captured the sociocultural meaning of the new structures of power.

Starting from what we have been analyzing, a key question returns: the cultural reorganization of power. It is a question of analyzing *what the political consequences are of moving from a vertical and bipolar conception of sociopolitical relations to one that is decentered and multidetermined.*

It is understandable that there is resistance to this displacement. The Manichaean and conspiratorial representations of power find partial justification in some contemporary processes. The central countries use technological innovations to accentuate the asymmetry and inequality between them and the dependent countries. The hegemonic classes take advantage of industrial reconversion to reduce workers employment, cut back the power of the unions, and commercialize goods—among which are educational and cultural ones—about which, after historic struggles, agreement had been reached that they were public services. It would seem that the big groups in which power is concentrated are the ones that subordinate art and culture to the market, the ones that discipline work and daily life.

A broader view allows us to see other economic and political transformations, supported by long-lasting cultural changes, that are giving a different structure to the conflicts. The crossings between the cultured and the popular render obsolete the polar representation between both modalities of symbolic development, and therefore revitalize the political opposition between hegemonics and subalterns, conceived as if it were a question of totally distinct and always opposed groups. What we know today about the intercultural operations of the mass media and new technologies, and about the reappropriation that makes of them diverse receivers, distances us from the theses about the omnipotent manipulation of the big metropolitan consortia. The classic paradigms with which domination was explained are incapable of taking into account the dissemination of the centers, the multipolarity of social initiatives, the plurality of references—taken from diverse territories—with which artists, artisans, and the mass media assemble their works.

The increase in processes of hybridization makes it evident that we understand very little about power if we only examine confrontations and vertical actions. Power would not function if it were exercised only by bourgeoisie over proletarians, whites over indigenous people, parents over children, the media over receivers. Since all these relations are *interwoven* with each other, each one achieves an effectiveness that it would never be able to by itself. But it is not simply a question of some forms of domination being superimposed on others and thereby being strengthened. What gives them their efficacy is the obliqueness that is established in the fabric. How can we discern where ethnic power ends and where family power begins, or the borders between political and economic power? Sometimes it is possible, but what is most important is the shrewdness with which the cables are mixed, and secret orders passed and responded to affirmatively.

Hegemonic, subaltern: heavy words that helped us to name the divisions between people but not to include movements of affection and participation in solidary or complicit activities in which hegemonic and subaltern groups are needed. Those who work on the border in constant relation with the tourism, factories, and language of the United States look strangely at those who consider them to be absorbed by the empire. For the protagonists of those relations, the interferences of English in their speech (to a certain extent equivalent to the infiltration of Spanish in the South of the United States) express the indispensable transactions in which everyday exchanges happen.

It is not necessary to look at those transactions as phenomena exclusive to zones of dense interculturalism. The ideological dramatization of social relations tends to exalt so much the oppositions that it ends by not seeing the rites that unite and connect them; it is a sociology of gratings, not of what is said through them or when they are not there. The most rebellious popular sectors and the most combative leaders satisfy their basic needs by participating in a system of consumption that they do not choose. They cannot invent the place where they work, the transportation that brings them there, nor the school where they educate their children, nor their food, nor their clothes, nor the media that supply them with daily information. Even protests against that order are made using a language they do not choose and demonstrating in streets or squares that were made by others. However many transgressive uses they make of the language, the streets, and the squares, the resignification is temporary and does not cancel the weight of the habits whereby we reproduce the sociocultural order, inside and outside of ourselves.

These realities—so obvious, but usually omitted in the ideological dramatization of conflicts—become clearer when nonpolitical behaviors are observed. Why do the popular sectors support those who oppress them? Medical anthropologists observe that in the face of health problems, the usual conduct of subaltern groups is not to attack the exploitation that makes it difficult for them to receive adequate care, but rather to accommodate themselves to the uses of the illness by private medicine or to take advantage as much as possible of deficient state services. This is not due to a lack of consciousness about their health needs, about the oppression that weighs them down, nor about the inadequacy or speculative cost of the services. Even when radical means of action are available for confronting inequality, they opt for intermediate solutions. The same thing happens in other scenarios. In the face of the economic crisis, they demand better salaries and at the same time limit their own consumption. Against political hegemony, the transaction consists, for example, in accepting personal relations in order to obtain individual benefits; in the ideological realm, in incorporating and positively valuing elements produced outside of their own group (criteria of prestige, hierarchies, designs, and functions of objects). The same combination of scientific and traditional practices—going to the doctor or to the healer—is a transactional way of taking advantage of the resources of both medicines, whereby the users reveal a conception that is more flexible than that of the modern medical system, so attached to allopathy, and of many anthropologists and folklorists who idealize the autonomy of traditional practices. From the perspective of the users, both therapeutic modalities are complementary and function as repertoires of resources starting from which they effect transactions between hegemonic and popular knowledge.[9]

The hybridizations described throughout this book bring us to the conclusion that today all cultures are border cultures. All the arts develop in relation to other arts: handicrafts migrate from the countryside to the city; movies, videos, and songs that recount events of one people are interchanged with others. Thus cultures lose the exclusive relation with their territory, but they gain in communication and knowledge.

There is yet another way in which the obliquity of the symbolic circuits allows us to rethink the links between culture and power. The search for mediations and diagonal ways for managing conflicts gives cultural relations a prominent place in political development. When we do not succeed in changing whoever governs, we satirize him or her in Carnival dances, journalistic humor, and graffiti. Against the impossibility of constructing a different order, we establish masked challenges in myths, literature, and comic strips. The struggle between classes or ethnic groups is, most of the time, a metaphorical struggle. Sometimes, starting from metaphors, new transformative practices slowly or unexpectedly invade the picture.

At every border there are rigid wires and fallen wires. Exemplary actions, cultural rodeos, rites are ways of going beyond the limits wherever possible. I think of the cunning of undocumented migrants in the United States, of the parodic rebelliousness of Colombian and Argentine graffiti. I remember the Mothers of the Plaza de Mayo walking every Thursday in a cyclical ritualism, holding photos of their disappeared children like icons, until they succeeded years later in having some of the guilty condemned to prison.

But the frustrations of human rights organizations makes us reflect also on the role of culture as a symbolic expression for sustaining a demand when political paths are closed. The day the Argentine Congress approved the Law of Ending (Ley de Punto Final), which absolved hundreds of torturers and murderers, two formerly disappeared persons put themselves into narrow booths, handcuffed and blindfolded, in front of the legislative palace, with posters that said "The end means returning to this"—the ritual repetition of disappearance and confinement as the only way of preserving memory of them when political failure seemed to eliminate them from the social horizon.

This limited symbolic effectiveness leads to that fundamental distinction for defining relations between the cultural and political fields that we analyzed in the preceding chapter: the difference between *action* and *acting*. A chronic difficulty in the political valorization of cultural practices is to understand them as actions—that is, as effective interventions in the material structures of society. Certain sociologizing readings also measure the utility of a mural or a film by its capacity to perform and generate immediate and verifiable modifications. It is hoped that the spectators respond to the supposed "conscientizing" actions with "consciousness-raising" and "real changes" in their conduct. As this almost never happens, one reaches pessimistic conclusions about the efficacy of artistic messages.

Cultural practices are performances more than actions. They represent and simulate social actions but only sometimes operate as an action. This happens not only in cultural activities that are expressly organized and acknowledged as such; ordinary behaviors too, whether grouped in institutions or not, employ simulated action and symbolic performance. Presidential discourses in the face of a conflict that cannot be resolved with the available resources, the criticism of governmental performance by political organizations without the power to reverse it, and, of course, the verbal rebellions of the common citizen are performances that are more understandable for the theatrical gaze than for that of "pure" politics. Anthropology informs us that this is not due to the distance that crises put between ideals and acts but to the constitutive structure of the articulation between the political and the cultural in any society. Perhaps the greatest interest for politics in taking into account the symbolic problematic lies not in the sure efficacy of certain goods or messages but in the fact that the theatrical and ritual aspects of the social make evident what there is of the oblique, the simulated, and the deferred in any interaction.

Notes

1. On Chile, see Lechner's *Notas sobre la vida cotidiana* and Brunner's *Un espejo trizado. Ensayos sobre cultura y políticas*, especially the first part. With respect to Argentina, see Landi.

2. The photos of this series of monuments were taken by Paolo Gori. The book that he did with Helen Escobedo is entitled *Mexican Monuments: Strange Encounters* (1989). A more extensive analysis of the problems treated here can be found in my article "Monuments, Billboards, and Graffiti," included in that volume. I am grateful to the Institute of Aesthetic Research of the National University of Mexico for having facilitated my access to photos by Gori that were not included in the book, and that were donated by the author to that institution.

3. Two historians of Chicano art, Shifra M. Goldman and Tomás Ybarra-Frausto, have documented this cultural production and reflected upon it in an original way. See, for example, the introductions to their book *Arte Chicano: A Comprehensive Annotated Bibliography of Chicano Art, 1965-1981*; see also the articles by both of them in Rodríguez Prampolini.

4. It should be clarified that the conception of life as a constant crossing of borders, although it remains adequate, is not as easy as Michel de Certeau pronounces it when it is a question of "second-class" North American citizens—for example, blacks, Puerto Ricans, and Chicanos.

5. The report of this investigation can be read in García Canclini and Safa *(Tijuana: la casa de toda la gente)*; photos by Lourdes Grobet. Jennifer Metcalfe, Federico Rosas, and Ernesto Bermejillo collaborated in the study.

6. With respect to the intercultural hybridization among rockers, *cholos*, and punks—who

produce magazines, records, and cassettes with information and music from various continents—see Valenzuela.

7. The second slogan involves a play on words that does not translate into English without losing the effect of the original Spanish: "Dios no cumple. Ni años." But the free translation given here captures more or less the sentiment of the original.—*Trans.*

8. This affirmation, like others I cite from Fontanarrosa, were obtained in a personal interview with him in Rosario, Argentina, on March 18, 1988.

9. I am using here the investigations carried out by Menéndez and Módena, who extensively analyze the practices of transaction.

Exit

I did not want to leave my conclusions for the end and therefore maintained a constant interaction between the theoretical and the empirical. In part, the conclusions were presented in every chapter. But although I attempted to sketch a general movement, the crisis of the notion of totality and the unequal empirical implementation of the changes described in the Latin American countries, and within each one, imposes an avoidance of broad generalizations.

Perhaps we could aspire to conclusions in the sense that the Council of the Ministers of Culture of the European Community does when it attempted to unify the administration and circulation of cultural goods on that continent by 1992. Conscious of the tension between the convergence of symbolic systems and the affirmation of regional identities, it distinguishes between conclusions and resolutions. The latter oblige countries to reorganize their management in order to be in tune with the rest; on the other hand, the conclusions—such as seeking a unified price for books or exempting them from the value-added tax—are recommendations, applicable in some places but unknown in others. It is in this sense that we might approach them here.

The pluralist perspective, which accepts fragmentation and multiple combinations among tradition, modernity, and postmodernity, is indispensable for considering the Latin American conjuncture at the end of the century. Thus the balance sheet attempted in this book verified how the four defining features or movements of modernity unfolded on our continent: emancipation, expansion, renovation, and democratization. All have been manifested in Latin America. The problem does not lie in our not having modernized but rather in the contradictory and unequal manner in which these components have been articulated.

Emancipation has occurred to the extent our societies achieved a secularization of the cultural fields, less widespread and integrated than in the metropolises but notably more so than in other underdeveloped continents. There was an early liberalization of political structures, beginning in the nineteenth century, and a rationalization of social life, although it has coexisted to this day with traditional (nonmodern) behaviors and beliefs.

Renovation is demonstrated by the accelerated growth of intermediate and higher education, by artistic and artisanal experimentation, and by the dynamism with which the cultural fields are adapting to technological and social innovations. On this point we also note an unequal distribution of benefits, an asynchronous appropriation of the changes in production and consumption on the part of different countries, regions, classes, and ethnic groups.

Democratization has been achieved in an astonishing way, with too many interruptions and with a different meaning from the one imagined by classical liberalism. It was produced in part, as that tendency foresaw, by educational expansion, the diffusion of art and science, and participation in political parties and unions. But the democratization of everyday culture and political culture that took place in the second half of the twentieth century was made possible above all by the electronic communications media and by nontraditional organizations—youth, urban, ecological, feminist—that intervene in the contradictions generated by modernization, where the old actors are less effective or lack credibility.

To what extent can these contradictions be attributed to the fact that *expansion,* particularly economic expansion, is the most stagnant aspect of our development? At the end of the 1980s, when the world growth rate was 4 percent, Latin America exhibited the recessive effects of the stagnation of the entire decade; the most dynamic countries of another time— Argentina, Brazil, Mexico—showed negative indices of growth, and in cases like Peru a decline of about 10 percent in real production. The consequent diminution of exports and imports brings along with it a decreasing participation in technological innovations and in new international strategies of capital accumulation (Castells and Laserna). Therefore, the possibility of cultural modernization is also deficient in dependent countries due to the low capacity to renew themselves by appropriating new technologies and inserting themselves in new rules for circulation and management of symbolic goods.

Nevertheless, the analysis presented in this book does not allow the establishment of mechanical relations between economic and cultural modernization. Nor does it allow this process to be read as one of simple backwardness—although it is, in part, with respect to the international conditions of development. This unsatisfactory modernization has to be interpreted in interaction with persistent traditions.

In sum, the whole crisis of modernity, traditions, and their historical combination leads to a postmodern problematic (not a phase) in the sense that the modern explodes and is mixed with what is not modern; it is affirmed and debated at the same time. Throughout this book we have analyzed why artisans continue to make pottery and textiles manually in industrial society; artists practice advanced technologies and at the same time look to the past in search of a certain historical richness or stimuli for their imagination. In both fields, culture is not believed to move in an ascending process, or certain ways of painting, symbolizing, or reasoning to be superior—although the market needs to reinvent often the hierarchies for renewing the distinction between groups.

There are those who continue to affirm their territorial identity, from indigenous peoples to ecologists. There are elite and popular sectors that reestablish the specificity of their patrimonies or search for new signs in order to differentiate themselves from others. The struggles to defend regional or national autonomy in the administration of culture continue to be necessary in view of the subordination that transnational corporations seek. But, in general, all of them reformulate their symbolic capital in the midst of crossings and exchanges. The hybrid sociability that contemporary cities induce leads us to participate intermittently in groups that are cultured and popular, traditional and modern. Affirmation of the regional or national is neither meaningful nor effective as a general condemnation of the exogenous: it should be conceived now as the capacity to interact with the multiple international symbolic offers on the basis of their own positions.

In this period, when history is moving in many directions, any conclusion is marked by uncertainty. More cultivated types of knowledge lead to more precarious decisions about how to enter or leave modernity, where to invert, how to invest, and how to relate culture to power.

To Enter or to Exit

The arc we follow in studying jointly the formation of historical patrimonies and their cultured, popular, and mass reconversion in migrations and intercultural transfers brings into view what the modernizing impulse prevented us from thinking about what it means to be modern. The compact version of the social given by the national museums of history and anthropology, which are put together through a fixed alliance between tradition and modernity, for that very reason becomes the perspective most adverse to decollection and deterritorialization. In dramatizing only the origin myths and the formation of collections that are apodictically constitutive of nationality, they do not allow the emergence of questions about the current recomposition of culture.

The Museum of Anthropology in Mexico City conceives of the originary patrimony as something essentially linked to the nation. Beginning with the arrival of migrants and their settling down, the construction of weighty proofs of their definitive settlement—pyramids, temples, cities—in territories that they would maintain up to today configures a static patrimony that is ratified by dehistoricized ethnography. The dramatization of this patrimony by the museum is achieved by guaranteeing its solidity with a nationalist discourse centralized in the Mexica room—which symbolizes the seat of power—and with a scientific discourse that orders ethnic groups according to the testimonies provided by their collections of ancient pieces.

Can a museum of anthropology today speak about the entrance into the territory across the Bering Strait and of its occupation and not mention the exit of the descendants through Zapata Canyon into the United States. How can we understand what is now Mexico if any of these movements is omitted: primordial migrations, the domestication of territories, the formation of collections of objects, and at the same time the reconstitution of those founding patrimonies by interethnic conflicts, migrations, and the changing identities of those who come from the countryside to the city, or leave Mexico for other countries?

It is possible, then, to assert that the cultural analysis of modernity requires putting together the methods of entering and leaving it. But putting it this way is incorrect because it suggests that modernity is a historical period or a type of practice with which one might connect oneself by choosing to be in it or not. It is often presented in these terms, and the entire discussion is reduced to what must be done in order to enter or leave—the artisan who *should* become a worker, the migrant who wants to improve by *going* to the city or to a developed country, the intellectual or artist who *incorporates* himself or herself into technological advance. These are situations of passage that suggest a change of state.

Something similar happens with those who want to leave: to flee to the megalopolises and *to return* to nature, to seek in a sacralized historical patrimony the *dis-solution* of modern conflicts, to liberate knowledge or art from the compulsion of progress.

The cultural reconversions that we analyzed reveal that modernity is not only a space or a state one enters into or from which one emigrates. It is a condition that involves us, in the cities and in the countryside, in the metropolises and in the underdeveloped countries. With all the contradictions that exist between modernism and modernization—and precisely because of them—it is a situation of unending transit in which the uncertainty of what it means to be modern is never eliminated. To radicalize the project of modernity is to sharpen and renew this uncertainty, to create new possibilities for modernity always to be able to be something different and something more.

In this sense, the modernizing movement—among whose contradictions is having contributed to engendering new fundamentalisms, strengthening them, and making them more threatening—is the adversary of all fundamentalism. It is the (uncertain) certainty that there is no dogma, no absolute foundation, that proscribes doubt and innovation.

Is this not what migrants discover when they go from the countryside to the city, or from one country to another, and have to renew their traditions? Is it not also what happens to contemporary art mixed with the popular and the primitive? And more clearly than to anyone else, it is what happens to mass-media producers who, in expanding their programs to new countries, where other tastes and cognitive systems reign, must reconvert their codes in order to communicate with different audiences.

At this point it can be perceived how wrong the notion of postmodernity is if we want to avoid having the *post* designate an overcoming of the modern. Can we speak critically about modernity and search for it at the same time that we are passing it by? If it were not so awkward, we would have to say something like post-intra–modern.

Where to Invest

Reconversion is, in part, an updating of the market. An updating of the biblical precept according to which many are called but few are chosen. Young people who enter the job market are warned that they have to leave behind their past life and the erroneous choices of their parents and dedicate themselves to something else. In becoming massified, the old professions no longer serve to guarantee the future of the individual—to the point of making it doubtful that following a university career is a path to social advancement. The middle and popular classes are beginning to internalize this knowledge, as is indicated by the decline in enrollment in higher education—for the first time in this century—during the 1980s.

In the face of this hegemonic tendency, many social groups—especially the culture professionals—believe it possible to resist the devaluation of laboriously worked educational investments. Among both the elites and the popular classes there are those who attempt to rehabilitate their modes of production and symbolic diffusion, restore the differences between the cultured and the popular (or between the popular and the cultured), and separate both from the massive. They seek new procedures for inscribing their works in institutional contexts and circuits of distribution that are still sensitive to traditional ways. It is conservatism that is opposed to neoconservatism.

Others think that there is no reduction in access and revenues but rather a radical change in the places where it is suitable to invest—no longer in crafts, or in art, but rather in the culture industry. All those who move from traditions to modernity, from the classical humanities to the social sciences, or better from the soft sciences to the hard sciences, will have their place. The symbols of prestige are found less in classical culture (books, paintings, concerts) and are displaced to technological knowledge (computers, systems), to sumptuary domestic equipment, to places of leisure that consecrate the alliance of advanced technologies with entertainment.

A third way is that of those who maintain that in the postmodern crisis of the links between traditions and modernity it has ceased to be mutually exclusive to be a painter or an advertising designer, to collect art or crafts, to seduce the elites in galleries and concert halls or the masses with television. Given the fact that a characteristic of contemporary symbolic structures is the constant slippage between the cultured, the popular, and the massive, in order to be effective and invest well it is necessary to perform on different stages at the same time, in their interstices and instabilities.

All three of these interpretations of how to adapt to reconversion are partially in effect, as is indicated by the fact that each one has representatives in the polemics on higher education, the spread of culture, and the administration of symbolic goods. Different social sectors and various aesthetic trends construct and renew their positions in the triangular relation that is established among these options. Of course this is not a mere coincidence; they compete for the legitimacy of cultural practices, for financial support, and for symbolic recognition.

The old contradiction between exuberant cultural development and the scarcity of economic resources, accentuated by neoconservative policies, lends a central role to this competition in many Latin American countries. The artistic and intellectual fields tend to reinforce their distinctive profiles and their demands for fidelity. If a university professor is successful in the mass media or an artisan is recognized in the art market, both encounter difficulties in remaining in their original fields. In the same way, the entrance of journalists into the university or artisans into art galleries is rejected.

The rise in legitimacy of the popular arts tends to be taken badly by artists. The polemics that occurred in Peru in 1975 are well known, when, in competition with famous painters, the National Art Award was won by the maker of altarpieces Joaquín López Antay; the Professional Association of Visual Artists declared that it could not accept "the thesis that handicrafts have greater significance for our cultural process than painting" (quoted in Lauer 1982, 136). In the same period, the visual artist Fernando de Szyslo quit a state commission to protest the Peruvian governments decision to send a crafts display to represent the country's art at the Bienal of São Paulo.

The need to protect the elite field by marking its difference from others is also seen in face of greater cultural recognition of mass artists. In 1985 two debates filled many pages of Mexican periodicals for weeks. One was started by the attempt of the organizers of the World Cup of soccer to hold the drawing for distributing the dates and locations of games in the Palace of Fine Arts. The other "scandal" was the holding in the same palace of the performance by one of the main representatives of New Song, Guadalupe Pineda, which was widely broadcast on television. Several artists and intellectuals objected to "our premier theater," which "represents culture at its highest level," being used for "events of a commercial character" or a musical trend that they doubted had sufficient "excellence of form." One of them summarized the incestuous character of the cultured aesthetic: "Fine Arts is for the fine arts." Singers of the offending style retorted that the palace should not be only for exhibitions of high art and opera, but rather "be extended to include other forms of popular expression that are also part of the history of music."[1]

The university and professional power of art historians and artists tends to be defended by exalting the singularity of the field itself and by devaluing the products of their competitors (handicrafts and the mass media). Inversely, specialists in "illegitimate" cultures—folklorists, mass communicators—seek to legitimize their spaces by attacking the elitist positions of those involved in high art and university learning.

The border between these fields has become more flexible. It is considered increasingly legitimate that university professors reconvert their symbolic capital into spaces of mass and popular culture, especially if they have characteristics equivalent to those of the intellectual world. Writing, for example. It is preferable for an intellectual to write in a newspaper—not as a common journalist but as an opinion columnist—than to appear on a television program. At the same time, on television it is more acceptable to participate as a panelist or an interviewee—that is, as a specialist—than as a permanent professional of the station. For the academy, the intervention of intellectuals in the media is more legitimate the less they share the logic of the media.

In exceptional cases, an intellectual is permitted to participate in mass communication, or in "extrauniversity" fields such as public policy, but on the condition that he or she not transfer to the intellectual field—let us say to his or her books—the spectacular style of the media or the passion of political struggle. The international validity of this rule is proved in societies as different as the United States and Italy. High-profile intellectuals are torn to pieces by the most orthodox sectors of their disciplines for being political (Chomsky) or because they continually appear in the media and achieve mass recognition (Umberto Eco).

In any case, the growing interaction between the cultured, the popular, and the massive softens up the borders between their practitioners and their styles. But this trend struggles against the centripetal movement of each field, where those who hold power based on rhetoric and specific forms of dramatizing prestige assume that their strength depends on preserving differences. The breaking down of the thin walls that separate them is experienced by those who hegemonize each field as a threat to their power. Therefore, the current reorganization of culture is not a linear process. On one side, the need to expand cultural markets popularizes elite goods and introduces mass messages into the enlightened sphere. Nevertheless, the struggle for control of the cultured and the popular continues to be waged, in part, through efforts to defend specific symbolic capitals and mark the distinction between themselves and others.

This conflictive dynamic is one of the causes of the frequent obsolescence of cultural goods. The artist who achieves popular acclaim but wants to maintain the recognition of specialized minorities must renew his or her repertory, introduce thematic and, especially, formal variations that allow his or her most exclusive followers to find again in his or her persona and products the sign of ultimate distinction. Such a requirement is at least as influential in changes as are the intrinsic necessities of creation. I am thinking of the collective passage of the conceptual and hyperrealist visual artists of the seventies to neo-Expressionism and the transvanguard of the eighties (even those who did not have the conditions for that shift) in New York, São Paulo, and Buenos Aires.

But there are also artists who are representative of what we call the third type of response to the requirements of reconversion. They are those who pursue their career simultaneously, without too many conflicts, in both the cultured and the popular-massive fields. Caetano Veloso and Astor Piazzola perform alternately in stadiums and concert halls, develop spectacular and experimental lines in their language, produce works where both intentions coexist, and can be understood and enjoyed on different levels by different audiences. Their success in one space does not disqualify them from continuing to be acknowledged in the other.

I already referred, in literature, to the case of Borges, who incorporated into his practice as a writer the image of him forged by the media, creating the genre of statements to the press in which he parodied the fictional relation of them with the real. In cinema, we find this ductility in European producers who came to the United States to shoot their films—for example, Roman Polanski, Milos Forman, Louis Malle, and Wim Wenders—or in North American filmmakers who are not culturally from Hollywood, such as Woody Allen and Francis Ford Coppola. In Latin America, Brazilian cinema achieved this duplicity in the seventies and the first half of the eighties: let us recall the aesthetic complexity and orgiastic popularity that are combined in Glauber Rocha's films, the light compositions that propose reflections on the hybrid character of Brazilian culture, such as *Macunaíma* by Joaquín Pedro de Andrade, *Doña Flor y sus dos maridos* by Bruno Barreto, and *Xica da Silva* by Cacá Diegues.

These are only a few examples of amphibious artists, capable of articulating cultural movements and codes of different origins. Like certain theatrical producers and the majority of rock musicians, they show that it is possible to fuse the cultural heritages of a society, critical reflection about their contemporary meaning, and the communicational requirements of mass diffusion.

How to Invest

The cultured and the popular, the national and the foreign, appear at the end of this journey as *cultural* constructions. They have no consistency as structures that are "natural" or inherent to collective life. Their verisimilitude was achieved *historically* through ritualization operations of essentialized patrimonies. The difficulty in defining what is the cultured and what is the popular derives from the contradiction that both modalities are organizations of the symbolic that are engendered by modernity, but at the same time modernity—by its relativism and antisubstantialism—is constantly eroding them.

It was necessary for the modern movement to bring these contradictions between essentialization and relativism to the extreme—almost to exhaustion—in order for it to be discovered to what degree the opposition between the cultured and the popular is unsustainable. The massive reorganization of culture made this clear. However, the academic difference of separate spaces for dealing with the cultured, the popular, and the massive, as well as the existence of diverse organizations for laying out their policies, reproduces the schism. The loss of the prescriptive efficacy of these institutions, which no longer succeed in having the hegemonic groups behave like cultured ones and the subaltern groups like popular ones, was discrediting the classification.

When it is a matter of understanding the intercrossings on the borders between countries, in the fluid networks that interconnect towns, ethnic groups, and classes, then the popular and the cultured, the national and the foreign, appear not as entities but as scenarios. A scenario—as we saw with regard to monuments, museums, and popular culture—is a place where a story is staged. It is necessary to include the restaging in reconversion—the procedures of hybridization through which the representations of the social are elaborated with a dramatic sense.

The study of cultural reconversion thus leads to a discovery in it of much more than an economic or technological restructuring. In the world of symbols, as we know from psychoanalysis, apart from investing financially we invest psychologically: we deposit psychic energy in bodies, objects, and social processes, and in the representations of them. How do we reinvest in the processes of cultural reconversion?

When a tradition or a form of knowledge no longer yields revenues, one cannot change to a different one the way one moves a deposit from a bank to a different lending institution, or from one branch of production to the next. There is an invested affective baggage, a mourning to go through when it is lost. This "investment" places us before the drama of temporality and gives us one more key for understanding the simultaneous persistence and obsolescence of the traditional forms of the cultured and the popular.

Mass industrial culture offers the inhabitants of postmodern societies a disorganizing-organizing matrix of temporal experiences that is more compatible with the destructurings that presuppose migration, the fragmented and heteroclite relation to the social. Meanwhile, elite culture and traditional popular cultures continue to be committed to the modern conception of temporality, according to which cultures are accumulations that are constantly enriched through transformative practices. Even in the most abrupt ruptures of the artistic and intellectual vanguards the assumption that wound up predominating was that these cuts were returns to a beginning or a renewal of a heritage that was continuing. (Therefore, it has been thought possible to write histories of the vanguards.)

In contrast, television, video games, videos, and disposable goods propose relations that are instantaneous, temporally full, and rapidly discarded and replaced. For this reason, the symbolic experiences favored by industrial cultures are opposed to those studied by folklorists, anthropologists, and historians. The media and new recreational technologies are not interested in traditions, except as a reference for strengthening the simultaneous contact between broadcasters and the public; what matters to them is not historical improvement but rather the possibility of full and brief participation in what is going on.

José Jorge de Carvalho says this more radically:

All those promises of happiness by the culture industry . . . are basically the experience of the transitory: it helps people in an increasingly hurried and changing life—as happens in the modern industrial metropolis—to free themselves from the weight and the responsibility of memory.

He then concludes that one of the reasons for the permanence of the other cultural fields—the cultured and the popular—is that

they always work inside a tradition, constantly commenting on and referring themselves to it, that is, establishing a hermeneutic practice basic for their dynamic of existence and contributing justly to the construction of a collective memory. (Carvalho, 22)

If there continues to be folklore—although it has been reformulated by the culture industry—it is because it still functions as a symbolic nucleus for expressing forms of coexistence and views of the world that involve a continuity of social relations. Since those compact relations almost no longer exist, could folklore then be a model, a utopia, among other accessible models for postmodern people?

In order to work out this tattered experience of temporal change, all cultures have used rituals. Because of its capacity for gathering together the affective meaning of social transformations, polarization, discrepancy, and condensation among meanings, ritualism, according to Turner, is more propitious than other practices: it serves as a way of living—and observing—processes of conflict and transition (1967, chapter 1). Symbolic and ritual thought has a "nodal function with reference to intersecting sets of classifications" (1969, 42).

According to the diverse responses to reconversion analyzed in this book, rituals are different. In a great many conflicts, there is a resort to funerary rituals. Of the many similarities indicated between high art and popular art—which invalidate their sharp separation—one is particularly astonishing: the one that exists between the folklorists' calls for help in saving handicrafts to the point of extinction, and the artists' and historians' statements about the death of art. A frequent reaction of artists and critics against the death of high art has been the celebration of its funeral rites. The first response of many artisans and researchers of popular art was, and continues to be, to ritualize, describe, and analyze its apparent extinction. I believe that insufficient comparative study has been done of this coincidence by which the representatives of the traditional cultured and popular, in speaking of the death of their objects, find a resource so that they continue existing in the symbolic market.

Perhaps nothing has been buried as many times as art. Its end—announced by almost all vanguards and favored by the demythifying criticism of politicians, moralists, and psychologists—never stops happening. On the contrary, it continues to be the "artistic theme of beautifully suicidal works," as Jean Galard wrote (9). Aesthetics and art history were also declared caducous. One of the last funeral ceremonies was conducted on February 15, 1979, in the Pompidou Center in Paris. After the inauguration of the Days of Body and Performance Art, organized by the Center of Art and Communication of Buenos Aires, Hervé Fischer announced the end of art history, as its cadaver was deposited in a metal box in the Lost and Found office of the Pompidou Center. Four years later, on April 14, 1983, at three o'clock, there continued to be relatives, survivors, and heirs: the artist Fischer, the critic Pierre Restany, and the "very subofficial" Denys Tremblay proceeded to the recovery, transfer, and definitive interment of the mortal remains of Art History in an anonymous gallery.[2]

The funerary declarations of art in Latin America tend to take the form of social critique. Art is said to have died upon losing its meaning and function in the face of social injustices. At least that was the prevailing interpretation in the sixties and early seventies, when artists stopped painting and attacked museums and galleries, especially those that represent modernity: the Di Tella Institute in Buenos Aires, the Bienal of São Paulo, the rituals of selection and consecration that brought peripheral art up-to-date with the art of the metropolises. The critique of cosmopolitan institutions questioned the imposition of visual patterns that were foreign to "our identity." Some of those artists went to look for that identity in unions and popular organizations; others became designers of posters and comic strips in which they attempted to express the sensual and imaginary habits of the masses.

If many of those artists returned twenty years later to painting and exhibiting works, and if things continue to be written about what they produce and exhibit, the insistent deaths of art and its institutions have not extinguished their social functions. Some of these functions survive; others are born in the ironic laboratories of postmodernity, and new paths of circulation appear in interacting with new audiences in commercial publicity and political propaganda and in urban and television visuality. The death of art, the resurrection of hybrid visual cultures.

In analyzing popular art, we also verified that its announced death is no such thing when we admitted that it has been transforming itself. A part of this change consists in the fact that handicrafts, folkloric music, and traditions no longer make up compact blocks with definitive contours. The potters who make devils in Ocumicho, the *amate* painters in Ameyaltepec, and the dancers in so many carnivals and fiestas appropriate modern languages, bring their ancient images to the cities, and multiply their diffusion among groups that discovered them and have been buying them for only a few years. Like the art that circulates in galleries and museums, the art that travels through markets and urban fairs is continually reformulating itself interdiscursively.

Therefore, funeral rites are not the only ones whereby contemporary cultures dramatize transitions. Artists and artisans reconvert their knowledge in ceremonies that search for new meanings for the intersections of the cultured and the popular, the national and international. They are postmodern officiants , "liminal personae," "threshold people," as Turner calls those who have been performing in rites of passage since antiquity, because "they elude or escape the system of classifications that normally establish situations and positions in cultural space" (1988, 102).

The artisans of Ocumicho and Ameyaltepec, the writers of the northern border of Mexico, Zabala and Borges, Fontanarrosa and a great many authors of graffiti are liminal artists. It is not by chance that some of them have taken the secularizing and transgressing impulse of the vanguards to the point of fusion with rituals of popular origin. Alfredo Portillos and Regina Vater reconstructed ceremonies of northern Argentina in Buenos Aires and of the Brazilian Mato Grosso in São Paulo. Felipe Ehrenberg and Antonio Martorell reinvest their experimental aesthetic in the Mexican capital and in cities in the United States in order to reconstruct the traditional altars that Mexicans make for the Day of the Dead. Young Cuban painters reformulate revolutionary iconography by mixing it with images of Santeria.

Liminal artists are artists of ubiquity. Their works renew the sociocultural function of art and succeed in representing the multitemporal heterogeneity of Latin America by simultaneously utilizing images of social history and of the history of art, of crafts, of the mass media, and of the multicolored urban patchwork.

Mediations and Democratization

This ubiquitous, multidimensional project of artists clashes with the trends toward stable reproduction of symbolic markets. Contradiction is produced with the conservative fringes of each cultured, popular, or mass field who refuse to lose their specificity. But this also happens with the more "advanced" sectors of the reconversion who seek to strengthen themselves by means of a centralized control of cultural decisions.

The effort of artists, journalists, or any cultural worker to operate as a mediator between the symbolic fields and in relations between diverse groups contradicts the movement of the market toward concentration and monopolization. High-investment technologies and the neoconservative economic dynamic tend to transfer the social initiatives of individual producers and grassroots movements to big corporations. Their conception of the rupture of borders—between cultural fields and between nations—is equivalent to subordinating local forms to transnational chains of production and circulation of symbolic goods. Those who control the market demand that artists move from the scattered exercise of individual vocations to corporately or institutionally programmed professionalization.

One of the few studies on the withdrawal of state organisms and the boom of private foundations in the financing of the arts—by Lourdes Yero in Venezuela—shows that democratizing conceptions of development and cultural promotion are replaced by the "flexible and efficient management of the sector." Unlike earlier forms of sponsorship, in which administrators and artists conceived of themselves as amateurs, the recent modalities of private organization modify the ethos of cultural actors. Cultural managers, supported by younger generations who are familiar with the new technologies, demand that artistic and communications producers be guided by criteria of efficiency and yield in designing their products, in their use of time and materials, that they meet schedules in executing their work, and that they set their prices by taking into account economic logic and not only the intrinsic necessities of creation. It is not strange that cultural producers tied to the mass media, with a corporate and sectored view of the symbolic fields, should be the ones who best adapt to this dynamic and whom the corporations choose to promote. In corporate organizations, more than in individuals, ubiquity and flexibility are valued, and not in relation to the democratization of culture but to the ability to insert their action in diverse circuits with the aim of multiplying profits (Yero).

Two main obstacles exist to the development in culture of alternative policies to this corporate reconversion. One is the inertia of romantic and individualist ideologies among cultural producers. Artists tend to organize collectively against threats to the autonomy of their creative work or the functioning of their field (to question censorship and reject political or religious interference), and in some cases for solidarity work (a mural or posters for a strike). But it is difficult, especially in disciplines where individual work is significant—the visual arts, literature—for them to join together in a permanent way to intervene in determining working conditions or in the constant defense of their rights, and even less so to systematize their function as critical mediators. The advance of unions and other types of organization happens more in theater, music, and the arts affiliated with mass communication.

The other obstacle is that almost all parties, unions, and groups dedicated to making cultural policy also have centralized and instrumental criteria of experimentation and symbolic practices. Their conception of historical processes and popular needs becomes even more rigid and one-dimensional than that of businesspeople. Their demands on artists, writers, and communicators are stricter and less up-to-date with respect to the industrial conformation of the cultural markets.

Nevertheless, all this has been reconsidered since the eighties as part of the postmodern debate. There is criticism, for example, of works of political art that trust in a unique meaning of History and are related to the social "under the corroborative mode of ideological subscription or under the illustrative mode of literary thematization." Their preferred organizing tactics are questioned: the "calls and convocations to events" in which art is nothing more than an instrument for mobilization. It is also objected that their dominant genres are figurative or narrative representation and "the overdramatizing of the imprint" of popular action and of its heroic meaning. The artistic practices subordinated to the rites of the left are seen as simple devices of self-affirmation:

> All the demonstrations planned for such fronts and alliances of democratic recovery (such as the—paradigmatic—case of "Chile creates") resort to the condensing power of antidictatorial symbols in order to consolidate the emblematic character of figures (referents, persons, institutions, etc.) charged with settling the political call from their militant histories, or else to decorate it with the illustrative power of motives that are deeply established in the "common sense" of solidary audiences. Intellectual debate and critical reflection have been systematically excluded from these festive calls or ceremonial pacts—everything that threatens to overturn the ritualized order of the phrases made by submitting dogmas and maxims to the liberating energy of a struggle of meanings and a competitiveness of readings. (Richard, 31-32, 34-35)

Artists who assume the new conditions of communication and verisimilitude of culture are suspicious of any historical account "governed by a homogeneous Truth (of class or nation)." Their works, fragmentary or unfinished, seek to "de-emphasize" social gestures. In choosing an interrogative or doubting relationship to the social, they produce a "counterepic." If there is no longer *one* coherent and stable Order, and if the identity of each group is not associated with a single territory but with multiple scenarios, and history is not directed toward programmable goals, then images and texts cannot be anything but a compilation of fragments, collages, an "irregular mix of textures and sources that cite each other in a scattered way" (ibid., 34).

Nelly Richard explains that antidictatorial Chilean art confronts the problem of how to admit the fragmentary meaning of the social without preventing itself from constructing resistant microstrategies adequate to the compact character of authoritarianism. She wonders how to transform "totalitarian projects (dictatorship) or totalizing frameworks (orthodox Marxism)" without the disappearance of subjects capable of mobilizing socially linking and interpellating forces (35).

For my part, I think that the fragmentary and scattered view of the experimentalists or postmodernists appears with a double meaning. It can be an opening, an occasion for again feeling uncertainties, when it maintains the critical preoccupation with social processes, with artistic languages, and with the relation that these weave with society. On the other hand, if this is lost, the postmodern fragmentation is converted into an artistic imitation of the simulacra of atomization that a market—in fact monopolistic and centralized—plays with dispersed consumers.

We can ask equivalent questions of the dominant conceptions in the new technologies when they present reconversion as a simple formal process, an opening of informative and communicational possibilities. Do the opening and the hybridization suppress the differences among cultural strata that cross, producing a generalized pluralism, or do they engender new segmentations? The technologists and technocrats tend to idealize communicational fluidity and decentralization, the multiplication of services afforded by videocassette players, television, parabolic antennas, computers, and fiber optics, as if these offerings were available to everyone. The effective dissemination of opportunities and transversalization of the power they generate coexist with old and new devices for concentrating hegemony.

Communicational *decentralization* is too often translated into *deregulation,* in other words the withdrawal of the state as a possible agent of the public interest. For neoconservative discourse, transferring initiative to civil society means concentrating power in monopolistic private corporations. The fact that the state is uninterested in information, art, and communications being public services means that they are converted chiefly into commodities and only become accessible to privileged sectors. In this framework, the *fragmentation* of the audiences, encouraged by the diversification of the offerings, reduces the expansion of symbolic goods. In fact, what is produced is an *unequal segmentation* of consumption practices (the individual subscription to cable television, the exclusive connection to data banks by means of fiber optics). Miguel de Moragas points to the present trend of accentuating and renewing stratification in separating "one model of information for action—reserved, secret, documented—and another informational model for the masses, in which the focus on spectacle predominates" (cited in Martín Barbero 1987b, 9).

Just as the privatized fragmentation of urban space permits a minority to reduce its dealings with "the masses," the segmented and commercial organization of communications specializes consumption practices and distances social strata from each other. To the extent that the role of public power as a guarantor of informative democratization and of the socialization of scientific and artistic goods of collective interest diminishes, these goods cease to be accessible for the majority. When culture ceases to be a public affair, information and intellectual resources on which the administration of power partially rests are privatized. And if power ceases to be public, or ceases to argue that it is something public, it can partially restore its verticality. Although in principle technological expansion and postmodern thought contribute to disseminating it, political development concentrates it. When these end-of-the-century transformations do not involve political and cultural democratization, the obliqueness they favor in urban and technological power becomes—more than pluralist dispersion—hermetism and discrimination.

Thus, this book does not end with a conclusion but with a conjecture. I suspect that thought on democratization; and innovation in the nineties will move along these two tracks that we have just crossed: the nonsubstantialist reconstruction of a social critique and the questioning of technocratic neoliberalism's claims to become the dogma of modernity. It is a question of verifying, in these two watersheds, how to be radical without being fundamentalist.

Notes

1. Anyone interested in reading more about the debate may consult *La Jornada* of November 8, 15, and 26, 1985, and *Unomásuno* of November 30, 1985.

2. For Hervé Fischer's reflections on this ritual, see his book *L'histoire de l'art est terminée*.

Bibliography

Acha, Juan. 1977. "El geometrismo reciente y Latinoamérica." In *El geometrismo mexicano*, ed. Jorge Adalberto Manrique. México: Instituto de Investigaciones Estéticas, UNAM: 29-49.

Aguilar Camín, Héctor. 1982 *Saldos de la revolución. Cultura y política de México, 1910-1980.* México: Nueva Imagen.

————. 1988. *Después del milagro.* México: Cal y Arena.

Altamirano, Carlos, and Beatriz Sarlo. 1983. *Literatura/Sociedad.* Buenos Aires: Hachette.

Amaral, Aracy A. 1985. "Brasil: del modernismo a la abstracción, 1910-1950." In *Arte moderno en América Latina*, ed. Damián Bayón. Madrid: Taurus. 270-81.

Anderson, Perry. 1984. "Modernity and Revolution." *New Left Review* 144 (March-April): 96-113.

Arantes, Antonio Augusto, 1984. *Produzindo o passado. Estrategias de construção do patrimonio cultural.* São Paulo: Brasiliense.

Arvatov, Boris. 1973. *Arte y producción.* Madrid: Alberto Corazón.

Avellaneda, Andrés. 1986. *Censura, autoritarismo y cultura. Argentina 1960-1983.* Vols. 1 and 2. Buenos Aires: Centro Editor de América Latina.

Bartra, Roger. 1987. *La jaula de la melancolía. Identidad y metamorfosis del mexicano.* México: Grijalbo.

Batallán, Graciela, and Raúl Díaz. N.d. *Salvajes, bárbaros y niños. La definición del patrimonio en la escuela primaria:* mimeograph.

Baudrillard, Jean. 1981. *For a Critique of the Political Economy of the Sign.* Trans. Charles Levin. St. Louis, Mo.: Telos Press.

Becerril Straffton, Rodolfo. 1982. "Las artesanías: la necesidad de una perspectiva económica." In *Textos sobre arte popular.* México: FONART-FONAPAS.

Becker, Howard S. 1982. *Art Worlds.* Berkeley: University of California Press.

Bellasi, Pietro. 1985. "Lilliput et Brobdingnag. Métaphores de l'imaginaire miniaturisant et mégalisant." *Communications* 42. Paris: Éditions du Seuil.

Belmont, Nicole. 1986. "Le folklore refoulé ou les séductions de l'archaïsme." *L'Homme* 97-98. Paris.

283

Benjamin, Walter. 1969a. "Unpacking My Library: A Talk about Book Collecting." In *Illuminations*, trans. Harry Zohn. New York: Schocken Books.

———. 1969b. "The Work of Art in the Age of Mechanical Reproduction." In *Illuminations*, trans. Harry Zohn. New York: Schocken Books.

Berger, John. 1980. *Modos de ver.* Barcelona: Gustavo Gili.

Berman, Marshall. 1988. *Todo lo sólido se desvanece en el aire. La experiencia de la modernidad.* Madrid: Siglo xxi.

Binni, L., and G. Pinna. 1980. *Museo.* Milan: Garzanti.

Blache, Martha. 1988. "Folclor y cultura popular." *Revista de Investigaciones Folclóricas* 3 (December). University of Buenos Aires, Instituto de Ciencias Antropológicas.

Bollème, Geneviève. 1986. *Le peuple par écrit.* Paris: Éditions du Seuil.

Bonfil Batalla, Guillermo. 1988. "Los conceptos de diferencia y subordinación en el estudio de las culturas populares." In *Teoría e investigación en la antropología social mexicana.* Iztapalapa, México: CIESAS-UAM: 97-108.

———. 1990. *México profundo.* México: Grijalbo.

———, ed. 1981. *Utopía y revolución. El pensamiento político contemporáneo de los indios en América Latina.* México: Nueva Imagen.

Bouchindhomme, Christian, and Rainer Rochlitz. "Prologue." In Habermas 1988.

Bourdieu, Pierre. 1967. "Campo intelectual y proyecto creador." In *Problemas del estructuralismo,* ed. Jean Pouillon. México: Siglo xxi 135-82.

———. 1970. *Le marché des biens symboliques.* Paris: Centre de Sociologie Européenne.

———. 1971. "Disposition esthétique et compétence artistique." *Les Temps Modernes* 295 (February): 1345-78.

———. 1977. "La production de la croyance: contribution à une économie des biens symboliques." *Actes de la Recherche en Sciences Sociales* 13 (February).

———. 1979. *La distinction—Critique sociale du jugement.* Paris: Éditions de Minuit.

——— 1980. "Quelques propriétés des champs." In *Questions de sociologie.* Paris: Éditions de Minuit.

———. 1982. "Les rites comme actes d'institution." *Actes de la Recherche en Sciences Sociales* 43 (June): 58-63.

———. 1983. "Vous avez dit populaire?" *Actes de la Recherche en Sciences Sociales* 43 (March).

———. 1990a. *The Logic of Practice.* Cambridge: Polity Press.

———. 1990b. *Sociología y cultura.* México: Grijalbo.

Bourdieu, Pierre, and Alan Darbel. 1969. *L'amour de l'art. Les musées européens et leur public.* Paris: Éditions de Minuit.

Bourdieu, Pierre, and Jean-Claude Passeron. 1977. *La reproducción—Elementos para una teoría del sistema de enseñanza.* Barcelona: Laia.

Brecht, Bertolt. 1983. *Escritos sobre el teatro.* Vol. 2. Buenos Aires: Nueva Visión.

Bricker, Victoria Reifler. 1973. *Ritual Humor in Highland Chiapas.* Austin: University of Texas Press.

Brunner, José Joaquín. 1982. *Vida cotidiana, sociedad y cultura: Chile, 1973-1982.* Santiago: FLACSO.

———. 1985. "Cultura y crisis de hegemonías." In *Cinco estudios sobre cultura y sociedad,* ed. J. J. Brunner and G. Catalán. Santiago: FLACSO.

———. 1988. *Un espejo trizado. Ensayos sobre cultura y políticas culturales.* Santiago: FLACSO.

Cabrujas, José Ignacio. 1987. "El Estado del disimulo." In *Heterodoxia y Estado. 5 respuestas, Estado y Reforma.* Caracas: n.p.

Calvino, Italo. 1983. *Punto y aparte. Ensayos sobre literatura y sociedad.* Barcelona: Bruguera.

Campra, Rosalba. *América Latina: L'identità e la maschera.* Rome: Riuniti, 1982 (*América Latina: La identidad y la máscara.* México: Siglo xxi).

Cardoso, R., ed. 1986. *A aventura antropologica*. São Paulo: Paz e Terra.

Carvalho, José Jorge de. 1989. *O lugar da cultura tradicional na sociedade moderna*. Brasília: University of Brasília Foundation, Anthropological Series 77.

Casar, José I. 1988. "La modernización económica y el mercado." In *México: el reclamo democrático*, ed. R. Cordera Campos, R. Trejo Delarbre, and Juan Enrique Vega. México: Siglo XXI-ILET.

Castells, Manuel. 1973. *La cuestión urbana*. 2d. ed. México: Siglo XXI.

Castells, Manuel, and Roberto Laserna. 1989. "La nueva dependencia. Cambio tecnológico y reestructuración socioeconómica en Latinoamérica." *David y Goliath* 55 (July): 2-16.

Castrillón, Alfonso. 1983. "Encuesta: pobres y tristes museos del Perú." *Utópicos* 2-3 (January), Lima.

Celant, Germano. 1979. Intervention in "El arte de la performance." *Teoría y crítica* (December). Buenos Aires: Asociación Internacional de Críticos e Arte.

Certeau, Michel de. 1981. "Californie, un théâtre de passants." *Autrement* 31 (April).

Cimet, Esther, and Julio Gullco. 1987. "El público de Rodin en el Palacio de Bellas Artes." In *El público como propuesta. Cuatro estudios sociológicos en museos de arte*, E. Cimet et al. México: INBA: 83-86.

Cimet, E., M. Dujovne, N. García Canclini, J. Gullco, C. Mendoza, F. Reyes Palma, and G. Soltero. 1987. *El público como propuesta. Cuatro estudios sociológicos en museos de arte*. México: INBA.

Cirese, Alberto. 1979. *Ensayos sobre las culturas subalternas*. Cuadernos de la Casa Chata 24. México.

Clifford, James, and George Marcus, eds. 1986. *Writing Culture: The Poetics and Politics of Ethnography*. Berkeley: University of California Press.

Cohen, Jeffrey H., and Harold K. Schneider. 1990. "Markets, Museums and Modes of Production: Economic Strategies in Two Zapotec Weaving Communities of Oaxaca, Mexico." West Lafayette, Ind.: Society for Economic Anthropology, vol. 9, no. 2.

Conde, Teresa del. 1988a. "Censura." *La Jornada* (January 28).

———. 1988b. "La Virgen, una madona del Apocalipsis." *La Jornada* (January 29).

Corbiere, Emilio J. 1982. *Centros de cultura populares*. Buenos Aires: Centro de Estudios de América Latina.

Coutinho, Wilson, 1989. "Esse teu olhar quando encontra o meu." In *Gerchman*. Rio de Janeiro: Salamandra.

Crimp, Douglas. 1983. "On the Museum's Ruins." In *The Anti-Aesthetic: Essays on Postmodern Culture*, ed. Hal Foster, Port Townsend, Wash.: Bay Press. 43-56.

del Paso, Fernando. 1989. "¿Al diablo la revolución francesa?" In *Les trois couleurs d'Ocumicho*. Paris: Centre Culturel du Mexique.

La dicotomía entre arte culto y arte popular (Coloquio internacional de Zacatecas). 1979. México: UNAM.

Duncan, Carol, and Alan Wallach. 1978. "Le musée d'art moderne de New York: un rite du capitalisme tardif." *Histoire et critique des arts* 7-8 (December).

———. 1980. "The Universal Survey Museum." *Art History* 3: 4 (December): 448-69.

Durand, José Carlos. 1989. *Arte, privilégio e distinção*. São Paulo: Perspectiva.

Durham, Eunice Ribeiro. 1986a. "A pesquisa antropologica com populações urbanas: problemas e perspectivas." In *A aventura antropologica*, ed. R. Cardoso. São Paulo: Paz e Terra.

———. 1986b. "A sociedade vista da periferia." *Revista Brasileira de Ciencias Sociais* 1 (June).

Eco, Umberto. 1981. *Lector in fabula*. Barcelona: Lumen.

———. 1986. "Viaje a la hiperrealidad." In *La estrategia de la ilusión*. Barcelona: Lumen.

Eder, Rita. 1977. "El público de arte en México: los espectadores de la exposición Hammer." *Plural* (July): 51-65.

———. 1981. *Gironella*. México: UNAM.

Ehrenberg, Felipe. 1988. Interview with García Canclini in Mexico City, June 6.

Fischer, Hervé. 1981. *L'histoire de l'art est terminée*. Mayenne: Balland.

Ford, Aníbal. 1986. *Ramos generales*. Buenos Aires: Catálogos.

———. 1987a. *Desde la orilla de la ciencia. Ensayos sobre identidad, cultura y territorio*. Buenos Aires: Punto Sur.

———. 1987b. *Los diferentes ruidos del agua*. Buenos Aires: Punto Sur.

———. 1988. "Las fisuras de la industria cultural." In *Alternativa latinoamericana*. N.p.: n.p.

Foucault, Michel. 1977. "Fantasia on the Library." In *Language, Counter-Memory, Practice*. Ithaca, N.Y.: Cornell University Press. 87-109.

———. 1980. *The History of Sexuality*. Vol. 1: *An Introduction*. Trans. Robert Hurley. New York: Vintage Books.

Franco, Jean. 1986. *La cultura moderna en América Latina*. México: Grijalbo.

———. 1987. "Recibir a los bárbaros: ética y cultura de masas." *Nexos* 115 (July), México.

Gabaldón, Iván, and Elizabeth Fuentes. 1988. "Receta para un mito." *El Nacional* (April 24), Caracas.

Galard, Jean. 1973. *La muerte de las bellas artes*. Madrid: Fundamentos.

García, Luz M., M. Elena Crespo, and M. Cristina López. 1987. Escuela de Bellas Artes, Facultad de Humanidades y Arte de la Universidad Nacional de Rosario: CAYC.

García Canclini, Néstor. 1977. *Arte popular y sociedad en América Latina*. México: Grijalbo.

———. 1987a. "Henry Moore o las barreras del arte contemporáneo." In *El público como propuesta. Cuatro estudios sociológicos en museos de arte*, E. Cimet et al. México: INBA. 106-9.

———. 1987b. "Las artes populares en la época de la industria cultural." *México Indígena* 19 (November-December).

———. 1987c. "Tapio Wirkkala: lo artístico, lo decorativo y lo útil." In *El público como propuesta. Cuatro estudios sociológicos en museos de arte*, E. Cimet et al. México: INBA. 139-57.

———. 1988. *La producción simbólica. Teoría y método en sociología del arte*. 4th ed. México: Siglo XXI.

———. 1989a. *Las culturas populares en el capitalismo*. 4th ed. México: Nueva Imagen.

———. 1989b. "Monuments, Billboards, and Graffiti." In *Mexican Monuments: Strange Encounters*, ed. Paolo Gori and Helen Escobedo. New York: Abbeville Press.

García Canclini, Néstor, and Patricia Safa. 1989. *Tijuana: la casa de toda la gente*. México: INAH-ENAH-UAM-Programa Cultural de las Fronteras.

García Canclini, Néstor, and Rafael Roncagliolo, eds. 1988. *Cultura transnacional y culturas populares*. Lima: IPAL.

Geertz, Clifford. 1983. "Introduction." In *Local Knowledge: Further Essays in Interpretive Anthropology*. New York: Basic Books.

Gilly, Adolfo. 1988. *Nuestra caída en la modernidad*. México: Joan Boldó i Climent Editores.

Goldman, Shifra. 1977. *Contemporary Mexican Painting in a Time of Change*. Austin and London: University of Texas Press.

———. 1989. "El espíritu latinoamericano. La perspectiva desde los Estados Unidos." *Arte en Colombia* 41 (September).

Goldman, Shifra M., and Tomás Ybarra-Frausto. 1985. *Arte Chicano: A Comprehensive Annotated Bibliography of Chicano Art, 1965-1981*. Berkeley: Chicano Studies Library and Publications Unit, University of California.

Gombrich, E. H. 1979. *Ideals and Idols: Essays on Values in History and in Art*. New York: E. P. Dutton.

Gómez-Peña, Guillermo. 1987. "Wacha ese border, son." *La Jornada Semanal* 162 (October 27).

González Casanova, Pablo. 1981. "La cultura política en México." *Nexos* 4:39 (March).

Good Eshelman, Catherine. 1988. *Haciendo la lucha. Arte y comercio nahuas de Guerrero.* México: Fondo de Cultura Económica.

Gori, Paolo, and Helen Escobedo, eds. 1989. *Mexican Monuments: Strange Encounters.* New York: Abbeville Press.

Gouy-Gilbert, Cécile. 1987. *Ocumicho y Patamban. Dos maneras de ser artesano.* México: Centre d'Études Mexicaines et Centraméricaines.

Granillo Vázquez, Silvia. 1986. "Nuestros antepasados nos atrapan. Arquitectura del Museo Nacional de Antropología." *Información científica y tecnológica* 8:21 (October), México.

Grignon, Claude, and Jean-Claude Passeron. 1982. *Sociologie de la culture et sociologie des cultures populaires.* Paris: Gides.

Gubern, Román. 1987. *La mirada opulenta. Exploración de la iconosfera contemporánea.* Barcelona: Gustavo Gili.

Gullar, Ferreira. 1980. "Cultura posta en questão." *Arte en Revista* 2:3 (March).

Gutiérrez, Leandro H., and Luis Alberto Romero. 1985. "La cultura de los sectores populares porteños." *Espacios* 2. Universidad de Buenos Aires.

Habermas, Jürgen. 1983. "Modernity—An Incomplete Project." In *The Anti-Aesthetic: Essays on Postmodern Culture,* ed. Hal Foster. Port Townsend, Wash.: Bay Press. 43-56.

———. 1985. "Walter Benjamin." In *Philosophical-Political Profiles.* Trans. Frederick Lawrence. Cambridge, Mass.: MIT Press.

———. 1987. *The Philosophical Discourse of Modernity.* Trans. Frederick Lawrence. Cambridge, Mass.: MIT Press.

———. 1988. *Le discours philosophique de la modernité.* Trans. Christian Bouchindhomme and Rainer Rochlitz. Paris: Gallimard.

Hadjinicolaou, Nicos. 1981. *La producción artística frente a sus significados.* México: Siglo xxi.

Hudson, Kenneth. 1975. *Museums for the 1980's.* London-Paris: Macmillan/UNESCO.

Hughes, Robert. 1989. "Art and Money." *Time* (November 27): 60-68.

Huyssen, Andreas. 1987. "Guía del posmodernismo." *Punto de vista* 10:29 (April-July), offprint: xx-xxvii.

———. 1988. "En busca de la tradición: vanguardia y posmodernismo en los años 70." In *Modernidad y posmodernidad,* ed. Josep Picó. Madrid: Alianza.

Iser, Wolfgang. 1978. *The Act of Reading: A Theory of Aesthetic Response.* London: Routledge & Kegan Paul and Johns Hopkins University Press.

Jameson, Fredric. 1989. "Marxism and Postmodernism." *New Left Review* 176 (July-August): 31-46.

Jauss, Hans Robert. 1978. *Pour une esthétique de la réception.* Paris: Gallimard.

Jelin, Elizabeth, and Pablo Vila. 1987. *Podría ser yo. Los sectores populares urbanos en imagen y palabra.* Buenos Aires: CEDES-Ediciones de la Flor.

Kerriou, Miriam A. de. 1981. *Los visitantes y el funcionamiento del Museo Nacional de Antropología de México* (February). México: mimeograph.

La Jornada. November 8, 15, and 26, 1985.

Ladislao, Ulises. 1986. "Evolución de la museografía en México." *Información científica y tecnológica* 8:21 (October), México.

Landi, Oscar. 1984. "Cultura y política en la transición democrática." In *Proceso, crisis y transición democrática,* vol. 1, ed. Oskar Oszlak. Buenos Aires: Centro Editor de América Latina.

Lauer, Mirko. 1976. *Introducción a la pintura peruana del siglo XX.* Lima: Mosca Azul.

———. 1982. *Crítica de la artesanía. Plástica y sociedad en los Andes peruanos.* Lima: DESCO.

———. 1984. *La producción artesanal en América Latina.* Lima: Fundación Friedrich Ebert.

Le Nouvel Observateur. 1987. (January 9-15): 43.

Lechner, Norbert. 1982. *Notas sobre la vida cotidiana: habitar, trabajar, consumir.* Vol. 1, Part 1. Santiago: FLACSO.

León, Aurora. 1978. *El museo. Teoría, praxis y utopía.* Madrid: Cátedra.

Lévi-Strauss, Claude. 1966. *The Savage Mind.* Chicago: University of Chicago Press.

Lyotard, Jean-François. 1993. *The Postmodern Explained: Correspondence 1982-1985.* Translation edited by Julian Pefanis and Morgan Thomas. Minneapolis: University of Minnesota Press.

Martín Barbero, Jesús. 1987a. *De los medios a las mediaciones.* México: Gustavo Gili.

————. 1987b. "Innovación tecnológica y transformación cultural." *Telos* 9, Madrid.

Martínez Luna, Jaime. 1982. "Resistencia comunitaria y organización popular." In *Culturas populares y política cultural,* ed. G. Bonfil Batalla. México: Museo Nacional de Culturas Populares/SEP.

Matamoro, Blas. 1979. *Diccionario de Jorge Luis Borges.* Madrid: Altalena.

Matta, Roberto da. 1980. *Carnavais, malandros e hérois.* Rio de Janeiro: Zahar.

McAllister, Ricardo. 1989. "Videoclips. La estética del parpadeo." *Crisis* 67 (January-February), Buenos Aires.

Menéndez, Eduardo. 1981. *Poder, estratificación y salud.* México: Ediciones de la Casa Chata.

Miceli, Sergio. 1979. *Intelectuais e classe dirigente no Brasil (1920-1945).* São Paulo-Rio de Janeiro: DIFEL.

————. 1984. *Estado e cultura no Brasil.* São Paulo: DIFEL.

Ministry of Culture of Spain. *Políticas culturales en Europa.*

Módena, María Eugenia. 1990. *Madres, médicos y curanderos: diferencia cultural e identidad ideológica.* México: CIESAS.

Monsiváis, Carlos. 1984. "Notas sobre el Estado, la cultura nacional y las culturas populares." *Cuadernos políticos* 30.

————. 1989. "De las finuras del arte rascuache." Graffiti 2 (July-August), Jalapa, Veracruz.

Monzón, Arturo. 1952. "Bases para incrementar el público que visita el Museo Nacional de Antropología." In *Anales del Instituto Nacional de Antropología e Historia.* Vol. 6, Part 2.

Moragas, Miguel de. N.d. *Opinión pública y transformaciones en el uso de la información.* Mimeograph. In Martín Barbero 1987b.

Morais, Federico. 1979. *Artes plásticas na América Latina: do transe ao transitorio.* Rio de Janeiro: Civilização Brasileira.

Mosquera, Gerardo. 1989. *El diseño se definió en octubre.* Havana: Editorial Arte y Literatura.

Moulin, Raymonde. 1985. "Le marché et le musée. La constitution des valeurs artistiques contemporaines." *Revue Française de Sociologie* 27.

Nieto, Raúl. 1988. "¿Reconversión industrial = reconversión cultural obrera?" *Iztapalapa* 8:15 (January-June).

Noé, Luis Felipe. 1982. "La nostalgia de la historia en el proceso de imaginación plástica de América Latina." In Foro de Arte Contemporáneo, Encuentro *Artes visuales e identidad en América Latina.* México: 46-51.

————. 1988. *El color y las artes plásticas.* Buenos Aires: Alba.

Ortiz, Renato. 1985. "Cultura popular: romanticos e folcloristas." *Textos* 3. PUC-SP: Programa de Pos-graduação en Ciencias Sociais.

————. 1988. *A moderna tradição brasileira.* São Paulo: Brasiliense.

Paternosto, César. 1989. *Piedra abstracta. La escultura inca: una visión contemporánea.* Buenos Aires: Fondo de Cultura Económica.

Paz, Octavio. 1979. *El ogro filantrópico.* México: Joaquín Mortiz.

————. 1987. *Los hijos del limo.* 3d ed. México: Joaquín Mortiz.

Pease García, Henry. 1988. "La izquierda y la cultura de la posmodernidad." In *Proyectos de cambio. La izquierda democrática en América Latina.* Caracas: Editorial Nueva Sociedad.

Piccini, Mabel. "Industrias culturales: transversalidades y régimenes interdiscursivos." *Diálogos* 17 (June), Lima.

Piglia, Ricardo. 1986. *Crítica y ficción.* Santa Fe: Universidad Nacional del Litoral.

———. 1987. *Respiración artificial*. Buenos Aires: Sudamericana.

Portantiero, Juan Carlos, and Emilio de Ipola. 1987. "Lo nacional popular y los populismos realmente existentes." *Nueva Sociedad* (May-June).

Poulot, Dominique. 1981. "L'avenir du passé. Les musées en mouvement." *Le débat* 12 (May), Paris.

Puente, Alejandro. 1988. Interview with García Canclini in Buenos Aires (March 14).

Ragon, Michael. 1978. "L'art en pluriel." In *Les singuliers de l'art*. Paris: Museum of Modern Art.

Ramírez, Juan Antonio. 1989. "Una relación impúdica." *Lápiz* 57 (March), Madrid.

Ramírez, Mari-Carmen. 1989. Interview in Austin, Texas (November).

Ratcliff, C. 1978. "Could Leonardo da Vinci Make It in New York Today? Not unless He Played by the Rules." *New York Magazine* (November).

Ribeiro, Berta G., Maria Rosilene Barbosa Alvina, Ana M. Heyer, Vera de Vives, José Silveira D'Avila, and Dante Luis Martins Teixeira. 1983. *O artesão tradicional e seu papel na sociedade contemporanea*. Rio de Janeiro: FUNARTE/Instituto Nacional de Folclore.

Richard, Nelly. 1989. *La estratificación de los márgenes*. Santiago de Chile: Francisco Zegers Editor.

Rockwell, Elsie. 1986. "De huellas, bandas y veredas: una historia cotidiana en la escuela." In *La escuela, lugar del trabajo docente*, ed. E. Rockwell and Ruth Mercado. México: Departamento de Investigaciones Educativas.

Rodríguez Prampolini, Ida, ed. 1983. *A través de la frontera*. México: UNAM-CEESTEM.

Romero, Luis Alberto. 1986. *Libros baratos y cultura de los sectores populares*. Buenos Aires: CISEA.

———. 1987. *Los sectores populares urbanos como sujetos históricos*. Buenos Aires: CISEA-PEHESA.

Rosaldo, Renato. 1989. *Culture and Truth: The Remaking of Social Analysis*. Boston: Beacon Press.

———. N.d. *Ideology, Place, and People without Culture*. Stanford University, Department of Anthropology.

Rouse, Roger. 1988. "Mexicano, Chicano, Pocho. La migración mexicana y el espacio social del posmodernismo." *Página Uno*, supplement to *Unomásuno* (December 31).

Rubin, William. 1984. "Introduction." In "*Primitivism*" *in 20th Century Art*, ed. William Rubin. New York: Museum of Modern Art. Vol. 1: 1-79.

Safa, Patricia. 1986. "Socialización infantil e identidad popular." Master's thesis in Social Anthropology, National School of Anthropology and History, Mexico City.

Sariego Rodríguez, Juan Luis. 1984. "La cultura minera en crisis. Aproximación a algunos elementos de la identidad de un grupo obrero." Paper presented at colloquium on worker culture organized by the National Museum of Cultures, Mexico City (September).

Sarlo, Beatriz. 1988a. "Políticas culturales: democracia e innovación." *Punto de vista* 11:32 (April-June).

———. 1988b. *Una modernidad periférica: Buenos Aires 1920 y 1930*. Buenos Aires: Nueva Visión.

Sazbón, José. 1987. "Borges declara." *Espacios* 6 (October-November), Buenos Aires.

Schmilchuk, Graciela. 1987. *Museos: comunicación y educación*. México: Instituto Nacional de Bellas Artes.

Schwarz, Roberto. 1977. "As idéias fora do lugar." In *Ao Vencedor as Batatas*. São Paulo: Duas Cidades. 13-25.

Seggerman, Helen-Louise. 1989. "Latin American Art." *Art and Auction* (September).

Signorelli, Amalia. 1980. "Cultura popolare e modernizzazione." *La ricerca folklorica* 1 (April), Milan.

Silva, Armando. 1987. *Punto de vista ciudadano. Focalización visual y puesta en escena del grafiti.* Bogotá: Instituto Caro y Cuervo.

———. 1988. *Graffiti. Una ciudad imaginada.* Bogotá: Tercer Mundo Editores.

de Slemenson, Marta F., and Germán Kratochwill. 1970. "Un arte de difusores. Apuntes para la comprensión de un movimiento plástico de vanguardia en Buenos Aires, de sus creadores, sus difusores y su público." In *El intelectual latinoamericano*, ed. J. F. Marsal. Buenos Aires: Editorial del Instituto.

Solanas, Fernando, and Octavio Getino. 1979. *Cine, cultura y descolonización.* México: Siglo XXI.

Stromberg, Gobi. 1985. *El juego del coyote. Platería y arte en Taxco.* México: Fondo de Cultura Económica.

Sullivan, Edward. 1989. "Mito y realidad. Arte latinoamericano en Estados Unidos." *Arte en Colombia* 41 (September).

Tibol, Raquel. 1969. *Historia general del arte mexicano. Época moderna y contemporánea.* México: Hermes.

Traba, Marta. 1982. "Preferimos los museos." *Sábado*, supplement of *Unomásuno* 247 (July 31), México.

———. 1969. *The Ritual Process: Structure and Anti-Structure.* Chicago: Aldine Publishing Company.

Turner, Victor W. 1980. *The Forest of Symbols: Aspects of Ndembu Ritual.* Ithaca, N.Y.: Cornell University Press.

Ulanovsky, Carlos. 1987. "El alma del país está en el interior. Conversación con Félix Coluccio." *Clarín* (November 22), Buenos Aires.

Unomásuno. November 30, 1985.

Valenzuela, José Manuel. 1988. *¡A la brava ese! Cholos, punks, chavos banda.* Tijuana: Colegio de la Frontera Norte.

Vega Centeno, Imelda. 1985. *Agrarismo popular: mito, cultura e historia.* Lima: Tarea.

Verger, Annie. 1987. "L'art d'estimer l'art. Comment classer l'incomparable?" *Actes de la Recherche en Sciences Sociales* 66/67 (March): 105-21.

Verón, Eliseo. 1985. "Discurso político y estrategia de la imagen. Entrevista de Rodolfo Fogwill." *Espacios* 3 (December): 59-65.

———. 1987. *La semiosis social.* Buenos Aires: Gedisa.

Walter, Lyn. 1981. "Otavaleño Development, Ethnicity, and National Integration." *América Indígena* 41:2 (April-June): 319-38.

Warman, Arturo. 1982. "Modernizarse ¿para qué?" *Nexos* 50 (February).

Williams, Raymond. 1977. "Plaisantes perspectives. Invention du paysage et abolition du paysan." *Actes de la Recherche en Sciences Sociales* 17-18 (November).

———. 1980. *Marxismo y literatura.* Barcelona: Península.

Yero, Lourdes. 1988. *Cambios en el campo cultural en Venezuela. Privatización y pluralidad.* Document developed for the project "Ciencias sociales, crisis y requerimientos de nuevos paradigmas en la relación Estado/Sociedad/Economía." Caracas: CLACSO-UNESCO-PNUD.

Yurkievich, Saúl. 1984. "El arte de una sociedad en transformación." In *América Latina en sus artes*, ed. Damián Bayón. 5th ed. México: UNESCO-Siglo XXI.

Zabala, Horacio. 1982. "Oggi, l'arte è una carcere." In *Oggi l'arte è una carcere?* ed. Luigi Russo. Bologna: Il Mulino. 95-103.

Index

Néstor García Canclini received his doctorate in philosophy from the University of Paris. He lived in Argentina until 1976, and since then has resided in Mexico. He currently directs the Program of Studies on Urban Culture in the Universidad Autónoma Metropolitana in Mexico City. In 1992 his book *Culturas híbridas* won the Premio Iberoamericano for the outstanding book on Latin America written in Spanish or Portuguese. He is also the author of *Transforming Modernity: Popular Culture in Mexico* (1993).

Christopher L. Chiappari is a doctoral candidate in the Department of Anthropology at the University of Minnesota.

Silvia L. López is a doctoral candidate in the Department of Cultural Studies and comparative literature at the University of Minnesota.

Renato Rosaldo is Lucie Stern Professor in the Social Sciences and chair of the Department of Anthropology at Stanford University. He is also president of the American Ethnological Society and author of *Ilongot Headhunting, 1883–1974: A Study in Society and History* and *Culture and Truth: The Remaking of Social Analysis*.